PRAISE FOR
THE FEAR-FREE ORGANIZATION

D0491930

"If you work in an organization, you already know this: fear runs the place. What you may not know is that fear is going to ruin it, too, sooner or later. This book tells us why. Then it tells us how to change that. It is a call to leaders to understand the neurobiology of fear, face the damage it is doing, say goodbye to it forever as a tactic, and replace it brilliantly – as in: see to it that your organization is teeming with joy, with relationships of dignity, with warranted trust. Make it full of energy, *not* adrenalin; focused on possibility, not profit; generating independent thinking, not obedience; and spawning meaning everywhere because what really matters there is what really matters.

"This book gives us all of that by being both academic *and* accessible, by being, in fact, friendly and in places quite eloquent. Most of all it hits the bullseye: fear is the problem and relationships of love are the solution. The sophisticated version of love, that is, the kind that creates intellectual and practical rigour and leaves us smarter and makes us better leaders. It's all in the brain, it turns out. And leaders need to understand this particular dimension of the brain and stop fooling themselves. The neurological fact is that fear destroys; trust creates. Even the title is worth a month of pondering: *The Fear-free Organization* – not an oxymoron after all. What a relief."
Nancy Kline, author of *Time to Think*

"Boy, I wish I had read something like this a long time ago. In my decades as a corporate leader, I observed and learned the hard way about a lot of themes in the book (eg building relationships, managing energy flow, fostering trust, triggering fear). I came to know these things were real over the years but never really understood *why* they were happening until reading this book.

"I believe many corporate leaders still believe triggering fear is more productive than triggering attachment – mainly because that's the only role modelling they've had and all they know how to do. For many, building relationships, managing energy flow, fostering trust and avoiding triggering fear is all hard and unfamiliar work. But the resulting increase in affiliation, work satisfaction, productivity – and yes, business results! – would be staggering if more leaders would roll up their sleeves and take the plunge."
Thomas M Botts, retired Executive Vice President, Royal Dutch Shell

"The jewel in the crown of all the recent books on this subject... Clear authoritative exposition of the emerging understanding that neuroscience has provided together with a practical common-sense approach. All leaders of complex organizations should have this book by their bedside and their office."
Professor Patrick Pietroni, Director, Centre for Psychological Therapies in Primary Care, University of Chester

"I cannot remember the last time I read such a creative, engaging, and absorbing book as *The Fear-free Organization*. Beautifully written, clearly structured and brimming with compelling case studies, this new work transports us into the psychological core of

organizational life and provides us with rich recipes for understanding the complex and often tortured dynamics of the workplace. Brown, Kingsley and Paterson deserve our congratulations for offering us an important set of solutions. This book will be essential reading for anyone who has ever worked in an office."
Professor Brett Kahr, Senior Clinical Research Fellow in Psychotherapy and Mental Health, Centre for Child Mental Health, London

"All organizations suffer from elements of dysfunctionality and all leaders will be familiar with the symptoms. This book *superbly* explains what is really going on together with fascinating insights on the fears that all of us have experienced in the workplace and which have such a destructive effect on culture. And then the authors provide some practical advice on how to change things for the better."
Charlie Geffen, Chair, London Corporate, Gibson Dunn and formerly Senior Partner at Ashurst

"*The Fear-free Organization* is the essential manual for effective management. It provides the practical methods needed to motivate people to do their best work. The authors explain, simply and understandably, how to apply the most advanced neuroscientific insights to business management. It is groundbreaking and indispensible."
Dotson Rader, Contributing Editor, *Parade*

"Fear pervades the workplace. It corrodes profits and stunts growth. This essential read equips CEOs with the tools to build a fear-free environment – and success."
Robin Morgan, CEO, Iconic Images

"Emotions are at the very of core of being human because they exert a powerful, often unconscious impact on how we think, feel and behave. There is a wealth of research highlighting how extended periods of stress, anxiety and fear can inflict a damaging effect on our physical and psychological health with significant consequences for our personal relationships and quality of life.

"Conversely psychological wellbeing is strongly correlated with greater energy, motivation and better cognitive function.

"There is a zeitgeist and not surprisingly progressive organizations are actively looking at how they can improve and maintain the psychological health and wellbeing of their employees to the benefit of all concerned.

"This book draws on robust psychological theory and the remarkable advances in neuroscience to provide the reader with fascinating and invaluable insights into how the human brain works. Most importantly it outlines a range of effective, practical strategies to help build a healthier environment that can deliver real and measurable benefits to the individual, teams and the organization – the fear-free organization.
Dr Brian Marien, Founder and Director of Positive

"Leadership is about making sense, and this book makes a lot of sense. I highly recommend it for leaders, and those who aspire to become one."
Rien Herber, former Shell Executive and currently Professor at Groningen University

The Fear-free Organization

The Fear-free Organization

Vital insights from neuroscience to transform your business culture

Paul Brown, Joan Kingsley, Sue Paterson

KoganPage

LONDON   PHILADELPHIA   NEW DELHI

First published in Great Britain and the United States in 2015 by Kogan Page Limited

2nd Floor, 45 Gee Street
London EC1V 3RS
United Kingdom
www.koganpage.com

1518 Walnut Street, Suite 1100
Philadelphia PA 19102
USA

4737/23 Ansari Road
Daryaganj
New Delhi 110002
India

© Paul Brown, Joan Kingsley, Sue Paterson, 2015

ISBN   978 0 7494 7295 5
E-ISBN   978 0 7494 7296 2

British Library Cataloguing-in-Publication Data

A CIP record for this book is available from the British Library.

Library of Congress Control Number: 2015021006

Typeset by Graphicraft Limited, Hong Kong
Print production managed by Jellyfish
Printed and bound by CPI Group (UK) Ltd, Croydon CR0 4YY

Paul says:
To Ketta with love,
and for understanding.

Joan says:
For Philip, Katherine and Anabel,
your love, support and belief
have been my inspiration.

Sue says:
In the words of an old song,
'this is dedicated to the ones I love'
– Steve, Dan and Eddie.

CONTENTS

LIST OF FIGURES

LIST OF TABLES

ABOUT THE AUTHORS

Dr Paul Brown is Faculty Professor, Organizational Neuroscience, Monarch Business School Switzerland; Honorary Chairman of the Vietnam Consulting Group, Saigon, and International Director of SIRTailors, Saigon. A clinical and organizational psychologist and executive coach, his main fascination is in creating a general theory of the individual and the organization based upon mapping how energy flows or gets blocked in the pursuit of profitable and other outcomes within the organizational system. He has recently co-authored *Neuropsychology for Coaches: Understanding the basics* (2012), *River Dragon* (a novel, 2014) and *Neuroscience for Leadership: Harnessing the brain gain advantage* (2015). He lives in Vietnam, teaches in the UK and consults worldwide.

Joan Kingsley is a Consultant Clinical and Organizational Psychotherapist. She has a private practice in London, is Honorary Consultant Psychotherapist at the National Hospital for Neurology and Neurosurgery, and is on the Psychotherapist register of the School of Life. Joan works with senior management in business organizations. She sits on the Board of Directors of two UK companies and is Vice President of a New York-based organization. Joan is a member of The New York Academy of Sciences, a Fellow of The Royal Society of Arts, and a member of the Royal Academy of Medicine and is registered with the UKCP. Joan has spent the past 25 years doing research into the links between brain systems and our psychological lives. A native New Yorker, Joan is based in London with her husband Philip. She is the proud mother of Katherine and Anabel.

Dr Sue Paterson is an oil and gas professional with over 30 years' UK and international experience. She worked for Shell International in exploration, new business development and JV management, as well as talent management, leadership development, learning and recruitment. She has led teams in-country and across continents. In 2010 she set up her own oil and gas consultancy, and in 2012 became the Director of an international management consultancy. She is a qualified IOD Chartered Director, and has board experience in the oil, public and voluntary sectors. Sue divides her time between Aberdeen and Amsterdam, where her husband Steve is currently working. Sue and Steve have two sons, Dan and Eddie.

PREFACE

This is a book that has been a long time in gestation. Joan and I started talking and writing a little about fear in the workplace almost 20 years ago. But the neuroscience was young and applied neuroscience was only just appearing. Since then a lot has happened in the scientific community and the wealth of information we have been able to draw on much greater. The 21st century has now established itself as the time when the workings of the brain will be understood. As with the genome in the 20th century, the mysteries of the brain and how it both manages the body and creates the person are yielding to systematic scientific enquiry.

One of the new certainties about human behaviour is that all actions of any conceivable kind, including all thoughts, are underpinned by their own specific neurochemistry. There is nothing that happens to us that is not triggered by, or itself creates, a specific chemical reaction. Fear continuously triggers the corrosive chemical cortisol – a substance very useful in short measures, for it wakes us up and directs attention, among other useful attributes. But triggered persistently, it destroys brain cells, causes ruminative early morning waking, and damages the immune system. Living under the executive pressures of continuous anxiety and uncertainty, the brain demands resources to cope with the pressures while an executive is simultaneously keeping the pressure on him- or herself for performance. It's like driving a car with one foot on the accelerator and one on the brake. The car shudders to a halt or something burns out. Organizationally it's called executive stress.

Exactly 50 years ago, in 1965, Abraham Maslow published a book that is now barely read or referenced. Called *Eupsychian Management* (and republished in 1998 by Wiley & Sons as *Maslow on Management*) it set out his humanist views as to how an organization might be run based on the strengths and potential of the people employed and the quality of relationship between them. It propounded 36 principles of enlightened management in five categories. Trust was the first category. The 36 principles now read like an exhortation to grown-up boy scouts to be responsible. But Maslow had seen a truth confirmed by the modern neurosciences, which is that trust is a critical variable in effective management and that relationships are the key carrier of the signals that create or destroy trust.

Over 15 years ago Sue joined in our discussions, and this book began to take shape as she brought to bear upon it an organizational lifetime as an oil explorer and organizational leader. Kogan Page liked the idea and put its very helpful editorial resources behind it. So here it is. *The Fear-free Organization* holds out the hope that managers and HR can begin to see people not just as performers, producers and paragons of productivity but people with a huge capacity to strive if their brains are free to direct their energies towards goals that are worth pursuing.

And, serendipitously, as the Endnote conveys, there is remarkable evidence emerging that fear-free systems produce extraordinary results and deliver sustainability of a completely credible kind.

Paul Brown
Saigon and Hanoi, Vietnam

Introduction

> I've learned that people will forget what you said, people will forget what you did, but people will never forget how you made them feel.
>
> Maya Angelou

Fear is one of the most powerful motivating forces in our working culture today. It is what an overwhelming majority of bosses use, deliberately or mindlessly, to keep order. Think about it. How often have you or someone you know felt one of these fears: the fear of being thought a slacker and fired; of being unfairly criticized; of being back-stabbed and passed over for promotion; of being left in the dark, excluded, left out of meetings, undercut, pre-empted; of being the last to know? The fear of not being wanted?

Fear easily overtakes excitement and enthusiasm as the primary driver of motivation at work. It is readily used as a management tool because there is simply nothing easier than tapping into another person's fear system.

But neuroscience shows us that a culture of fear is unhealthy and invariably destructive of both people *and* businesses. Fear costs human beings their physical and emotional well-being. It costs companies money and time to deal with the damage done to employees. A culture of fear produces companies that are increasingly inefficient, non-competitive and uninventive. They may survive, but they may not thrive.

The challenge to business organizations is how to break out of this vicious cycle of fear. To meet this challenge we look to the brain sciences to understand the progressively devastating effects of fear, in all its aspects, on the individual. We then look at how relationships impact the brain, and investigate the biology of trust, which is the effective antidote to fear and, we believe, the essence of the new organizational paradigm that will replace the greedy, performance-driven models that have shown themselves so destructive of the common good.

The first quarter of the 21st century is going to be defined by the remarkable advances in biology that are taking place. Nowhere is this more apparent than in the brain sciences, which can now see the direction from which an understanding of the neurobiology of the 'Self' – an understanding of the way the brain constructs the person – will come.

This has huge implications for all aspects of our social existence, among which will be the way we think of people at work, their relationship to the workplace, their relationships with each other, what the workplace will be, and how human energy will be focused on the pursuit of profit in monetary and social terms.

The new science of the mind deepens our understanding of how relationships build brains and the continuing emotional impact that relationships have on the brain – for better or worse – throughout the lifespan.

The application of this knowledge is crucial for leaders and managers. It has important implications for the way human energy will drive goals in organizations, and what the whole field of human relationships at work really is about. The brain-savvy organization will put high value on a relationship culture and become wary of simplistic, performance-driven and transactional values.

It is the purpose of this book to present, in a highly accessible form, the basis upon which the application of human energy to profitable activity – social as well as financial – can be pursued. It offers the advantage of knowledge from the modern brain sciences in establishing the fear-free organization.

In the fear-free organization there are no panic rooms, no internal enemies, no bad guys. The fear-free organization has zero tolerance for bullies, for back-biting, vicious gossip, tittle-tattle, undermining behaviours, hijacking tactics, political jockeying for position, favouritism, and fascist-style policies. In the fear-free organization leaders understand that scared people spend a lot more time plotting their survival than working productively. In the fear-free organization people work on inspiration. They are encouraged to take risks, to think out of the box, to challenge the status quo, to explore new frontiers, to stand up and be counted.

We set out the argument for condemning fear within organizations, and explain why fear makes absolutely no sense in any organization, and why running on fear has no profit in it. We explain the new frontiers in neuroscience that are beginning to teach us how we become who we are, how we are not stuck in a mould, how we can adapt ourselves to become who we want to be, how we can lead ourselves and become leaders who inspire others.

We examine businesses that operate using fear as their fuel, presenting interviews with current and former employees. We show and discuss the negative results of the culture of fear in real businesses. We present scientific evidence of the destructive nature of fear in the workplace, and we show managers new, efficient, cost-effective, healthy ways to restructure and successfully run their businesses based not on fear but on the emotions that create energy and direct cooperation.

This book will *not* set forth a step-by-step model of behaviour that will guarantee your success as a leader. *The Fear-free Organization* considers how each individual develops and grows. We do not evolve out of cookie-cutter moulds. There is no guarantee that if we do x then y will follow. We are each born with highly complex systems and structures that comprise the brain: a brain that is underpinned by genetics and sculpted by experience; a brain that is dynamic and driven by energy. Both nature and nurture combine and interact to determine our ways of thinking, feeling and acting.

Excessive and persistent levels of fear create changes in brain function that then interfere with decision-making processes. We show how those levels of excess can be recognized and corrected. We show how to bring neuroscientific knowledge about the 'Self' into the heart of the organization in order to develop robust models of leading and managing in a sustainable business culture free from fear. Above all, we raise a banner for the working idea that fear-free organizations are what the future of work at its best will be about.

PART ONE
The person

Fear essentials and the development of the Self

01

We all know, from what we experience with and within ourselves, that our conscious acts spring from our desires and our fears. Intuition tells us that that is true also of our fellows and of the higher animals. We all try to escape pain and death, while we seek what is pleasant. We all are ruled in what we do by impulses; and these impulses are so organized that our actions in general serve for our self-preservation and that of race. Hunger, love, pain, fear are some of those inner forces which rule the individual's instinct for self-preservation. At the same time, as social beings, we are moved in the relations with our fellow by such feelings as sympathy, pride, hate, need for power, pity, and so on. All these primary impulses, not easily described in words, are the springs of man's actions. All such action would cease if those powerful elemental forces were to cease stirring within us.

Einstein (1938)

Fear... is the most depressing of all the emotions; and it soon induces utter, helpless prostration, as if in consequence of, or in association with, the most violent and prolonged attempts to escape have actually been made. Nevertheless, even extreme fear often acts at first as a powerful stimulant. A man or animal driven through terror to desperation is endowed with wonderful strength, and is notoriously dangerous in the highest degree.

Darwin (1872)

Introduction

Fear is the most primitive of all the emotions and pivotal in the development of brain and mind, from birth and throughout our lifespan. Thus, fear plays a major role in the development of the 'Self'. Fear is essential to our survival, but persistent fear can destroy us. Advances in brain science show just how devastating and long-lasting the effects of trauma and abuse (mental as well as physical) can be on the structure and function of the brain. Fear experiences can produce dramatic changes in the brain's architecture, resulting in profound alterations in our assumptions and perceptions.

In this chapter we explore the role that fear plays in our development from birth and throughout life. The chapter describes what fear is and how it is perceived; that is, what's happening in our brain when we are overcome by it. We consider why fear is so easily triggered and why it is so readily used as a management tool. We set fear in the context of the eight basic emotions, and discuss how our psychological growth and development is in large measure shaped by the emotional experience of relationships.

We are our emotions

Human beings are very complex. We are also very simple. Even more importantly, we are immensely adaptable. This gives us the remarkable evolutionary advantage that humans have gained over all other mammals.

Starting with the simple, we have three – only three – main operating components. *We think, we act,* and *we feel.*

Underpinning all three are eight emotions. They are the results of at least 2 million years of evolution. They are what make us complex.

The emotions are hard-wired in. In consequence the architecture of the human brain has evolved with emotions in mind. Emotions create the dynamic interpersonal energy upon which our whole social system – our whole existence as humans – relies. Emotions are real, physiological events and they exist *whether we recognize them or not in conscious awareness.* Emotions also happen whether we like them or not. Emotions stir us to act.

Emotions create our psychological lives. In that sense they create 'us' through our psychological growth and development, which is parallel to, but much less visible and understood than, our physical growth and development.

The main drivers of bodily growth and development are genetic endowment and the supply of food. The main drivers of our psychological growth and development are the emotions and those who create the emotional environment around us during our development. That is the essence of nurturing: parent to child. We are psychologically sculpted by the emotional qualities of our relationships from minute one, day one. What happens emotionally in the womb also has a profound effect upon the developing brain and its non-conscious assumptions of the world it will inhabit. Experience sculpts and shapes the brain in order to make it the brain it is – unique to each individual, but with each brain structured from the same materials as every other brain.

Emotions are the primary colours from which the patterns of our lives are created and upon which our feelings, mindset and attitudes develop. We are continuously emotional. The bedrock of everything we do and are is emotional. Emotions underpin all our thoughts and actions. Without emotions we would be androids.

Emotions, basically speaking

The eight basic emotions are (see Table 1.1):

> *fear, anger, disgust, shame and sadness*
> *surprise/startle*
> *excitement/joy, trust/love*

Without trust would we invest ourselves in intimate relations? Without joy would we find life bearable? Without fear would we recognize danger? Without anger would we fight for what's important? Without disgust would we know what's poisonous? Without shame could we ever know what's right? Without sadness could we ever know who or what is important to us? Without surprise would we feel excited by all the possibilities in the world?

Of the eight basic emotions, five keep us safe and let us know about danger (top of Table 1.1), two get us closely involved positively with people and objects and action (bottom of Table 1.1), and one pushes us in either direction (centre of Table 1.1). The emotions of *fear, anger, disgust, shame* and *sadness* keep us safe or make us ready to deal with danger. They are the flight/fight/fright/freeze emotions related to escape/avoidance. *Excitement/ joy* and *trust/love* are the two emotions to do with growth through attachment and belonging. *Startle/surprise* can take us in the direction of either escape/avoidance or attachment. If the likelihood is that it's going to go in the direction of avoidance, then surprise appears as 'shock-horror' *startle*. If on the other hand the likelihood is that surprise is going in the direction of attachment, then it appears as 'oh-my-gosh' *delight*.

The numerical balance of the emotions is strongly in favour of the escape/ avoidance emotions: five avoidance emotions as against two attachment, and one falling on either side of the fence. In the wilds, fighting, fleeing or

TABLE 1.1   The eight basic emotions

8 basic universal emotions	Responses	Key biology
Fear Anger Disgust Shame Sadness	SURVIVAL Escape/Avoid/ Fright/Fight/Flight	STRESS Cortisol
Startle/ Surprise	SURVIVAL OR ATTACHMENT?	
Excitement/Joy Trust/Love	ATTACHMENT Wonder Frolic Growth	REWARD/PLEASURE Dopamine Noradrenaline Serotonin Oxytocin

freezing is, to put it mildly, very useful. Through fright we survive. In the sophisticated human jungle those responses can both be very useful but also cause big problems.

Socially we have come a long way from our distant social origins. But it's still our biological origins that drive us. When we understand that not surprisingly, but very confusingly, the escape/avoidance emotions are easier to trigger than the attachment/growth emotions, then we can easily see the single simple reason why organizations find it easier to run on fear than anything else. It's the emotion easiest to trigger *because* it's the one most closely connected with survival. It's also the fastest route to burnout.

From an organizational perspective, leaders who understand the eight emotions underpinning how we all think, act and feel can be much more effective. This is because they are conscious about their own emotions and consequently their behaviour, and they are also aware how their behaviour can trigger emotions in others. We will see that it is much more productive in an organization to trigger the attachment emotions of *excitement/joy* and *trust/love* than it is to encourage any of the fright/flight/fight emotions, with *fear* being the most destructive. These emotions will cause people to pay more attention to their own survival than to any business they have been asked to deliver. High-quality creativity takes place best when the *surprise* emotion is present, swinging into *excitement/joy*.

The next step is to understand how emotions underpin our feelings, but first we need to get a high-level understanding of how the brain works. We will go into the emotional underpinning of feelings in much more detail in Chapter 2.

What is the brain?

Until the late part of the 20th century it used to be thought that the brain was a switching system receiving and sending messages like a complex telephone switchboard. Now we know that that's much too simple a way of understanding how the brain is organized.

We are born with highly complex brain structures organized in many different parallel systems. This is probably true of non-human animals too, but the area of the brain concerned with complex thinking, logic and rational decision-making is probably only present in human brains. And even if some animals are capable of making choices, mammalian brains of other species have reached nowhere near the levels of sophistication of the human brain because they lack the capacity to represent experience through an adaptable language.

All non-human animals are endowed with instinctive reflex behaviours: nest-building or migration in birds, for instance; Atlantic salmon unerringly seeking out the rivers where they first hatched after three years away; honey bees collecting pollen and returning to the hive and communicating location and distance to other bees through a complex dance. Human brains, on the other hand, with their ability to be creative, contemplate the past, consider the future, make plans and change the environment to suit those plans, have developed along evolutionary lines that *maximize on the capacity to adapt*. This is an extraordinary evolutionary advantage. It is the basis of all human endeavours. It is what gives shape to hope and to despair, to dreams and to destruction. We will discuss more about this in Chapter 10.

Built from around 86 billion brain cells (neurons), the brain is a set of parallel systems, each with different functions. Though different parts of the brain have specific purposes, there are an almost infinite number of possibilities for making pathways through the brain along which messages can travel. Messages are transmitted through electrochemical signals across the gaps between the cells (synapses). The gaps are managed by particular chemicals called neurotransmitters (Figure 1.1).

FIGURE 1.1 The synapse: Where nerve impulses convert to chemical messages (neurotransmitters)

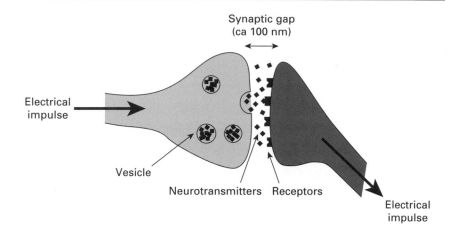

In various states, such as fatigue, depression or being in love, the synaptic neurochemicals facilitate or impede message transmission. This is also especially the case during all strong emotional reactions.

As neurons can be at rest or in a state of discharge there is a frequency and *pattern* to the electrical signals that constitutes the *code* used by neurons to transfer information from one location to another. So every simple and complex thing we human beings feel, think, and do is managed by these systems in the brain; systems which are continuously being fed by the monitoring of information from within the body itself as well as from the external world, and for most of which we have no awareness at all.

The main drivers for turning on or switching off these processes come from the emotions that are attached to the actual experience of relationships.

Let's get physical: what are feelings?

An emotion is *always accompanied by physiological reactions*. A quickening of the heartbeat, a churning stomach, sweating palms, trembling muscles are familiar to us all. We may laugh or weep, run for cover or be frozen to the spot, pound our fists in fury, strike out in defence, or make love with great and thoughtful passion. But these are only the ones that are strong enough for us to notice. For the hundreds of thousands of reactions and interactions that we have every day we will not have any awareness of the physiological reactions at all, *even though they are happening, and are managing our behaviour, forming or re-forming the basis of our future actions.*

What we all call 'feelings' are the refined combinations in conscious awareness of the underlying and usually non-conscious emotions. Here we are not referring to the 'feelings that get hurt' type of feelings, but to the combinations of emotions that generate a physiological reaction. They continuously underpin 'mindset' or 'attitude'. At a feeling level we may have physiological reactions so brief we hardly perceive them at all, such as when choosing what to wear for the day ahead and discriminating between one blouse and another, one tie or another. Feelings, often of a hardly-perceived kind, are the refinements and combinations of emotions that underlie all our choices. Our body's physiology has patterns for them all. If we paid more attention to these feelings we would connect more deeply with the emotions underpinning them.

I smell a rat

Of all the emotions, fear is the most basic and profound.

As Chapter 2 explains in more detail, human beings have essentially three parts to their brain: the thinking (neocortical) brain: the emotional (limbic system) brain; and the brain that keeps all our body systems working (the old – or reptilian – brain). Long before the evolution of brains that could think, let alone think about thinking, there were brains that sensed and felt and sniffed out danger. That was good for survival.

The brain is a hierarchical structure that has evolved ever so slowly over millions of years. In the beginning was the brain stem, out of which grew the olfactory lobe made up of cells 'that take in and analyse smell' (Goleman, 1995). That is how primitive forms of life knew what to eat, and what to avoid. The olfactory lobe, the smell-sensitive brain that is linked to the probing forked tongue of the snake and is sometimes called 'the snake brain', is the root of the emotional brain.

Further down the evolutionary road emerged the 'rhinencephalon', which literally means 'the nose brain'. This elegant piece of brain design was equipped with memory. Species could not only differentiate fish from fowl, and both from foul, but could *remember* as well.

With memory came the ability to make rudimentary decisions. Once this happened the evolutionary stage was set for the next leap forward in brain design, the neocortex: the thinking brain. This started using memory as the basis for conscious as against just reflex decisions. Thus emotion precedes, informs, and is inextricably linked to thinking, logic and decision-making and, above all, memory.

In his seminal work *Descartes' Error*, the neuroscientist Antonio Damasio shows how, when emotional centres of the brain are destroyed, the ability to be rational, to make decisions, and to make sense of the world is lost. To underline this one only has to think of Alzheimer's disease, in which the essential signs are loss of memory. And, sadly, once memory goes so does the 'Self' that it created.

With our sophisticated thinking brain informed by, and working in parallel with, our emotional brain, we humans can sniff out danger, respond to it, and come up with strategies to stay out of harm's way. Organizationally speaking it's pretty useful to be able to 'smell a rat'. But that means we have to be smart enough to pay attention to the signals picked up by our emotional radar system. All too often we push emotional signals out of the way, or discount them as being less important than our thoughts. *But it is the emotions that give us the data so that our thinking can create a rationality for our experience.* It is profoundly wrong thinking to believe (itself a feeling) that emotions will cloud our clear thoughts. In fact, the reverse happens – we lose essential information. The very best strategies are those informed by feelings as long as the feelings themselves are clear. If we have learned to suppress feelings and emotions then they will create confusion; *but they will be no less in play for having been suppressed.*

It may be an uncomfortable reality, but it is feelings, the product of our emotional system, not thinking, that rule our decision-making (Goleman, 1995; Brown and Hales, 2012). The best-quality decisions made in organizations all have an emotional component.

Born to be afraid

Fear plays an important part in how we develop into the person we are. We are all born to feel afraid: it is part of our hard-wiring. There are some scary things we're probably genetically *prepared* to be afraid of: big bangs; heights; snakes and spiders; lions, tigers and bears. Scientists call this 'preparedness theory' (LeDoux, 1996). Then there are the things we *learn* to be afraid of. That's where our parents come in (although they may get ignored pretty quickly).

Whatever the source of fear – learning or genetics – there is circuitry in the brain to ensure we not only learn what to be afraid of, but to *never ever* forget it; whether we're consciously aware of it or not. Some memories we are aware of (explicit memories) whilst some memories we are not (implicit memories); and some hidden memories may pop up into awareness – like when our memory is jogged.

The things we remember or can recall to memory are symbolically represented in a seahorse-shaped structure in the brain called the hippocampus. Buried deep inside the brain along with the hippocampus, behind the nose and eyes, are two little almond-shaped interconnected structures called the amygdala. They are perched above the brainstem in the ancient corridors of our emotional brain. One of the main roles of the amygdala is to keep us safe and ensure our survival. The amygdala receives information from the external world and processes it.

> The amygdala gets sensory information directly from the various sensory
> systems that process the external world. So the visual system, the auditory
> system, olfactory, touch, pain, and so forth. All of these kind of come together,
> or converge, in the amygdala.
>
> LeDoux (2010)

When the information received indicates imminent threat the amygdala immediately swings into action 'on the output side with all the systems involved in the emotional reactivity. So, when you encounter sudden danger, you might freeze, your blood pressure and heart rate begin to rise, stress hormones are released, all of these things happen as a result of outputs of the amygdala' (LeDoux, 2010).

The amygdala are like extraordinarily efficient radar scanners and air-traffic controllers combined, checking out in nanoseconds where trouble lies and commanding whatever action is necessary. The amygdala and hippocampus are also responsible for the release of hormones into the whole of our mind/body system. 'Although these are independent memory systems, they act in concert when emotion meets memory' (Phelps, 2004).

When it comes to fear, it is the amygdala that play the central role in the survival of all mammals – including us.

> Escaping from danger is something that all animals have to do to survive...
> What is important is that the brain has a mechanism for detecting the danger
> and responding to it appropriately and quickly... This is as true of a human
> animal as of a slimy reptile. And... evolution has seen fit to pretty much leave
> well enough alone inside the brain when it comes to these functions.
>
> LeDoux (1996)

When danger appears in whatever shape or guise – the hooves of a bull suddenly pounding in what was thought to be a safe field full of cows, or the sight of a boss we don't trust – messages are sent coursing through the brain along two different messaging systems. The 'quick and dirty route', or the 'low road' in Figure 1.2, is traversed in nanoseconds to the amygdala. The amygdala turn on all sorts of emergency bodily systems which activate the release of the body's fight-or-flight hormones; set off autonomic nervous system responses (racing heart, sweating palms, tightening stomach muscles); and inform the movement centres of the body to engage in appropriate behaviour (run, walk, crawl, hide, hit, bite, snarl, scream, freeze, close down and don't respond socially until the bastard has gone). Adrenaline cascades through the body, returns to the brain and, for reasons not fully understood, but certainly connected with survival, has an influence on *strengthening the memories being created there* (LeDoux, 1996).

In parallel with the quick and dirty route, danger signals are also sent through another neural system to the thinking brain, which takes a few moments to figure out what is going on. This is the process of making sense of something, and is the 'high road' in Figure 1.2. The signals are then forwarded on to the amygdala, but this time they arrive at the amygdala informed by thought. What follows is the ability to come up with some survival strategies or good decisions based on reason and logic. That's where the human animal has the evolutionary edge.

FIGURE 1.2 Tracing emotional pathways

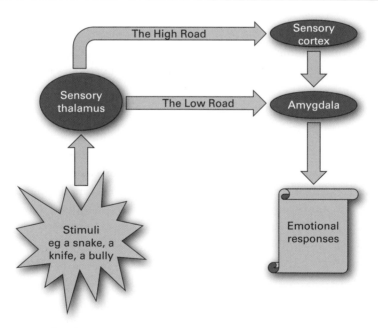

SOURCE: LeDoux (1996)

So the fear mechanisms in the brain function exactly the same whether you are threatened by a poisonous snake, a sharp knife, or the proverbial snake-in-the-grass of a boss. It is in these kinds of interpersonal environments where we get tripped up by evolution. The amygdala are not built to distinguish reality from metaphor. Dangers really do lurk in organizational corridors. But they are the kind of dangers that are best dealt with by clear thinking and calm emotions that have been integrated with thought – with intelligent emotions indeed.

Memories

One of the most basic and vital jobs the brain does is to capture, encode and store the simple and complex details of every single experience we have. What becomes a great wealth of learning and knowledge, which begins at birth and continues throughout life, forms every individual's unique auto-biographical memory (Damasio, 1999) and creates the unique patterning of each person's brain. Patterning is activated through the emotional transmissions that take place in the first minutes, days and months of life. It goes on being developed in exactly the same way *and it happens within the context of relationships.*

So the emotions, the primary colours of our feeling system, start laying down their patterns. They do so even before birth, but they are at their most powerfully effective in the active mother–child relationship. *What* we learn depends upon our experiences. *How* we learn is largely determined by the emotional quality of this relationship.

Early learning is suffused with emotional learning. There is simply no separating out experience from emotion. Our every experience is accompanied by basic emotions upon which our physical survival depends and eventual emotional maturity, through the capacity to regulate emotions appropriately, is based. And, most importantly, how we come to feel about ourselves, our sense of self, arises out of the emotional experiences of our earliest relationships.

The process most crucial to becoming an autonomous adult through psychological growth and development *is* the experience of relationships. This is where the simplicity and the complexity of being human always reside.

In this process fear is a powerfully effective learning tool. It's easier to let loose than love; and of the eight emotions it is the most basic and essential to survival. Like all emotions, fear is contagious; it can be caught with never a voice raised nor a word spoken. Looking into the face of fear, it is impossible not to feel fear for one's self, even if for a fleeting moment. Neuroscientific research suggests that across species the amygdala is prepared to respond to species-relevant cues (calls, facial expressions, body language) (LeDoux, 1996). In the animal kingdom non-verbal communication is essential for survival. In the human mother–baby relationship, non-verbal messages play a key role in early learning. An emotionally expressive face is worth a thousand words.

Much of what is learned and experienced early in life is unlikely to be remembered – consciously that is. But embedded in the amygdala are all the fear-based events we've ever experienced; stored as neuronal patterns, available to be triggered at any time throughout life – the most basic and powerful learning of any that we have. Each individual's experience of fear is vital in how we develop into the person each of us becomes.

We will go into more detail about how memories shape us in Chapter 3.

Becoming a person: Change and adaptability

> Fertile minds: from birth, a baby's brain cells proliferate wildly, making connections that may shape a lifetime of experience. The first three years are critical.
>
> Nash (1997)

The human brain is profoundly more complex and more sophisticated than the brains of any other species. The human baby is born with a brain consisting of 86 billion neurons. In the first days of life *trillions* of new connections are produced: many more than a person will need. Is it any wonder that babies sleep so much?

While the brain's hard-wiring provides the framework, the human brain itself is endowed with great plasticity, which means the brain is capable of adapting, learning and intellectually growing throughout the lifespan. Genetics, brain anatomy and inherited personality traits may be finite, but the possible range of human differences appears to be infinite (Posner and Levitin, 1997).

Through the first 10 years of life the 'use it or lose it' principle operates. By a process of pruning, probably commencing in the earliest days of life and continuing through adolescence, the brain loses those neuronal connections that are not being used, and forms and strengthens connections that are of particular importance in the growing brain of babies and children (Goleman, 1995). These are critical periods of development. The physical shape and design of the brain is significantly affected by emotional experience. Essentially, the crucial attachment relationship between mother and child helps sculpt the growing brain. If the emotional food of life is not provided or is withdrawn at critical developmental periods the emotional growth of the brain is likely to be stunted.

The expression and experience of all eight emotions gets played out throughout childhood; but it is the early experience of fear that takes centre stage in determining the internal feeling world of a person. Fear is the primary emotion overriding all others – and with good reason. If presented with a choice when your life is threatened, there is no choice to be made – saving your life is paramount. The decision is not made by your thinking brain, but by your emotional brain; the amygdala swings into survival mode before you even have time to understand what's happening. This is entirely relevant to organization life and survival as well. When fear is triggered at work, survival strategies take precedence over creativity, independent thinking, decision-making, attachment to the organization, and doing what's right vs doing what will please the boss. In a 'yes man' culture you can bet there's fear running rampant.

Because fear sticks in our memory systems long after the danger has receded, it is also an easy and powerful tool for both teaching and controlling. As we saw earlier, fear is accompanied by potent chemical surges from brain to body and back to brain again. Thus the laying down of fear-related memories in the amygdala is strengthened. We will explore the corrosive effects of persistent and pervasive fear in Chapter 4.

Of course it is essential in the natural course of a childhood to learn about dangers and to remember them throughout life: playing with fire, talking to strangers, eating poisonous substances, leaping before looking. The Grimm Brothers' fairy tales were written with survival in mind. For German children living on the edge of a forest The Big Bad Wolf was not just a metaphor.

Learning what to fear doesn't just start at the beginning of life. Scientific research on the developing foetus has established that the brain is a working operational system in the womb – subject to the same external stimuli that affects the brain circuitry of a newborn (Nash, 1997). Traumas to the mother undoubtedly affect the amygdala-linked systems in the developing foetus. A seriously anxious or depressed mother-to-be risks her child-to-be becoming suffused with some of the same emotions.

For the baby and pre-verbal toddler, learning happens in the non-conscious realm of brain and mind. Memories laid down in the amygdala are symbolic, implicit (out of awareness) and, if graspable at all, would be more in the nature of images. To retrieve memories and be consciously aware requires the ability to think and be verbal.

It can be quite difficult to understand the difference between conscious awareness and non-conscious memories. A basic tenet of brain/mind/emotions/physiology/psychology is that consciousness is just the tip of the mental iceberg. Everything that is available to conscious awareness is in the first instance non-conscious; but most everything in the realm of the non-conscious will never be available to conscious awareness.

There are an infinite variety of things that occur in the internal milieu moment by moment that support our survival but of which we may never be aware. Although all our bodily organs and functions are regulated and monitored by the brain we generally have no awareness of them – unless something goes wrong.

> The brain accomplishes its behavioural goals in the absence of robust awareness. And absence of awareness is the rule of mental life, rather than the exception, throughout the animal kingdom. If we do not need conscious feelings to explain what we would call emotional behaviour in some animals, then we do not need them to explain the same behaviour in humans. Emotional responses are, for the most part, generated unconsciously.
>
> LeDoux (1996)

With the acquisition of language comes the beginning of accessible (explicit) memories and, in parallel, of self-awareness. The memory system of the brain is hierarchical: the implicit amygdala-based memory storage is connected to the primitive emotional brain; the explicit hippocampal-based memory storage system is connected to the sophisticated thinking brain. And both are connected to each other. But it is entirely possible, and happens not infrequently, that fear-based emotional reactions can arise from the non-conscious and be entirely to do with experiences of which the person has no memory. That's why sometimes we can have emotional reactions that don't seem to make any sense at all. They do to the brain, of course, but not to the conscious self. The brain operates on the 'What You See Is All There Is' principle (Kahneman, 2011).

Saying that early life experiences help shape the person is perhaps stating the obvious. It's a long way from agreeing with that statement, however, to being certain about cause–effect consequences in any particular person. Babies do not come into the world entirely as a blank slate, for intra-uterine life has been preparing them for the world their mother inhabits; but they also need an enormous amount of input to develop the potential that is there when they do emerge into the world. Whatever the nature of a person, the quality of nurture cannot be understated in its effects upon the developing person. The foundations of self-esteem, self-reliance and self-confidence are built upon the experience of fear contained within the mother–child relationship. A bullying father is bad news for any child; a tyrannical, vengeful mother is a recipe for disaster. Neuroscientific studies on the brains of babies strongly suggest that the experience of verbal and physical displays of violence leave indelible scars on the developing brain.

> There is now no doubt that the dendritic growth and synaptogenesis of the post-natally developing brain is 'experience-sensitive'... and 'experience-dependent'... It should be emphasized that the primary caregiver is the most important source and modulator of stimulation in the infant's environment and the primal wellspring of the child's experience... Scheflen (1981) argues that the neurodevelopmental processes of dendritic proliferation and synaptogenesis, which are responsible for post-natal brain growth are critically influenced by events at the interpersonal and intrapersonal levels.
>
> Schore (1994)

Yet inherited potential will remain and be just that if the emotional fuel of growth is corrupted. Or it will find awkward ways of presenting itself to the world.

Christian was the son of the boss and would one day run a large organization, a kingdom. It was his birthright. It was not a question of 'if', but 'when'. Christian was two years old when his mother died. His father, King Christian VI, was a drunk and a womaniser. He took no interest at all in his son's upbringing; that was left to his advisors whose only interest in the young prince was to rob him entirely of his will and power. Their methods were humiliation, subjugation, and degradation. Their tools were whips and words and terror. Shortly before his 17th birthday Christian VII became king. By this time he was considered mad. For those who encountered him as an adult it was considered that beneath the chaos there was an undeveloped but fine intellect. If only...

Enquist and Nunnally (2002)

King Christian VII is a rather dramatic example of the damage fear can do. Early fear is more typically of a less intense kind with less drastic, but certainly quite debilitating, results. Constant nagging and criticism can do the same damage on the developing mind as careless slips of the sculptor's chisel on marble. Pervasive low levels of fear permeate the developing psyche and dampen the creative spirit. And subtle use of fear messages can resonate through life:

You lost your ability for doing things in childhood... It all began with your inability to put on your socks and ended by your inability to live.

Goncharov (1859)

Whatever the form fear takes in early life, it sets up patterns that resonate throughout life. Because the kind of fear we're especially interested in here – the kind that creeps around the corridors of organizations – is relationship-led, the patterns that relationships have set up have profound implications for the quality of our relationships as adults. After all, the first bosses we ever have are called parents.

Patterns

Me and my patterns

How many times have you told yourself that next time you're going to do things differently; that you're not going to fall into the same old traps; that you're going to learn from past mistakes; that you're going to choose relationships that are good for you; that you're not going to let someone else's bad behaviour get you down? And despite all these inner determinations and promises to yourself, how many times have you found yourself falling into the same old patterns? Why are patterns so difficult to break?

Brain, mind and body are all cut from the same genetic cloth: they operate by the same principles of physiology and biology. For that matter, so does our psychology, which arises from the extraordinary neural patterns created by systems in the brain.

Patterning is a basic function of brains – human or otherwise. Very systematic patterns of interactions between neurons in various brain areas create order where chaos could reign by connections made by billions of neurons. These are called *neural* patterns (LeDoux, 1996).

Neural patterns, for reasons neuroscientists do not yet understand, give rise to *mental* patterns or 'images'. The neuroscientist Antonio Damasio (Damasio, 1999) uses the term 'images' in a metaphorical sense in that they include sensory input from the body (tone, touch, smell, colour, shape); emotional input; spatial and temporal relationships; actions and movement; processes and entities both concrete and abstract.

Because there is no one word to describe highly complex neural processes that result in the thoughts we have running through our minds every second of every day, Damasio has adopted the phrase 'the movies in our minds'; this is what neuroscientists think about when they are exploring the neural basis of object representation (how people, places and things get represented in our minds).

Patterns – whether they are related to neural and mental processes or to human relationships – provide stability. And stability is essential to the survival of any organism.

> Life is carried out inside a boundary that defines a body. Life and the life urge exist inside a boundary... that separates the internal environment from the external environment... If there is no boundary there is no body, and if there is no body, there is no organism. Life needs a boundary.
>
> Damasio (1999)

Embedded in our patterns are our perceptions. How we perceive things is by and large built upon memories – some consciously remembered but the majority of which are stored away for use on an as-, when- and if-needs-be basis. Part and parcel of our memories and perceptions are emotions, the whole gamut of them, with fear at the top of the list. The way we perceive things, people, places and events is based on what we believe to be so. If we have a frightening experience then it is highly probably we will view any similar experience as a threat.

But if we are likely to avoid fearful people, places and things then why is it that we keep repeating behaviours that are potentially damaging to us? Well here's where things get a little tricky.

When we are young we learn how to survive. Children are brilliant at coming up with good survival strategies. If the name of the game is survival, then successful strategies are crucial. Children don't have a choice about the world they're born into, and if the world a child inhabits is fraught with peril, then the child will find ways to survive in that world. As night follows day, dangerous places and threatening people become ordinary commonplace events. They create the familiar terrain of life.

Stability and familiarity are entwined; you simply can't have one without the other. Any variation in the environment, any change, threatens stability and feels plain scary. Venturing into the unknown is potentially dangerous. We're not just talking people here. Even amoebae are wired for life – for staying alive – they just don't know it.

We are creatures of habit and habits are not easy to break.

As we move from childhood into the adult world of work, the familiar beckons. Often without knowing it, we are drawn like magnets to environments that we perceive to be safe; that feel familiar. And if familiar = danger, then people can unwittingly find themselves in places permeated by fear and filled with danger.

Patricia's patterns

A case in point is Patricia.

Patricia grew up in a suburban community with traditional, old-fashioned family values. Unfortunately those values were not lived out in any real sense within her family. Patricia's mother was doting and attentive. She was also highly stressed, depressed, disillusioned, frightened and very angry. Patricia's father was a womaniser. He adored Patricia but he was rarely at home; never on Sundays and rarely at mealtimes. Patricia's mother said that the most important thing in the world to her was family. But she would, on a daily basis, bemoan how marriage had ruined her life; how men were worthless cads; how you could never trust a man – not even as far as you could throw him; she also suffered from frequent panic attacks. She remained in the marriage to provide security for Patricia. She was forever reminding Patricia that she'd sacrificed her own happiness for Patricia's well-being.

Patricia was torn between feeling trapped by responsibilities to her mother and her wish to run away. In addition, she looked up to her father, revered him, and resented her mother's attempts to make her hate him. Patricia envied her father's freedom. Patricia was bright, clever, crafty and beautiful. She excelled at school. And she had a way with words – they provided her with an escape clause. But at the age of 16 Patricia's world collapsed. She arrived home from school to find her mother in turmoil, clutching photographs of Patricia's father in compromising positions with another woman. Patricia ran to her father's shop and proceeded to tear everything off the shelves. Her rage knew no bounds. She didn't speak to him again for 40 years – not until he was on his deathbed.

At the first possible opportunity, Patricia escaped to live and work abroad. When she returned home several years later she took up a career in a field dominated by men at the top and women underneath; the men called the shots and the women did all the work. The men were bullying, crude, arrogant and dismissive of women. They turned up for meetings to dictate policies and procedures and then disappeared. Patricia was incredibly successful. She knew how to work around these men. And then, at the height of her career, she challenged her chairman – raged at him actually just as she had done to her father, wrecking his shop – and was unceremoniously parachuted out of the organization. But she picked herself up, continued to build her career and enjoyed even greater success in another organization in the same kind of business.

Patricia never married; she considered it a fate worse than death. She suffered debilitating agoraphobia, which could only be controlled by anti-depressants. She hung around with men who destroyed other women's lives; they were her best friends and she liked them; they were bright, fun, interesting and incredibly good company. She was one of the boys. Patricia had a wonderful group of women friends but she failed to grasp how they could stay in what she perceived as hopeless marriages. Patricia hated making lunch and dinner commitments – especially on Sundays. And if she did make dates, she'd often fail to appear. She was constantly disappointed in love. She was often imprisoned by agoraphobia.

Once bitten, twice shy

If patterns are so deeply imbedded in our brains, does that mean we are stuck with them for life? Whilst it's true that you may not be able to teach an old dog new tricks, fortunately we human beings have highly sophisticated brains that are hard-wired to adapt to changing environments. It is likely that we are the only species evolution has equipped with a brain that both thinks and feels and tries to integrate the two; the only species that is capable of knowing what we are thinking and feeling as we are thinking and feeling it. We are the only species who can be deliberately adaptive, who can creatively express ourselves in words, through art, and in music.

Emotions are very powerful but so is our ability to look inside ourselves, to learn from experience, to make sense of the world, to figure out new strategies, and to find new ways of doing things.

'We can't solve problems by using the same kind of thinking we used when we created them' (Einstein, 1938). Albert Einstein, in his infinite wisdom, applied the scientist in him to come up with some truisms about life. And, in a sense, we are all scientists forming hypotheses about the world we live in and the relationships we form.

In childhood, when patterns are being formed and taking shape, the assumptions we make about the world – our hypotheses – are based on experience and learning. We learn what is safe and what is to be feared. If a child is attacked by a dog, he or she will assume all dogs are dangerous; that's much the safest thing. Consequent behaviours are based on predictions of future events; predictions are based on experience; experience forms perceptions; perceptions are infused with emotion. In other words – once bitten, twice shy.

Patterns, assumptions, hypotheses and predictions determine behaviour throughout the lifespan. Logic enables us to adapt – to come up with new ways of coping and surviving.

Organizations have patterns too

In hierarchical business organizations, policies, procedures and strategies are determined and driven by the people at the top. But when we're talking about people the exact reverse is true. And business organizations would do well to think more about the real drivers of business – the emotions that charge a person with energy or drain a person dry.

Organizations have patterns too.

> Culture implies some level of structural stability in the group... When we say that something is 'cultural' we imply that it is not only shared but deep and stable. By deep I mean less conscious and therefore less tangible and less visible. The other element that lends stability is *patterning* or integration... that lies at a deeper level. Culture somehow implies that rituals, climate, values and behaviours bind together into a coherent whole. This patterning or integration is the *essence* of what we mean by culture.
>
> Schein (1992)

As organizations attempt to become global, diverse and highly adaptive, leadership development and change programmes abound. Attention is being focused, and rightly so, on 'organizational culture'. But there is a misguided belief that if you write a mission statement, set forth organizational values, change your leader, and put some new HR policies and procedures in place, then culture change will follow.

When we talk about 'culture' what we're really talking about is the emotional climate: 'how things feel around here'. Which in turn affects 'the way we do things around here' (Schein, 1992). And just like with people, organizational change is an awesome undertaking that can destabilize and be potentially destructive.

Adaptation

Adaptation is about modifying internal processes so that they become better suited to the external environment. Change is about becoming something altogether different. We are not hard-wired to change, but we are built to adapt. Adaptation is a natural process and essential to survival. And that holds true for organizations as well as people.

In the hierarchical organization of the brain the main drivers are contained in systems at the bottom. Evolution built the brain from the bottom up, not from the top down. And no matter how brilliant, gifted and educated a person may be, if the internal milieu is flooded with fear and loathing, those destructive emotions have the potential to cause mayhem and havoc – internally and externally. Bullying bosses may rise through the organization on their cunning and know-how, but oh, the damage these people do to anyone who gets in their line of fire. Nerds have feelings too, and safety in cyberspace is continually threatened by angry techies bent on destruction and acting out their rage on a global scale.

When we're thinking about tackling disruptive behaviour patterns, the best place to start is at the source – the emotions. The creation of adaptive behaviours is a bottom-up strategy.

Many management gurus will happily charge you great sums of money to teach you how to build self-confidence by changing your thinking. They'll advise you to talk to yourself, tell yourself how wonderful you are, tell yourself how powerful you are, and tell yourself you're a truly happy person. If you've ever tried 'the power of positive thinking' you'll know that whilst it does have some instant feel-good results, at the end of the day you're left feeling just as you did at the beginning. Instant gratification does feed immediately into the reward system in the brain, but real shifts in sense of self – in self-confidence – are built on insight. Insight means looking inward, knowing what you're feeling when you're feeling it, and why.

The major airlines figured out a long time ago that people afraid of flying were not going to be won over by relaxation exercises and lectures on the safety of flying, and thinking positively. No amount of chanting 'flying is safe, I'm not afraid to fly' rids anyone of their fears – irrational or not. So airlines instituted programmes to teach people concrete facts about how planes are built, what keeps them up there, and what all those scary sounds mean (Watson, 2001). Knowledge is power and the same sorts of understanding about what makes you tick will set the stage for adaptation, and for creating different patterns of behaviour to suit a changing world.

Behaviour patterns have been given a bad rap and patterns are essential tools in our survival kit. So it's as important to know what is working as it is identifying and tackling the patterns you're tripping over. A sound operating principle is to build on strengths rather than operate from weaknesses.

Scientists examine the world through a magnifying glass to see as much detail as possible. Patterns also need that kind of metaphorical microscopic examination to identify the emotions underlying them and the assumptions they're operating from:

- When the pattern was in the making, usually quite early in childhood, what was going on in the external world to trigger the emotions that motivated the behaviour pattern?

- As patterns are there to create safety and promote survival, what was good about the pattern, what benefits did you accrue, what value did it have?

If patterns are part and parcel of who we are, is it realistic to think we can make the significant adaptations necessary to think, feel and act differently? The fatalistic view would be acceptance of the status quo – but that could be fatal. The belief that no amount of knowledge actually ever changes anything is likely to be a self-fulfilling prophecy: will and determination, whether directed towards positive or negative outcomes, is a prediction about the future. Prediction is a function of brain.

The miraculous evolutionary design of brains (human and otherwise) includes an internal emulator – mechanisms that make predictions, nanosecond by nanosecond, of the body in the world out there.

> The 'Self' is very much tied to what [Patricia Churchland] terms an internal emulator. This emulator uses a cognitive image of the body in the environment to give us the ability to try out possible actions in response to various situations. We use our emulators all the time – from deciding what to order in a restaurant to debating the outcome of US military action. The evolution of the emulator might have been the crucial leap that gave rise to human consciousness.
>
> Volk (2003)

In other words, when deciding what to buy for dinner your brain is imagining what the food will taste like, visualizing how it will look, imagining how you will feel eating it, imagining how hungry you're going to be, deciding if you want to buy enough to have left-overs, imagining how your friends or family might feel about the food. Your decisions will be based on predictions of how the meal will be.

Some predictions we are aware of, whilst many we are not. Memory is built on the storage of vast numbers of emotionally coloured patterns that inform everything we do; from driving a car, to baking a cake, to tying a knot, to making holiday plans. Predictions of the future – and that future may be only an intake of breath away – are based on learning and memory. (You'll choose your menu based on prior experience of the food you're going to eat.) Our perceptions, based on past experience, inform the choices we make. If you've had a bad experience somewhere, you are likely to associate that place with bad luck; it's unlikely you'll want to return to the scene of an accident.

We tend to think of memory as connected to things that have happened and people we have met. But memory is concerned with ever so much more than mental states of mind. Memory is a biological necessity. Our cells have memories too.

Contained within every living organism is a vast amount of knowledge that is used throughout the lifespan to promote survival.

> This fact – that enormous amounts of information can be carried in an exceedingly small space – is, of course, well known to the biologists, and resolves the mystery which existed before we understood all this clearly, of how it could be that, in the tiniest cell, all of the information for the organization of a complex creature such as ourselves can be stored. All this information – whether we have brown eyes, or whether we think at all, or that in the embryo the jawbone should first develop with a little hole in the side so that later a nerve can grow through it – all this information is contained in a very tiny fraction of the cell in the form of long-chain DNA molecules in which approximately 50 atoms are used for one bit of information about the cell.
>
> Feynman (1999)

Inside each of us are more than ample resources to facilitate adaptation: innate and accrued knowledge we don't even know we know. Looking inward, gaining insight, understanding patterns and the emotions contained within them is fundamental to self-development.

Adaptation and learning go hand in hand. Self-development, becoming self-made, is a learning process. Much of what we 'know' is inherent, and much acquired through experience, but whether the learning is at a cellular level, has its origins in genetics, is connected to environment and culture, is enforced by parents and teachers, or voluntarily chosen, our brains evolved by learning and for learning. Learning modifies our neural networks. And whilst hard-wiring and software are useful metaphors to help us understand what we're born with vs the things we are taught, our brains are far more complex than computers and we individuals entirely more complicated, interesting, malleable and unique than computers. There are a myriad of influences that can act upon and modify functions of the brain. Some of those, like mind-altering substances, we can choose whilst others, like hostile take-overs, just happen.

Of utmost importance in becoming self-made – developing the leader in you – is your management of self-knowledge. That is, the things you know that you may or may not even know you know and that can inform your choices, decisions and relationships on a daily basis.

References

Brown, PT and Hales, B (2012) Neuroscience for neuro-leadership: Feelings not thinking rule decision-making, *Developing Leaders*, issue 6, pp 28–37

Damasio, AR (1994) *Descartes' Error: Emotion, reason and the human brain*, 1st edn, GP Putnam's Sons, New York

Damasio, AR (1999) *The Feeling of What Happens*, 1st edn, Houghton Mifflin Harcourt, New York

Darwin, C (1872) *The Expression of the Emotions in Man and Animals*, new edn, ed P Ekman, HarperCollins, London

Einstein, A (1938) Albert Einstein's commencement address: Swarthmore College Sesquicentenial, available at http://swat150.swarthmore.edu/1938-albert-ein-steins-commencement-address.html [accessed 5 December 2014]

Enquist, PO (2002) *The Physician's Visit*, trans T Nunnally, The Harvill Press, London

Feynman, R (1999) *The Pleasure of Finding Things Out*, ed J Robbins, Basic Books, New York

Goleman, D (1995) *Emotional Intelligence*, Bantam Books, New York, Toronto, London, Sydney, Auckland

Goncharov, I (1859) *Oblomov*, trans N Duddington, Everyman's Library

Kahneman, D (2011) *Thinking, Fast and Slow*, Farrar, Straus and Giroux, New York

LeDoux, J (1996) *The Emotional Brain*, Simon and Schuster, New York

LeDoux, J (2010) The amygdala in 5 minutes, *Big Think*, available at http://bigthink.com/videos/the-amygdala-in-5-minutes [accessed 6 December 2014]

Nash, JM (1997) Fertile minds, *Time*, 3 February 1997

Phelps, EA (2004) Human emotion and memory: Interactions of the amygdala and hippocampal complex, *Current Opinion in Neurobiology*, **14**, pp 198–202, available at: www.sciencedirect.com [accessed 13 April 2014]

Posner, MI and Levitin, DJ (1997) *Mind and Brain Sciences in the 21st Century*, ed RL Solso, A Bradford Book, MIT Press Cambridge, MA; London, UK

Schein, EH (1992) *Organizational Culture and Leadership*, 4th edn, Jossey-Bass, San Francisco, CA

Schore, AN (1994) *Affect Regulation and the Origin of the Self: The neurobiology of emotional development*, Lawrence Erlbaum Associates, Hills Dale, NJ

Volk, Tyler (2003) *The Self: From soul to brain*, eds J LeDoux, J Debiec and H Moss, New York Academy of Sciences, New York

Watson, C (2001) 'Fear of flying' class helps even the unafraid, *Star Tribune*, available at http://www.startribune.com/lifestyle/travel/11285421.html

The brain

02

Introduction

> Emotions, after all, are the threads that hold mental life together. They define who we are in our own mind's eye as well as in the eyes of others. What could be more important to understand about the brain than the way it makes us, happy, sad, afraid, disgusted, or delighted.
>
> LeDoux (1996)

This chapter is about what happens in our brain when we're afraid. Fear, along with all the eight basic emotions (trust/love, excitement/joy, fear, anger, disgust, shame, sadness and surprise), causes changes in the brain. These changes may happen throughout the brain; they affect the make-up of brain chemistry, create changes in mental states and are experienced physically in the body.

In this chapter we explore brain structures and their functions; the cells that comprise the brain; neural pathways and wiring; the hierarchical make-up of the brain; brain systems and their connections; and brain chemistry and its role in our emotional experiences.

Using stories from organizations, we explore what might be happening in the brain when fear shakes our very sense of self.

Pure imagination

The capacity of the human brain to turn imagination into magic is not a miracle. It is neuroscience, plain and simple, tapping into the complexities of the human brain and turning dreams into reality.

When John Donaghue graduated from Brown University in 1976 he thought he'd like to pursue postgraduate studies into how the brain works. This big idea got honed down to the study of how thoughts become actions. John Donaghue is now a professor of engineering and neuroscience at Brown University. The technologies created in his laboratory allowed him to make a machine he called BrainGate. This clever bit of kit is implanted into the motor cortex of a paralysed patient. A tiny sensor detects and decodes brain signals and their relationship to movement. As the patient imagines movement the corresponding signals, via a plug attached to the scalp, are sent to a computer that is programmed to turn the instructions into actions (Dreifus, 2011).

On 12 June 2014 a paraplegic teenager got up from his wheelchair in midfield and kicked a ball to open the 2014 World Cup in Brazil. He was wearing a mind-controlled robotic exoskeleton suit developed by neuro-engineer Miguel Nicolelis of Duke University, North Carolina (Nicolelis, 2012; Sample, 2014). Like BrainGate, the exoskeleton suit turns brain waves into action. Miguel Nicolelis believes that in the not-too-distant future wheel-chairs will become a thing of the past.

In September 2014 researchers at Harvard University reported that brain-to-brain communication between humans based in India and France had been achieved. The signals were sent by binary code thousands of miles via the internet electromagnetically. Through non-invasive brain stimulation the person receiving the messages saw flashes of light in their peripheral vision corresponding to the signals that were transmitted (Anon, 2014).

Welcome to your brain on emotion

To understand how fear and other emotions affect an organization, we must know how the seat of the emotions – the brain – works. And to do that, we have to examine the impact of fearful experiences on human brain development.

Neuroscientists tracking the human brain are developing detailed models of how our 86 billion brain cells fire and wire. Increasingly sophisticated brain scanners produce vivid images of our brains at work. Brain-imaging techniques track the workings of the brain in real time – as we think, learn and remember. Cell biologists are demonstrating how experience modifies perception, which in turn changes the neurochemistry controlling the way genes express themselves behaviourally.

The new science of the mind deepens our understanding of how human relationships build brains and the lifelong emotional and behavioural impact that relationships have on the brain – for better or worse. A study reported in the *Washington Post* on 12 September 2013 found that childhood abuse and neglect can so shape a child's brain that the effects can last a lifetime (Schulte, 2013).

The application of this knowledge is crucial for leaders and managers. It has important implications for the way we think about people at work, their relationship to the workplace, and their relationship to each other and to customers too. The brain-savvy organization will put high value on a relationship culture and become wary of simplistic, performance-driven and transactional cultures.

Advances in understanding the development of the human brain mean that 21st-century neuroscience puts emotion right at the heart of the effective functioning of the human brain.

Contextually speaking

How does the brain work? What is the mind? Does the brain create the mind? What is the 'Self'? What is consciousness? Can consciousness be reduced to neurons? Where do feelings come from? What are emotions and why do we have them? What links the brain to emotions, feelings, thoughts and behaviours? Through the millennia, answers to such questions have proved elusive at best. Scientists, philosophers, doctors, psychologists, artists, poets, playwrights and writers have sought to understand mind and brain. It has been a long, difficult journey.

Scientists and doctors tried to understand the brain through explorations of neuroanatomy and to draw links between brain and body. Written in 1700 BC and based on texts dating back to 3000 BC, the Edwin Smith Surgical Papyrus is the earliest known medical document and contains the first known written reference to the brain, its anatomy and the effects of brain injury on different areas of the body (Anon, nd). In the 1st century BC Hippocrates was the first to speculate that the left and right halves of the brain were endowed with 'mental duality' and capable of working independently (Anon, nd).

Philosophers have grappled with trying to understand the nature of mind and the relationship between mind and body. Born in 427 BC, Plato believed the brain to be the seat of mental processes (Anon, nd). Born in 384 BC Aristotle believed that the heart, not the brain, was the centre of sensations and movement (Gross, 1995). René Descartes was born in France in 1596 and is considered to be the father of modern philosophy. His belief in 'dualism' – that mind and body are split – formed the basis of understanding the brain from the 17th century to the present day. For Descartes, psychological processes were not rooted in the physical brain but were nonphysical processes of soul and mind (Churchland and Sejnowski, 1992).

In 1859 Charles Darwin published *On the Origin of Species by Means of Natural Selection*. Darwin's theories caused a revolution in the way people thought about themselves, the natural world and the universe. His theories serve as the foundation for modern biology, neurophysiology and psychology (Wiley, 1998). In *The Expression of Emotions in Man and Animals* (1872) Darwin set forth his thesis that there is a set of specific fundamental emotions that are universal in human beings and animals; and that the emotions are expressed overtly through behaviour in all species.

Darwin gathered his information from both personal observations of the world around him and from information from colleagues working with people around the world. His sources reported on how emotion was expressed by infants, children, those suffering from physical ailments and mental illness, and also included animals. Darwinian theory profoundly changed scientific thinking and the nature of scientific exploration in the latter part of the 19th century, as it continues to do today.

Following Darwin, John Hughlings Jackson, the 'father of British neurology', developed his theories on the workings of the brain along evolutionary lines (Morrish, 1999), linking evolutionary ideas to an understanding of neural function (Gillett and Franz, 2013).

Born in 1835, Jackson was a simple man with straightforward ideas about the brain. His interest in brain organization was his great passion and his theories were to revolutionize scientific and medical understandings of the brain. By 1878 he had created a conceptual framework for scientific neurology.

He achieved international scientific acclaim based on his research into the diagnosis of epilepsy. Ironically, his wife Elizabeth suffered a series of epileptic seizures that led to her death. Through the course of her illness Jackson carefully observed the patterns of the seizures. He was to identify the movement of seizures from one brain region to another as being connected to a corresponding series of body parts (York and Steinberg, 2007; Sweeney, 2009).

Jackson was a pioneer – his ideas were radical. The prevailing thinking of the time was informed by Descartes' belief that all that happens in the realm of the human mind is quite apart from mechanistic bodily functions (Damasio, 1994). Jackson understood that there must exist a relationship between brain and mind; the sophisticated human brain consisting of psychical and physical systems acting in concert; that neural systems involved in emotions, thoughts, feelings and actions are linked. He grounded the functions of the nervous system as a sensorimotor machine hierarchically arranged according to Darwinian theory. Drawing from the work of Herbert Spencer, he believed that higher life forms evolved from lower ones (York and Steinberg, 2011).

Jackson understood the complexities of the highly sophisticated human brain as a product of neural evolution and development; that mind emerged from physical brain systems; that everything in the psychological realm had its basis in the physical.

For Hughlings Jackson mental processes were functions of the brain. Thus, psychology emanates from neurobiological systems. He crucially identified that specific areas of the brain are connected to specific areas of the body. He described the brain as having three distinct evolutionary levels. Contained at every level and through to the highest levels of brain systems are all the components of the lower levels; as each level evolved it incorporated functions of the lower levels (Hughlings Jackson, 1884; York and Steinberg, 2011).

The three Jacksonian brain levels are:

- lower level: anterior spinal horns and motor nerve nuclei;
- middle level: motor cortex and basal ganglia;
- highest level: 're-re-represents the body', consisting of the premotor (frontal) cortex.

Jackson hypothesized that speech underlies thinking and reasoning as well as being intricately connected to action. He further connected emotions to action.

Jacksonian ideas are critically important. They are the foundations of current neurological thinking. They now inform every area of neuroscience, including the disciplines of neurology, psychiatry and psychology. His papers are the basis of the discipline of clinical neurophysiology. It was Jackson's research that paved the way for the development of Sigmund Freud's theories.

Hughlings Jackson developed his theories from direct observation of neurological patients. Today, neuroscientists have the benefit of modern technology that allows them to peer directly into the human brain as it thinks, feels and acts.

The emotion connection

Late in the 19th century conceptual models of self, underpinned by psyche and soma (mind and body), were hypothesized separately by two giants of psychology, Sigmund Freud and William James. Their innovative ideas radically changed our understanding of the human mind and the role of emotions in thinking and acting (Deigh, 2001). They linked the development of personality and self to the relationships human beings have with other people – for example, how people relate to each other in an organization. Through the 20th century these theories have been further developed and elaborated upon by psychotherapists, psychologists, sociologists and, most recently, neuroscientists.

Born in 1842, William James is known as the 'father of American psychology'. Following Darwin, James considered links between mind and emotions, and how emotions were expressed by the body and in behaviours. He puzzled over how contemporary physiologists, exploring the brain's associations between sensation and motor elements, ignored the emotions in their investigations; how psychologists were mainly concerned with processes underlying perception and volition; how philosophers failed to include emotion in their dispassionate treatises.

For William James, emotions arise in mind and body; the bodily responses accompanying emotions are intrinsically linked:

> Objects of rage, love, fear etc not only prompt a man to outward deeds, but provoke characteristic alterations in his attitude and visage, and affect his breathing, circulation, and other organic functions in specific ways... fear betrays itself in voice and colour, though one may suppress all other sign.
>
> James (1981, p 1058)

William James grew up in a family surrounded by the intellectual elite of the time. His father was a wealthy theologian, his brother the novelist Henry James, his sister the diarist Alice James, and his godfather Ralph Waldo Emerson. Trained as a physician, James spent most of his career at Harvard turning to the disciplines of physiology, philosophy and psychology. He introduced the first psychology course in the United States, at Harvard. Spending most of his career at Harvard, in 1890 James published *The Principles of Psychology*. In his 1,200-page masterpiece James set forth his ideas about theory of mind, stream of thought, consciousness of self, attention, perception, memory, imagination, instinct, will and the emotions.

Following Darwin and Hughlings Jackson, James considered the hierarchical structure of the brain – brains that evolved from lower and higher centres.

In the latter part of the 19th century Freud developed a theory of psychoanalysis drawn from his early work as a neuroscientist; his hypothesis was that psychological mental processes arise from non-conscious neurobiological systems. His theories were informed by Darwin's *On the Origin of Species* and *The Expression of Emotions in Man and Animals*, and the writings of Hughlings Jackson.

Freud was first and foremost a neurologist. In *Project for a Scientific Psychology* (Freud, 1895), he attempted to reconcile neurophysical knowledge of brain functioning and neuroanatomy with his revolutionary ideas about neuropsychic processes. Freud believed that, one day, neuroscience would be able to describe the dynamics of psychological processes. 'We must recollect that all our provisional ideas in psychology will presumably some day be based on an organic substructure' (Freud, 1914, p 78 quoted by Solms and Saling, 1986, p 413).

For most of the 20th century scientists and psychologists did not really know what to make of emotions; they couldn't be measured, seen, observed, experimented on or assigned to brain systems. And there was something mythical and mystical about emotions that was unappealing to scientific research. Emotions were seen as 'soft', not observable, subjective and not subject to scientific scrutiny. Psychologists, psychiatrists, neurologists and philosophers of the mind focused instead on theories of cognition, perception, computation and appraisal (de Sousa, 2003).

For example, in the 1890s Russian psychologist Ivan Pavlov's experimental work with dogs led to his discovery of the processes of classical conditioning. Pavlov showed how dogs could be conditioned to salivate to the sound of a bell – not a stimulus that would usually make a dog salivate – when the sound of the bell had been regularly paired with food. The spotlight fell on the way experience creates connections that control behaviour.

Following Pavlov, the American psychologist James Watson hypothesized that behaviour rather than consciousness was the foundation of human psychology; that all human psychology could be explained by patterns of stimuli and response; that there is no such thing as mind and consciousness (McLeod, 2007). In the 1950s the behaviourist and Harvard professor of psychology, B F Skinner, developed his theories of operant conditioning or reward-related behaviour. Whilst recognizing the existence of internal mental states, Skinner understood behaviour by looking at its causes and consequences. Operant conditioning changes behaviour through reinforcement; behaviours are likely to be repeated if there is positive reinforcement; behaviours are likely to be weakened or extinguished through punishment.

Following behaviourism, came the cognitive revolution. Cognitive psychological theories are concerned with internal mental states; how information is received, processed and stored; attention, perception, language, memory, acquisition of knowledge, decision-making and thinking (McLeod, 2007). Cognitive neuroscientists focus on the biological basis of cognition linking brain mechanisms to processes of thinking, memory, perception and attention (LeDoux, 2002).

The influence of the cognitive revolution was, and continues to be, far-reaching in the sciences, mathematics, information processing, artificial intelligence (AI) and the social sciences.

The behavioural schools and cognitive schools have formed the basis of therapeutic techniques used in psychotherapies as well as in organizational and executive coaching, maximizing the efficiency and effectiveness of organizations. How do they do this?

- Behavioural therapies seek to modify maladaptive behaviours through reinforcement, extinction, counter-conditioning etc.

- Cognitive therapies focus on identifying and correcting irrational beliefs.

- Cognitive behavioural therapeutic (CBT) techniques are a blending of the two disciplines and seek to change the thinking underpinning maladaptive mental and behavioural habits. CBT has become the therapeutic model of choice within the UK's National Health System, though treatment results are proving immensely variable.

Cognitive science only goes so far. It is not a science of the whole mind; it does not account for how perception, memory and thinking work together; it does not consider how mind emerges from the various cognitive processes; it fails to give insights into what makes an individual unique; it does not address the nature of the Self. Where all these theoretical models fall short is that they fail to incorporate the very human qualities that make us who we are. Emotions get left out of the equation, and feelings are seen as encumbrances (LeDoux, 2002). This must be addressed if we are to create fear-free organizations.

Putting it together: The role of the emotions

Towards the end of 19th century some neuroscientists were beginning to think about the building blocks of the brain; how certain structures in mammalian brains might connect ancient primitive areas of the brain to the neocortex; how emotions might be generated in neurobiological structures. In 1878 Paul Broca identified the 'limbic lobe', an area in the brain surrounding the brainstem and which contains structures related to emotion (Purves *et al*, 2001). In 1937 James Papez, a Cornell University anatomist, set out to identify neural circuitry involved in the subjective experience of emotions through a flow of information (LeDoux, 1996).

Paul D MacLean was a leading brain scientist and physician of the 20th century. Puzzling about the conflicting nature of human behaviour – on the one hand rational and on the other aggressive and violent – he sought answers from neuroanatomy and from the evolution of the human brain

(Pearce, 2008). Based on the work of Broca and Papez, MacLean put the pieces together conceiving a three-in-one hierarchical model of the brain of mammals. He called this the Triune Brain (Figure 2.1 and Appendix 2A). Not surprisingly, MacLean's model links to Hughlings Jackson's description of the human brain as hierarchical, containing three levels and evolving from one to the next:

1 The Reptilian Brain: the oldest part of the brain that ensures survival and regulates bodily functions.

2 The Mammalian/Limbic Brain: the emotional brain – the brain that is charged with emotion and memory (see Appendix 2B).

3 The Neocortex or New Brain: the thinking or cognitive brain – highly evolved in humans, the brain that is the seat of language, imbued with logic, and has the capacity to think about itself.

FIGURE 2.1   The triune brain

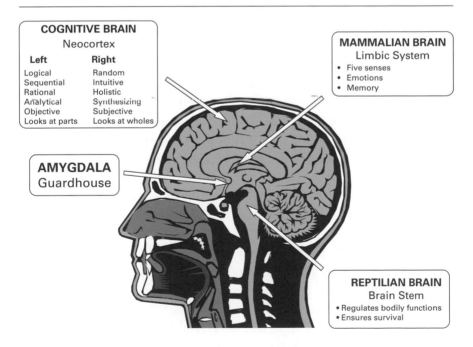

MacLean understood the crucial role emotions played in the evolution of the human brain. He posed the questions: 'Where do subjective emotional experiences reside in the brain?' and 'Is the functional circuitry of the brain inherited in the evolution of vertebrates and, if so, how did these circuits evolve?' (MacLean, 1990, p 247; Newman and Harris, 2009). Recognizing that the limbic brain developed in parallel with the evolutionary development of family life in mammals, MacLean placed family – the capacity to manage relationships, which is not present in reptiles at all – as central to the evolution of the brain in mammals.

> ...the evolution of the limbic system is the history of the evolution of mammals, whereas the history of the evolution of mammals is the history of the evolution of the family.
>
> MacLean (1990); Newman and Harris (2009)

MacLean's three-in-one model is based on a brain that evolved from the bottom up. The bottom layers are the more ancient parts with the higher centres elaborating on the lower ones. The human brain grows from the bottom up – which is what is seen in the way the brain in the human embryo grows (Goleman, 1995).

From an evolutionary perspective the design of the human brain is a rather inelegant affair, patched together as needs be, much as a quilt is stitched together with whatever fabric is at hand. MacLean likened the evolution of the brain to a house with wings added on over time, the finished product functioning as a seamless whole (MacLean, 1990; Newman and Harris, 2009).

MacLean believed, as do many modern neuroscientists and psychologists, that the thinking brain and the emotional brain, while operating in parallel, function independently, using different neural codes. Thus, they do not necessarily communicate with each other. Neuroscientist Joseph LeDoux is of the view that this goes a long way towards explaining why oftentimes emotions seem to be disconnected from, and act independently of, the thinking brain; and why some psychiatric illness might arise from the emotional brain working in isolation from the rational thinking brain (LeDoux, 1996). It may, on the other hand, be the case that the emotional brain has primacy and overrides the thinking brain. It is the basis of the destruction of many a marriage or non-rational behaviour when alcohol has temporarily impaired cognitive mechanisms. What is certainly true is that without emotions informing thinking there is no meaning or moral judgement possible, though decisions can still be made.

The 1990s were named 'The Decade of The Brain' by the US Congress and then-President George W Bush. But the breakthroughs occurred 20 years earlier. In the 1970s there was a seismic shift in neuroscientific explorations: focus began to shift to study the role of emotion in thinking and acting. The two key neuroscientists provoking this shift were Antonio Damasio and Joseph LeDoux. They introduced neuroscientific concepts about the role of emotions in the brain and their research has created a neuroscientific revolution. MacLean's Triune Brain theory provided an extremely useful starting model.

Born in Portugal in 1944, Antonio Damasio is professor of neuroscience at the University of Southern California. In the 1970s Damasio was professor and head of neurology at the University of Iowa Hospitals and Clinics. He was studying patients with prefrontal lobe damage. The damage to the prefrontal lobe in every instance had robbed patients of their free will or capacity to make informed choices. Damasio noted similarities with a much-studied neurological patient from the middle 1800s named Phineas P Gage (Damasio, 1994).

Phineas Gage was a construction foreman helping to lay new tracks for the Rutland & Burlington Railroad in Vermont. It was the summer of 1848 and Gage was 24 years old. About to tamp down sand on powder and a fuse in preparation for blasting rocks, he was momentarily distracted. The iron rod he used made direct contact with rock and created a spark. The explosion blew the rod through his left cheek, the base of his skull, the front of his brain and out through the top of his head. Incredibly, he not only survived, but remained conscious and was able to speak about what had happened to him. Gage went on to make a complete physical recovery. But there was a radical change in Gage's character and astonishing changes in his personality, including engaging in inappropriate behaviours. His employers, family and friends reported that Gage would be disrespectful, use profane language, be extremely restless, wilful and make grandiose plans which were quickly abandoned (Damasio, 1994).

Damasio noted that his prefrontal patients engaged in similar disruptive behaviours, did not seem to experience a wide range of emotions, and were unable to make decisions informed by reason. Crucially, Damasio began to draw links between emotions and the inability to concentrate, make rational decisions, learn from mistakes, and to plan for the future. He concluded that reasoning requires emotion (Damasio and Hustvedt, 2010; Damasio, 1994).

In 1995 Damasio joined forces with Joseph LeDoux to organize the first international symposium on emotion at the Society for Neuroscience in New York.

Joseph LeDoux became interested in emotion in the 1970s. LeDoux chose to research the neural underpinnings of emotion using animal models. His work has focused on the underlying brain mechanisms of emotion – 'how the brain detects and responds to emotionally arousing stimuli, how emotional learning occurs and emotional memories are formed, and how our conscious emotional feelings emerge from unconscious processes' (LeDoux, 1996).

LeDoux's research on fear has identified pathways in the brain that link to and from the amygdala: how the system involving the amygdala triggers the body's vast array of survival mechanisms when apprehending fearful stimuli; how the amygdala store emotional memories; and how neurochemicals released in response to the amygdala's appreciation of any situation pre-empt our thoughts and behaviours. The amygdala links the reptilian brain and the thinking brain in that it has direct pathways from the sensory thalamus (reptilian brain) as well as pathways from the sensory cortex (thinking brain) whilst itself being located in the mammalian part of the brain where meaning is made emotionally too (LeDoux, 1996).

The 1970s saw the introduction of imaging technologies that allow snapshots of the brain to be taken while its owner thinks, feels and acts. On 3 July 1977, five hours after the start of the first MRI test, the first human scan was made as the first MRI prototype. Since that time there have been, and continue to be, great advances in understanding the inner workings of the living brain. Neuroimaging machines are increasingly sophisticated. Neurologists and neuroscientists are gaining deeper and more sophisticated understandings of what's happening inside the brain.

17 billion miracles

What puts everything together is the wiring. Bit by bit, neuron by neuron, connections are constantly being made throughout the brain and through the entirety of the nervous system (Figure 2.2 and Appendix 2D).

FIGURE 2.2 Neuronal connections

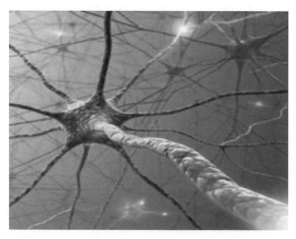

SOURCE: Lieff (2012)

Of the 86 billion neurons, 69 billion of them are located in the cerebellum (the structure at the back of the brain that helps refine motor control). Of the 86 billion neurons, a mere 17 billion of them are located in the cortex, the area of the brain thought to be responsible for thought, culture and creativity. The frontal lobes and prefrontal cortex, which are involved with memory, planning, cognition, abstract thinking, initiating and inhibiting behaviours, and learning, have many fewer neurons than the visual and other sensory areas and the motor cortex. It's not the numbers that count but the number of possible connections that make the difference between being human and being a member any other species. The tree-like terminal branchings (aka aborization) of the dendrite tips of neurons make many connections to neuronal networks, creating new networks, which in turn make many connections to other neuronal networks creating more new networks, and on and on it goes. The result is a vast number of possible increased connections (Gazzaniga, 2011). What all this adds up to is approximately an awesome 100 trillion connections. How cool is that! (Zimmer, 2011).

So, what makes people different?

The development of the human brain is unique. No other species has evolved with the extraordinarily adaptive, learning capacity of the human brain. A human is the only animal that has the capacity to imagine a future and then to set about creating that future whilst simultaneously communicating, more or less successfully, a vision of that future to itself and to other members of the tribe. In one strangely developed form it is called politics. In another it is essential to business organizations.

There is a phenomenal growth of the brains of human babies after birth, with a baby's brain probably forming a million new neurons every 20 seconds. So you can see why experiences from birth through adolescence have such a critical effect on brain development and the developing person. The maturation of neural wiring in humans is not complete until approximately 24 years of age when the executive centres of the thinking brain come into their own (Bainbridge, 2008).

The frontal part of the cortex – the prefrontal cortex – is known as the executive region. It is 'the master control centre' coordinating, balancing and linking different brain areas. Through the teenage years and early twenties the executive region is in a period of maturation. It is believed that this explains why teenagers and young adults are liable to engage in risk-taking behaviours.

They may not be the biggest brain in terms of observable size and weight but human brains are by far the largest in terms of size-to-body ratio, and they are more complex and diverse than the brains of any other mammals. Encased in the confined and rather small area of the skull, cortical folding has allowed brains to increase markedly in volume and to expand in surface area (Sun and Hevner, 2014). 'Two-thirds of the human cortex is buried in the grooves' (Bainbridge, 2008).

The brains of vertebrates contain all the basic structures and major neural pathways. As species evolved, different species-specific neural areas of specialization emerged in each one to adapt to its peculiar needs and circumstances. From fish to fowl, from lions to tigers and bears, from monkeys to men, evolution has created neural systems that give each species the greatest chance for survival (LeDoux, 1996).

The main thing that sets us apart from all other species is the one area of neuroscientific research that has yielded few, if any, satisfactory answers. This is called *the problem of consciousness*. 'The overwhelming question in neurobiology today is the relation between the mind and the brain...' (Crick and Koch, 1992).

Antonio Damasio identifies the big questions as: 'First: how does a brain construct a mind? Second: how does the brain make that mind conscious?' (Damasio, 2010). Neuroscientists agree that answers reside in the science and will come from the brain itself, with explanations couched in terms of brain activity. There is no doubt, scientists believe, that mind and consciousness will follow the same rules that other brain functions obey (Bainbridge, 2008). The best that can be said at present is that mind is an emergent property of the brain. In the way that when hydrogen and oxygen combine they form water, and then if heated create steam, so some process happens in the brain from which mind gradually emerges – though the quality of the functioning of the mind depends a great deal on what has gone into the brain. But, crucially linked to the Self, the human mind is vital in creating a self-directing organism, apparently purposeful, that can imagine and create a future and not simply just respond to stimuli in the present – an idea that is critical to understanding how business organizations succeed.

As neuroscientific research yields more knowledge it is increasingly clear that central to the forging of neural connections are the day-to-day relationships that give life purpose and meaning. We are our brains, and our brains grow, develop, thrive and bloom in the context of the quality of the relationships we experience throughout our lives as well as defining much of what we are through the way our own particular brain was constructed during its early embryonic development. The social context in which we find ourselves is where our brains tell us who we are as we slowly discover our adult identity through all our developmental stages. Our social circumstances shape specific cultural ways of expressing who we are, but the core of the Self comes from early brain development (Swaab, 2014).

Emotions deep down inside: Your business card

> Your smile is your logo, your personality is your business card, how you leave others feeling after an experience with you becomes your trademark.
>
> Jay Danzie, nd

Relationships make us, can break us and change us in a myriad of ways.

Andrew had been given a project. He spent hours researching and then writing up his findings for his team. 'I took great pride in everything I did. It was important that I be given feedback and recognition for a job well done.' And all of that happened. But. A few months later Andrew overheard Helen, his manager, on the phone with the client. The client was clearly happy to have received the information Andrew had prepared. 'I couldn't believe what she was saying – taking all the credit for the work I'd done.' He thought it pretty pathetic, didn't say anything to Helen, and went about his day. This little event was to reverberate in Andrew's system in bad ways. His confidence was knocked. He felt humiliated. Once highly motivated to do his very best, Andrew had now lost his edge – projects seemed just that little bit harder to begin. A little voice in his head kept popping up saying, 'What's the point in working so hard?'

This seemingly inconsequential event of a manager stealing credit had a striking impact on Andrew. 'I started seeing Helen differently. I just didn't trust her as much. I found myself looking for ways to make sure I was appreciated.' His enjoyment at work was diminished. He was hesitant to contribute his ideas for fear that Helen would adopt them as her own. A low level of resentment seemed to pervade his system when he was in meetings with Helen. Then Andrew started being hard on himself for his bad feelings towards Helen. 'I felt guilty for being judgemental.' His energy, instead of being directed at doing his work, was depleted and his creativity suffered.

Unwittingly Helen had tapped into emotional systems in Andrew's brain, setting off a flurry of signals and a cascade of neurochemicals. Helen had no idea of the harm she had done and if asked she would certainly have said this was the last thing she intended to do. All she was trying to do was impress the client. Helen would not have known that she had headed right into the heart of Andrew's fear system – the amygdala. When it comes to fear, the role of the amygdala is crucial.

The amygdala is the place where all emotions, but especially fear, are based and remembered, and from where neurochemicals are triggered that cascade through brain and body evoking fear responses (LeDoux, 1992; Bainbridge, 2008). And that's the last place in an organization to which you want to take someone. Unless, that is, you want them to freeze up, fight with you, or call in sick.

As we saw in Chapter 1, there are eight basic emotions: trust/love, excitement/joy, fear, anger, disgust, sorrow, shame and surprise. The attachment emotions are trust/love and excitement/joy. The avoidance emotions are fear, anger, disgust, shame and sadness. Surprise can trigger into either side depending upon the nature of the surprise. In the hierarchical developmental architecture of the human brain emotions come before cognition. And because emotions are concerned with our moment-to-moment survival they can, and oftentimes do, override thinking and logic. In any event they always inform thinking and logic in decision-making processes.

Human experience is suffused with emotion. As the brain of an infant evolves it becomes hierarchically organized (Schore, 1994). While DNA and genetic make-up determine much of the potential organization of the brain, a great deal of the actual organization is affected by the experience of our relationships. Think of a house. The bricks (neurons) define the structure. The internal decoration and furnishings (experience) define the quality of the way it is inhabited.

From the earliest moments of life the human brain is sculpted by the experience and the quality of relationships, with emotions key as to how we develop. It is the emotions that organize the pathways of the brain. So relationships, which cover the whole range of the emotions, affect the forging of brain connections, neurochemistry and brain functioning throughout our lives. How people treat us in our own development has a profound impact, sometimes a massively bad impact, on how good or bad we feel about ourselves. As in the case of Andrew, thoughtless words and behaviours leave their mark. At its extreme, bullying and abuse carve emotionally painful wounds from which many people never properly heal. The wound is there to be reopened under stress.

As we grow and develop into adulthood, the brain retains its ability to learn, develop and adapt. Brain connections are rather malleable because they are endowed with Hebbian plasticity, so named after the Canadian psychologist Donald Hebb. In 1949 Hebb hypothesized that interconnected and collaborative synaptic pathways permanently modify the effectiveness of the activated pathways (Haider, 2008). Hebb proposed that learning occurs when two neural cells fire at the same time. 'Cells that fire together wire together.' But herein lies a double-edged sword: brains don't discriminate about what they learn. The brain does not have a template as to what it 'should' be like. That is what a culture provides. Brains take on board the good, the bad and the ugly.

The leader's low road

Leaders and managers typically rise up the corporate ladder based on output and delivery to the bottom line. The higher you climb the more distanced you risk becoming from what you're good at: the 'work'. With increased management responsibility you are expected to manage what you may have no expertise or experience in: the management of people. It is inevitable to focus on what you excel at and to leave the people stuff to chance and guess-work. Unfortunately that often means taking 'the low road' to manage and motivate – 'the low road' being the quick and dirty route to the amygdala. And, as we saw in Chapter 1, nothing will get you faster to the amygdala than fear (Goleman, 1995; LeDoux, 1996). The trouble is however, that nothing will de-motivate someone faster than fear.

Relationships at work and in social life take time and effort to develop. The world of work often encourages the adoption of short-term strategies in pursuit of goals. As the brain responds quickly to threats, fear tactics give the appearance of getting people to work harder, faster and longer. But what they are really working at – because the brain works this way – is protecting themselves. A lot of the rest is show.

Words count

So News Corp's demand for success at all costs was passed down from Andy Coulson's office through Kuttner and Wallis to the news desk and the features department and then onwards to the journalists beneath them, and with it came a certain style of management, simply and repeatedly described by those who experienced it as 'bullying'. This was a rough place to work.

Davies (2014)

Some work environments are so brutal and perverse that they defy imagination.

> Marsha was a star athlete at school and then at Cambridge she was awarded a blue for rowing. Marsha went on to represent the UK internationally. Clearly Marsha had everything going for her and was full of confidence and bonhomie. She wanted a career that was connected to her sporting life and was thrilled to be offered a job at a top sports management company in New York. She grabbed it.
>
> Nothing in Marsha's experience prepared her for what was coming. She'd never confronted bully-boy behaviour and was shocked at the way men in her new organization talked to her – or, to be more precise, at her. Marsha's boss expected her to know how to do everything from the get-go. There was no one to train her, not even to tell her where the stationery cupboard was. 'I had a lot of questions to ask and I certainly didn't shy away from speaking up. That is until I was shot down so many times I just wanted to hide under my desk. And the language used was appalling. My boss – I nicknamed him Barry Bigshot – called me every name in the book. His language was appalling, shocking. It was a male-dominated culture and the men took their tone from Mr Bigshot. Those that didn't were considered wimps.
>
> 'Honestly, I didn't want to resign – this was my dream job. And I was never one to throw the towel in. I tried to see this as a challenge. To say it wasn't easy is an understatement.' Marsha's logical side thought she could turn things around. But her emotional side suffered badly from the onslaught of so many assaults.

Threatening words take their toll. Because the emotional neural systems, and the amygdala in particular, are concerned with survival, we are programmed to give priority, and respond instantly, to perceived threats. Words associated with verbal or physical attack tap instantly into the amygdala and put us on high alert. We are biased to attend to bad words, bad behaviour, bad relationships, and bad events. In numerous studies bad consistently trumps good (Baumeister *et al*, 2001; Kahneman, 2011; Sutton, 2011).

Given the architecture of the human brain it is no wonder that Marsha was bumping up against her own conflicted thoughts and feelings. Not only do we have three brains in one, we also have a brain with two distinct halves: the left hemisphere (left brain) and the right hemisphere (right brain).

The hemispheres are connected by a bundle of 300–800 million fibres (the corpus callosum) (McGilchrist, 2009; Gazzaniga, 2011). In brains of addicts, fMRI scans suggest impaired structural integrity to the corpus callosum (Arnone *et al*, 2008).

There is increasing evidence that the two systems (left brain/right brain) differ in their physiology and chemistry and consequent control of behaviour. Therefore, the left brain and right brain process similar types of information in different ways (Schore, 2012 and see Appendix 2C). The left brain is primarily concerned with all things logical and what is known. The right brain thrives on emotion and keeping a continuous scan for the unknown.

Much of what is understood about the functional lateralization of the human brain is down to the work of cognitive neuroscientist Michael Gazzaniga who is known as the 'godfather of modern split-brain science'. He has studied split-brained patients whose corpus callosum was severed to treat severe epileptic seizures. This drastic procedure has been replaced today by drug therapies. The split-brain patients provided a perfect study group for the ways in which the two hemispheres of the brain work together as well as functioning separately. For instance, Gazzaniga's studies have revealed differences in the two halves such as that the left side usually specializes in speech and language comprehension while the right side specializes in visual–spatial processing and facial recognition (Wolman, 2012).

Marsha's logical side – left brain – was trying to make sense of the loutish behaviour, the anger that was permeating the atmosphere, as well as trying to dampen down any right-brain emotional responses. Always a team player, Marsha sought to be objective about what was happening and to try and not take things personally. But for the right brain *everything* is personal.

Marsha felt under threat. 'All I could focus on was how to defend myself. I was not used to operating on a verbal battleground – I found myself at a loss for words.' Although she loved working with the clients and felt really connected to them, the team meetings in the office became increasingly difficult. Her preferred method of coping was to try and find reasons not to attend. She felt disrespected. The danger was that clients would pick up on her loss of self-faith and start to question how competent she was.

Marsha's boss and male colleagues just didn't get it. As some of their clients were very high-profile women sports stars they'd gone out of their way to recruit Marsha, a woman. What they saw as harmless banter was just the way of the world they worked in. They thought Marsha was overly emotional and over-reacting – if she couldn't take it, maybe she should rethink her job choice? They didn't understand that equality of opportunity in the workplace does not mean that there can be no differences of style.

It was difficult work they did – they had to be nice and charming and good at schmoozing while at the same time driving deals forward, managing prima donna personalities, smoothing over PR nightmares. The culture of the organization was left-brain-driven.

The angry words (left brain in action) were a way to let off steam – and to maintain hierarchical structures of implied dominance and leadership. Young stags in the animal kingdom know all about that, locking horns to work out who will eventually challenge the leader of the herd. They could not have cared less that bullying words may often be taken literally and were particularly wounding to someone who had not had cause to develop the skills of defending against them. In her rowing, Marsha had been in all-women crews. In the awards she had gained, she was the respected equal of men and admired by them for her achievements, which were real and tangible and on the record. In this job none of that was true. And Marsha was an easy target. In fact they enjoyed tormenting Marsha, some of them envying her sporting record. People who predominantly operate from their left brain are not known for empathy or compassion.

The problems Marsha was experiencing may seem insurmountable, but they're not. Underneath the words and aggression were people trying to do their best, and, in most cases, with good intentions. But the way forward must be paved with good intentions that get acted on: developing respectful relationships; understanding that different people use words differently; understanding that aggressive words may be perceived as real threats; understanding the culture you're working in.

Cult as in culture

A newly-appointed MD of a three-country consulting group was told by his chairman, the owner, that he wanted the company to be run like a family. The MD liked that concept. He had been appointed after a boardroom bust-up had broken the original three-man partnership, leaving just the chairman in control. It took the new MD more than a year to work out that the chairman came from a very dysfunctional family. He thrived on rows, splitting people into factions, and creating conditions where no one trusted anyone. 'Family' meant very different things to the chairman and his MD.

It's a really good idea to try and suss out as much as you can about the culture of an organization before deciding to accept a job. We're not talking about the promises and platitudes contained in published mission statements – but about the realities that lie beneath and between the words. You may not be able to pick your family but you can certainly choose where to work. It just requires some research.

In the following story, the name of the company and the wording of the mission statement have been changed to protect the identity and ensure anonymity.

Atlantic Crossing is a global financial services company. They are leaders in their field and recruit people from the top echelons of business and government. Their graduate recruits come from top universities. They offer an excellent employment package including many perks, profit-sharing incentives, high salaries, good bonus scheme and health insurance.

Here is an extract from their mission statement:

At Atlantic Crossing, we strive for excellence and to that end we look to be constantly improving. We believe the pursuit of excellence is connected to knowing what is true and verifiable. We are principled about how we work and deal with people. We foster a culture of innovation and independent thinking, understanding that disagreements and making mistakes are inevitable. Truth involves radical openness that can be difficult and uncomfortable. We expect the people we employ to be assertive, open, and willing to engage in honest debate.

James was headhunted to interview at Atlantic Crossing. It seemed an amazing opportunity. He read their mission statement and was very taken with what seemed to be a special job at a unique kind of company. The recruitment process was different from anything he'd experienced before. The questions were direct and non-traditional. The recruitment process took 15 months. 'I had eight interviews and a day of shadowing.' James took the job.

Four years later, battered, bruised and on the brink of a breakdown, he resigned.

'The problem was there was one truth – if you didn't see it then you had a synthesis problem,' James said. 'The 'openness' turned out to be constant criticism. But I learned how to fit in. We all felt very arrogant, great. We had each other's back. In my second year there everything changed, including management. Once great risk-takers, as their success grew and with more on the line, they became increasingly risk-averse. The new MD was running scared. I was told I wasn't good enough – that I had to be more like someone else. It was very destructive. They never fire anyone, they'd just demote people and it's very demeaning. They shrink your universe so you can't do anything. In the guise of truth, I was told off publicly in meetings, in front of my colleagues. I was told to just trust in the culture – open and honest. Just tell them what's on your mind. And then I discover it's all a trap – information seeking.

'I saw a very senior person in the organization completely humiliated at a management meeting. You watched him age while he was working there. You felt if they can do it to him, nothing is going to stop them from doing it to you. People were always taking medical leave – stress, eating disorders, panic attacks, depression. Everyone was overwhelmed with responsibility. The other side of the coin was that they did things for you – it was very seductive. There were lots of grand gestures. Medical plan was spectacular, holidays paid for, private jets offered for personal use. We were based outside of London on what was once a grand country estate. They had brilliant sports facilities, tennis courts, swimming pool, and two good staff restaurants. You arrived in the morning and never had to leave. It seemed ideal but quickly it began to feel like we were cut off and controlled.

'I finally asked for help and was berated for not asking in the right way. I tried not to be emotional because management said emotions pull you down – we're all about thinking and logic. I've never seen so many grown men cry. The CEO went to a seminar about emotional intelligence and came back talking about the amygdala. We were told to operate from the prefrontal cortex – to use our logic. He told us everyone had to be comfortable with big emotional reactions. Outbursts were normal – the amygdala reacting to something. But we must learn to use our logic to control our emotions.'

James went on to say that something akin to the Stockholm Syndrome took over and people were literally terrified to leave. They were told they were unemployable and they believed it.

It's a shocking story, but as more companies watch their earnings rise into the hundreds of billions, the stakes get higher, greed runs out of control and values and principles are compromised.

Atlantic Crossing presented itself as an innovative, forward-thinking organization, breaking ground in global markets, and setting the trend for all other financial service businesses. James bought into the promise of excitement, adventure and creativity, all within a caring, entrepreneur-led, family-type business. He felt like he was invited into an exclusive club that would provide safety and sanction. The culture James found himself working in was quite different.

Atlantic Crossing runs on pure, unadulterated fear. There is only one truth and that is the truth of the founder. Transparency translated into ratting on your colleagues, engaging in gossip, never questioning how things were done. In a money-driven business, money was never talked about; it was *verboten*, un-discussable. The great pretence was that the organization was driven by values, not the bottom line. People were led to believe that the only things that mattered were trust, loyalty and the truth.

Fear started to take its toll, and Atlantic Crossing began to pay the price. Many of their best people decided to bite the bullet, risk all, and leave. The year James resigned, the organization had an astonishing 50 per cent attrition rate. Many who stayed were falling sick, both psychologically and physically. Fear is a killer. The culture of fear and paranoia is the foundation of the organization and nothing kills creativity, motivation and productivity faster than having to watch your back all the time. When the brain is operating in full fear mode it is completely and solely concerned with survival. Forget about concentration, creativity, teamwork. When neural systems are on red alert attention must be paid, and focusing on anything else is just not possible.

James got out just in time. It took almost a year for him to recover and move on to launching his own business.

What's trust/love got to do with it?

What are brains for? Sex... in short, everything that constitutes the intricate web of life that we have constructed around ourselves with our amazingly large brains – serves a very simple purpose. Sex.

Gazzaniga (1997)

There's anatomy – and then there's neurochemistry.

Brain chemistry is built on love, fear and the whole gamut of emotions combined into an infinite landscape of feelings. Neurotransmitters are central to foetal brain development – the switching on of genetic potentials. Gender identity and eventual choice of which gender will attract us sexually is determined before we are born, for instance. Those chemical influences continue after birth into infancy, childhood, adolescence, and right through the lifespan. Neuroplasticity means that learning, experience and emotions change the brain (see Chapter 1). Neurons are flexible and can make, break and remake relationships with other neurons. The brain can and does rewire itself, though not without a bit of difficulty (LeDoux, 1996; LeDoux, 2002). You could learn Mandarin if you don't already know it, but it's hard work getting the brain to forge the new pathways. But you could do it if you really wanted to. Learning new emotional behaviours is not easy either.

Love, care and kindness suffuse the brain with a healthy balance of chemicals that promote robust physical and psychological development. Fear does the reverse. Extreme levels of fear can do permanent damage. Traumatic experiences change the release of neurotransmitters, electrical signalling, and changes in neurons themselves. When the delicate balance of neurochemistry is upset the effects on the internal milieu can result in disruptions to your well-being (LeDoux, 1996).

In James's story we can see how he had lost his confidence, his sense of self, his ability to think clearly and to make sense of what was happening to him. The toxic environment at Atlantic Crossing resulted in an imbalance in neurochemicals taking their toll emotionally and physically. James said, 'I felt like the rug had been pulled out from under me. My confidence took a big hit. I felt panicked, paranoid, sad, and was avoiding people I'd been close to.'

Neurochemicals impact everything from personality to memory, mood, thinking, concentration and behaviour. As we discussed in Chapter 1, relationships are crucial to the mix of brain chemicals. In an organizational culture defined by fear the collective neurochemistry has an inhibitory effect on productivity, motivation, problem-solving, trust, and energy. Fear is the enemy of effective individual and organizational energy.

How the brain uses energy

Although energy will be discussed later in Chapter 7, let us give you a brief overview of what we have learned about brain energy.

Early in the 19th century discoveries by Ampère and Faraday led to an understanding that electricity was a physical phenomenon. Their discoveries allowed neuroscientists to understand the electrochemical mechanisms underpinning brain signalling.

In the middle of the 19th century the German scientist Herman von Helmholtz discovered that the transmission of electrical signals in the brain was biologically generated. In the 1920s it was discovered that electrical impulses carrying signals in the brain and throughout the nervous system involve the release of neurochemicals called neurotransmitters.

Neurotransmitters are released across synapses, synapses being the intensely small gaps between the axonal ends of neurons.

We have already noted that there are *trillions* of synaptic connections with billions of synapses active at any given time. Synapses regulate the flow of information in the brain. It's a one-way system – the neuron releasing the neurochemical is called presynaptic and the neuron receiving the neuro-chemical is called postsynaptic. The point at which it receives the signal is called a dendrite. A neuron receiving a signal (postsynaptic) then becomes a neuron sending a signal (presynaptic). It takes 'an electrical storm', many presynaptic neurons bombarding many postsynaptic neurons, to create an action potential.

> 'An action potential occurs when a neuron sends information down an axon, away from the cell body... The action potential is an explosion of electrical activity that is created by a depolarizing current.' When the explosion of electrical activity reaches a critical threshold level in a neuron '... the size of the action potential is always the same... all action potentials are the same size. Therefore, the neuron either does not reach the threshold or a full action potential is fired – this is the "ALL OR NONE" principle'.
>
> Chudler, nd

The sending and receiving of messages via neurotransmitters requires highly coordinated complex split-second timing. The whole process is electrical-chemical-electrical, or electrochemical.

> As hard as it may be to imagine, electrochemical conversations between neurons make possible all of the wondrous (and sometimes dreadful) accomplishments of human minds.
>
> LeDoux (2002); Kaku (2014)

Walking on air

Fear is one of the most powerful (de-)motivating forces in our working culture today. It is what an overwhelming majority of bosses use, deliberately or mindlessly, to keep order. Performance-driven cultures are frequently full of it.

Fear easily overtakes excitement and enthusiasm as the primary driver of (survival) motivation at work. It is readily used as a management tool because there is simply nothing easier than tapping into another person's fear system.

Excessive and persistent levels of fear create changes in brain function that then interfere with decision-making processes and the ability of people to get their work done. We know these levels of excessive fear can be recognized and corrected. It is imperative that organizational leadership and management bring neuroscientific knowledge about the self into the heart of the organization in order to develop robust models of leading and managing in a sustainable business culture free from fear.

There should be zero tolerance for bullying, brutish and belittling behaviour. Bullying, brutish and belittling behaviour is fairly easily observed, difficult to deal with though it is.

Fear is insidious in all sorts of ways that stem from what is actually happening and what an individual perceives to be happening. What may seem true to one person, may not seem true to others. Individual perceptions based upon interpersonal experience and corporate culture can sometimes be in serious conflict with each other. The difficult cultural task for business leaders is to orchestrate and conduct the emotional responsivity of others. Later chapters give some clues to that.

References

Anon (nd) A short history of brain research: 1st century to 1872, available at http://www.mybrain.co.uk/public/learn_history1.php [accessed 8 May 2014]

Anon (2014) Brain-to-brain 'telepathic' communication achieved for first time, *Daily Telegraph*, 8 September 2014, available at: http://www.telegraph.co.uk/news/worldnews/northamerica/usa/11077094/Brain-to-brain-telepathic-communication-achieved-for-first-time.html [accessed 8 September 2014]

Arnone, D, Barrick, TR, Chengappa, S, Mackay, CE, Clark, CA and Abou-Saleh, MT (2008) Corpus callosum damage in heavy marijuana use: Preliminary evidence from diffusion tensor tractography and tract-based spatial statistics, *NeuroImage*, **41** (3), pp 1067–74, doi:10.1016/j.neuroimage.2008.02.064

Bainbridge, D (2008) *Beyond the Zonules of Zinn*, Harvard University Press, Cambridge, MA; London, UK

Baumeister, RF, Bratslavsky, E, Finkeanauer, C and Vohs, KD (2001) Bad is stronger than good, *Review of General Psychology*, **5** (4), pp 323–70 available at: http://bobsutton.typepad.com/files/bad-is-stronger-than-good.pdf [accessed 9 August 2014]

Bear, MF, Connors, BW and Paradiso, MA (1996) *Neuroscience: Exploring the Brain* 3rd revision, Lippincott Williams and Wilkins, Baltimore

Chudler, EH (nd) *Neuroscience For Kids: Action potential*, available at: https://faculty.washington.edu/chudler/ap.html [accessed 4 September 2014]

Churchland, PS and Sejnowski, TJ (1992) *The Computational Brain*, 5th edn, The MIT Press, Cambridge, MA; London, UK

Crick, F and Koch, C (1992) The problem of consciousness: The hidden mind, *Scientific American*, pp 11–17, available at http://codatest4.library.caltech.edu/329/1/Crick-Koch-92-Sci_Am.pdf [accessed 15 August 2014]

Damasio, AR (1994) *Descartes' Error: Emotion, reason, and the human brain*, 1st edn, GP Putnam's Sons, NY

Damasio, A (2010) *Self Comes To Mind: Constructing the conscious brain*, Pantheon Books, NY

Damasio, A and Hustvedt, S (2010) A legacy of behavioralism in the neurology of emotion, *Big Think*, available at: http://bigthink.com/videos/a-legacy-of-behavioralism-in-the-neurology-of-emotion [accessed 27 May 2014]

Danzie, J, Jay Danzie quotes, available at http://www.goodreads.com/quotes/792897-your-smile-is-your-logo-your-personality-is-your-business [accessed 11 December 2014]

Davies, N (2014) *Hack Attack*, Chatto and Windus, London

Deigh, J (2001) Emotions: The legacy of James and Freud, *International Journal of Psychoanalysis*, **82** (6), pp 1247–56, available at: http://doi.wiley.com/10.1516/J91T-TEJB-Q1Y5-K0RW [accessed 25 May 2014]

Dreifus, C (2011) A conversation with John P Donoghue: Connecting brains to the outside world, *New York Times*, available at: http://www.nytimes.com/2010/08/03/science/03conv.html?_r=0 [accessed 3 May 2014]

Freud, S (1895) *Project for a Scientific Psychology* (The Standard Edition, 1957), ed J Strachey, The Hogarth Press and The Institute of Psycho-Analysis, London

Freud, S (1914) *On Narcissism: An introduction* (The Standard Edition, 1957), ed J Strachey, The Hogarth Press and The Institute of Psycho-Analysis, London

Gazzaniga, MS (1997) What are brains for? in *Mind and Brain Sciences in the 21st Century*, ed RL Solso, pp 157–71, A Bradford Book, The MIT Press, Cambridge, MA; London, UK

Gazzaniga, MS (2011) *Who's in Charge?: Free will and the science of the brain*, 1st edn, Harper Collins, NY

Gillett, G and Franz, E (2013) John Hughlings Jackson: Bridging theory and clinical observation, *The Lancet*, **381** (9866), pp 528–29, available at http://www.thelancet.com/journals/a/article/PIIS0140-6736(13)60268-8/fulltext [accessed 1 May 2014]

Goleman, D (1995) *Emotional Intelligence*, Bantam Books, New York, Toronto, London, Sydney, Auckland

Greenfield, S (1997) *The Human Brain*, 1st edn, Basic Books, NY

Gross, CG (1995) Aristotle on the brain, *The Neuroscientist*, available at http://www.princeton.edu/~cggross/Neuroscientist_95-1.pdf [accessed 8 May 2014]

Haider, B (2008) Contributions of Yale neuroscience to Donald O Hebb's organization of behavior, *The Yale Journal Of Biology And Medicine*, **81** (1), pp 11–18, available at http://www.pubmedcentral.nih.gov/articlerender.fcgi?artid=2442722&tool=pmcentrez&rendertype=abstract [accessed 4 August 2014]

Hughlings Jackson, J (1884) John Hughlings Jackson evolution and dissolution of the nervous system III, *Croonian Lectures*, available at http://www2.psykl.med.tum.de/klassiker/hughlings_jackson_croonian_III.html [accessed 1 May 2014]

James, W (1981) *The Principles of Psychology*, Harvard University Press, Cambridge, MA; London, UK

Kahneman, D (2011) *Thinking, Fast and Slow*, 1st edn, Farrar, Straus and Giroux, New York

Kaku, M (2014) *The Future of the Mind*, Doubleday, New York, London, Toronto, Sydney, Auckland

Keenan, JP, Gallup, GC and Falk, D (2003) *The Face in the Mirror: The Search for the origins of consciousness*, Harper Collins, New York

LeDoux, J (1992) Parallel memories: Putting emotions back into the brain, *Edge.org*, available at http://edge.org/conversation/parallel-memories-putting-emotions-back-into-the-brain [accessed 29 May 2014]

LeDoux, J (2002) *Synaptic Self: How our brains become who we are*, 1st edn, Viking, NY

LeDoux, J (1996) *The Emotional Brain*, Simon and Schuster, New York

Lieff, J (2012) *A Cell Becomes a Neuron*, available at www.jonLieff.md/blog/neuronal-plast/city-blog/a-cell-becomes-a-neuron [accessed 10 April 2015]

MacLean, P (1990) *The Triune Brain in Evolution*, Plenium Press, New York

McGilchrist, I (2009) *The Master and his Emissary*, Yale University Press, New Haven and London

McLeod, SA (2007) Cognitive psychology, available at http://www.simplypsychology.org/cognitive.html [accessed 26 May 2014]

Morrish, P (1999) John Hughlings Jackson: Father Of English Neurology, *Brain*, **122** (6), pp 1199–1200, available at: http://brain.oxfordjournals.org/content/122/6/1199.full [accessed 30 April 2014]

Newman, JD and Harris, JC (2009) The scientific contributions of Paul D MacLean (1913–2007), *The Journal of Mental Disease*, available at http://udn.nichd.nih.gov/pdf/Paul_D_MacLean_Contributions.pdf [accessed 21 June 2014]

Nicolelis, MAL (2012) Mind in motion, *Scientific American*, available at http://www.nicolelislab.net/wp-content/uploads/2012/11/SciAm2012_Nicolelis.pdf [accessed 6 May 2014]

Panskepp, J (1998) *Affective Neuroscience: The foundations of human and animal emotions*, Oxford University Press, Oxford

Pearce, J (2008) Paul MacLean Obituary, *New York Times*, available at http://www.nytimes.com/2008/01/10/science/10maclean.html?_r=0 [accessed 21 June 2014]

Purves, D (2001) *Neuroscience*, 2nd edn, eds D Purves, GJ Augustine, D Fitzpatrick, LC Katz, A LaMantia, JO McNamara and SM Williams, Sinauer Associates, Sunderland, MA, available at: http://www.ncbi.nlm.nih.gov/books/NBK11060/ [accessed 24 June 2014]

Sample, I (2014) Mind-controlled robotic suit to debut at World Cup 2014, *The Guardian*, available at: http://www.theguardian.com/technology/2014/apr/01/mind-controlled-robotic-suit-exoskeleton-world-cup-2014 [accessed 6 May 2014]

Schore, A (2012) *The Science of the Art of Psychotherapy*, WW Norton and Company

Schore, AN (1994) *Affect Regulation and the Origin of the Self: The neurobiology of emotional development*, Lawrence Erlbaum Associates, Hills Dale, NJ

Schulte, B (2013) available at http://www.washingtonpost.com/local/new-report-finds-that-untreated-the-effects-of-child-abuse-and-neglect-can-last-a-lifetime/2013/09/12/1edc0bdc-1bc7-11e3-82ef-a059e54c49d0_story.html

Schutz, LE (2005) *Neuropsychology Review*, **15** (15), pp 11–27

Solms, M and Saling, M (1986) *A Moment of Transition: Two neuroscientific articles by Sigmund Freud*, The Institute of Psychoanalysis, Karnac Books, London

De Sousa, R (2003) *Emotion*, available at: http://plato.stanford.edu/entries/emotion/ [accessed 26 May 2014]

Sun, T and Hevner, RF (2014) Growth and folding of the mammalian cerebral cortex: from molecules to malformations, *Nature Reviews Neuroscience*, **15** (4), pp 217–32, available at http://dx.doi.org/10.1038/nrn3707 [accessed 15 July 2014]

Sutton, B (2011) Bad is stronger than good: Why eliminating the negative is more important than accentuating the positive, available at http://bobsutton.typepad.com/my_weblog/2011/10/bad-is-stronger-than-good-why-eliminating-the-negative-is-more-important-than-accentuating-the-posit.html [accessed 9 August 2014]

Swaab, DF (2014) *We Are Our Brains: A neurobiography of the brain from womb to Alzheimer's*, Penguin Random House, New York

Sweeney, MS (2009) *Brain – The Complete Mind: How it develops, how it works, and how to keep it sharp*, The National Georgraphic Society, Washington, DC

Wiley, JPJ (1998) Expressions: The visible link, *Smithsonian.com*, available at http://www.smithsonianmag.com/science-nature/expressions-the-visible-link-153844951/?no-ist [accessed 29 April 2014]

Wolman, D (2012) The split brain: A tale of two halves, *Nature*, **483** (7389), pp 260–63, available at http://www.nature.com/news/the-split-brain-a-tale-of-two-halves-1.10213 [accessed 8 August 2014]

York, GK and Steinberg, DA (2007) An introduction to the life and work of John Hughlings Jackson: Introduction, *Medical History*, Supplement, (26) p 3, available at: http://www.ncbi.nlm.nih.gov/pmc/articles/PMC2640105/ [accessed 1 May 2014]

York, GK and Steinberg, DA (2011) Hughlings Jackson's neurological ideas, *Brain: a journal of neurology*, **134** (Pt 10), pp 3106–13, available at: http://brain.oxfordjournals.org/content/134/10/3106.abstract [accessed 30 April 2014]

Zimmer, C (2011) 100 trillion connections, *Scientific American*, **304** (1), pp 58–63, available at: http://www.scientificamerican.com/article/100-trillion-connections/ [accessed 27 May 2014]

APPENDIX 2A

The triune brain

The reptilian brain/old brain

The **brainstem**: also called the Reptilian Brain, it surrounds the top of the spinal cord and is the most primitive part of the brain. It is present in all species with more than a minimal nervous system and in all vertebrates. It regulates basic life functions, breathing, the metabolism of the body's other organs, semi-reflex rhythmic movements, the co-ordination of movement with visual and sensory information, balance, mediation of movement of individual limbs, and fine movement of the fingers. It keeps the body running smoothly and is not concerned with conscious thinking or learning. The emotional centres of the brain have their origin at the top of the brainstem. The olfactory lobe, consisting of thin layers of cells, is the most primitive of the emotional centres. It comprises cells that take in and analyse smell allowing primitive species to identify enemies and avoid danger. In reptiles the olfactory lobe is particularly well developed (Goleman, 1995).

The emotional brain/limbic brain

The **limbic system**: comprises the emotional centres and systems of the brain; also called the Mammalian Brain as it is the step in brain evolution associated with the appearance of the first mammals where an effective working relationship between parent and young becomes crucial to survival. The limbic system has links from the reptilian brain (and particularly the smell centres) and upwards through to the neocortex. Although primarily concerned with emotion, the limbic system is implicated in behaviour, memory, and motivation. The limbic system is a group of pre-cortical and sub-cortical structures and linked systems that ring and border the brainstem and which runs through specific neural circuits. The limbic system added emotional processes to the brain's repertoire. It 'is an arching, re-curved structure – a long detour around some of our newer evolutionary acquisitions...' (Bainbridge, 2008).

The cognitive brain/the neocortex/the new brain

The **neocortex**: the seat of thought that adds thinking and comprehending to the emotional layers of the brain. It is found only in mammals (Bear *et al*, 1996; Goleman, 1995) and includes a series of circuits that register and analyse information. It comprehends the information and, through the prefrontal lobes, orchestrates a reaction. Because it receives information through an involved circuitry, the neocortex can calculate responses in a thoughtful, judicious and considered manner at great speed. The prefrontal cortex is capable of acting as an efficient emotional manager by weighing reactions before acting. The left prefrontal lobe, which functions as a neural thermostat, can switch off distressing emotions, keeping raw emotions in check and inhibiting the right lobe which is the seat of escape/avoidance feelings like fear and aggression. Any damage to the prefrontal lobes means that the ability to process feelings becomes impaired. When there is damage to the prefrontal lobes much of emotional life is deadened (Bear *et al*, 1996; Goleman, 1995). When the emotional centres kick in (as in times of grave danger) they have the capacity to influence the function of the rest of the brain, including cognitive centres (Goleman, 1995).

APPENDIX 2B

The emotional brain: Key ingredients

The amygdala are located in the forebrain and so named because they comprise two almond-shaped structures (the Greek word for 'almond' is 'amygdalon' and 'amygdala' is the plural, though like the word 'data' it is often used in the singular form referring to the whole system), one in each half of the brain, positioned on the inner surface of the temporal lobe, inwards from the ear. Together are referred to as 'the amygdala'. When it comes to fear, the role of the amygdala is crucial. The amygdala is the place where fear is learned and remembered, as are all the basic emotions; and from where neurochemicals are triggered that cascade through brain and body evoking fear responses. Most of what is known about the amygdala comes from animal research or from people who have suffered damage to these structures. In people who suffer from the rare Urbach-Wiethe disease, the amygdala degenerates. These people do not feel fear or anger and are unable to read emotional expressions in others. It has been discovered that the amygdala complex has many inputs gathering information from the neocortex, and from the olfactory system (Bainbridge, 2008; LeDoux, 1996).

The rhinencephalon ('smell brain') is the rudimentary basis of the thinking brain, the neocortex. It is apparently involved in the perception of odours as well as controlling behaviours that are guided by smell (Bear *et al*, 1996).

The thalamus, which is often referred to as the gateway to the cerebral cortex, relays incoming sensory information onto the cortex and, it is believed, contributes to the consolidation of memories (Greenfield, 1997).

The hypothalamus is located at the base of the forebrain and 'forms the interface between the psychological sophisticated forebrain and the more primitive lower area' (LeDoux, 1996). The hypothalamus makes up less than 1 per cent of the brain's mass but its influence on body physiology is enormous. It is involved in the control of the autonomic nervous system (ANS) and the pituitary gland, and is also involved in transmission of the hormone adrenaline (Bear *et al*, 1996; LeDoux, 1996).

The hippocampus is thought to play an essential role in the laying down of new memories. 'The hippocampus has... come to be thought of as a key link to one of the most important cognitive systems of the brain, the temporal lobe memory system. The hippocampal system runs in parallel with the implicit emotional memory system and is responsible for holding explicit memories and emotional situations' (LeDoux, 1996).

The basal ganglia is a collection of areas in the sub-cortical forebrain having to do with physical movement. It is believed that the interactions between the amygdala and the basal ganglia are implicated in emotional actions (LeDoux, 1996).

APPENDIX 2C

Left brain/right brain

Left brain

- Thrives on language.

- Uses words to its advantage and won't hesitate to engage in some white lies to get what it wants.

- Seeks certainty.

- Suppresses escape/avoidance emotions, the exception being anger.

- Deals in a world of objects and things (McGilchrist, 2009; Panskepp, 1998). If the world is a forest, the left hemisphere doesn't look beyond the trees.

- Breaks things down into units.

- Sees body as a thing detached.

- Accepts a single either/or solution.

- Abstract reasoning.

Right brain

- Locus of the emotional brain.

- Compels the mind to immediately attend to crisis.

- The language of the right hemisphere is metaphor.

- Engaged in the narrative – the story.

- Engaged in personal meaning.

- Empathy, compassion, morality, creativity emanate from right brain.

- Most sophisticated and highly evolved part of the brain.

- Sees 'The Big Picture' – the forest – and takes things in context.

- In problem-solving the right brain will consider an array of possible solutions.

- Makes perceptual links between words.

- Attends to emotional tones and recognizes the body language of emotion.

- Unified self: the sense of having a self – the embodied self – resides in the right hemisphere.

Keenan, Gallup and Falk (2003); Schutz (2005); McGilchrist (2009); Schore (2012)

APPENDIX 2D

Neurotransmitters and hormones

Neurotransmitters

Acetylcholine	Makes your muscles move and contract.
Dopamine	This causes feelings of pleasure and reward; addiction results from imbalances in dopamine levels.
Endorphins	Powerful opiates, block pain.
GABA (gamma-aminobutyric acid)	Quiets neurons.
Glutamate	This one is responsible for learning and memory.
Norepinephrine	Regulates mood, blood pressure, heartbeat and arousal.
Serotonin	Links to depression and anxiety; crucial for proper sleep and appetite.
Cortisol	Stress hormone.
Oxycotin	Social bonding; secreted during labour and falling in love, as well as in more general social engagement.

Hormones

Adrenaline	The fear hormone; prepares the body for fight or flight, stimulates heart rate.
Prolactin	Most generally attributed to milk supply during breast feeding, but has more than 300 known effects throughout the body, including social bonding.
Vasopressin	Raises blood pressure.
Testosterone	A steroid hormone from the androgen group. It is a male sex hormone produced in men by the testes; women have small amounts produced by the ovaries. It is found in mammals, reptiles, birds and other vertebrates.
Oestrogen	A steroid hormone produced primarily by the ovaries; a female sex hormone present in all vertebrates and some insects.
Progesterone	A hormone secreted by the pituitary gland that stimulates milk production.

Memories are made of this

03

Introduction

This chapter is about the power of memory and, in particular, memories suffused with fear.

Memories are essential to our sense of self. They are the basis of the stories we tell ourselves; our experience of self in relation to others. Memories underpin our perceptions, assumptions and attributions. Neuroscientists believe that although everything we experience throughout life is stored at a neural basis in brain structures and systems, only 10–20 per cent will be available to conscious awareness. Memory is located throughout the nervous system with some brain structures featuring prominently in the storage and retrieval of memories.

This chapter addresses the impact memory has on our feelings and relationships. We consider how memory helps form the chemistry between people. We discuss how memories are not static things but subject to the context in which they are brought to mind. We will show how memories triggered from earlier experiences and relationships get played out in an organizational setting. In this chapter we will show how the organizational bully instinctively knows who and how to push around by tapping into another person's fear systems.

What are memories?

There is no such thing as memory of the present while present, for the present is the object only of perception, and the future of expectation, but the object of memory is the past. All memory, therefore, implies a time elapsed; consequently, only those animals which perceive time remember, and the organ whereby they perceive time is also that whereby they remember.

Aristotle

In Chapter 1 we discussed memory in relation to our sense of self:

- the making of memories;
- the storage of memories in hierarchical brain systems;
- the power of memories suffused with emotion, and particularly fear;
- how decision-making is built on memories;
- how memories are embedded in brain systems;
- how our sense of self relies upon memory.

In this chapter we will discuss, with the brain in mind, how memories affect all aspects of our lives and particularly our decision-making. We will consider the fleeting nature of memories and how memories are subject to distortions, misinterpretations and editing. Accessing memories is essential to creativity and we look at the underlying neural processes at play in creative insights. We discuss Eric Kandel's research on the physiological basis of memory storage in neurons and how memories can echo down through the generations.

Memory plays a crucial role in the life of an organization as well as the individuals who populate it. People come to work with a lifetime of learning, knowledge and experience. Personal history – memory – impacts on how we perceive colleagues, managers, leaders; how work gets done, how well it gets done, how quickly it gets done.

Organizational culture incorporates the collective customs, ideas and social behaviours that underpin the way things get done. Organization culture is underpinned by the history of the organization – the organizational memory. It is intensely valuable though, unlike branding, has not yet been the object of formal accounting valuation. Perhaps it should be. As a guide and touchstone for organizational behaviour it is vital to corporate efficiency.

Once upon a time

'This is a true story. The events depicted in this film took place in Minnesota in 1987. At the request of the survivors, the names have been changed.
Out of respect for the dead, the rest has been told exactly as it occurred.'
Great opening. And not a word of truth to it.

Snopes.com

It starts with a true story that gets edited, sometimes many times a day, until finally it bears little relation to the reality. It works a bit like Chinese whispers.

Each time the tale is told it changes slightly until it bears only some resemblance to reality. That's how memory works.

Memory is not foolproof, is often inaccurate, and cannot be absolutely relied upon. Because brain storage of memories involves many different neural systems, recollections are not objective. Recall is subjective and influenced by subsequent personal perceptions, judgements, cognitions, interpretations and emotions. Like the brain itself, memory is fluid. One person's experience of an event is not the same as another's and one person's memory of another is coloured and perhaps clouded by emotional content and one's own history (Churchland, 2012).

As an example, consider this story:

Eloise and Joseph, now both 32, are reminiscing about a 6th birthday party they both attended when they were at school. Eloise recalls what fun the party was and how silly Clem the Clown was. Joseph recoils in horror. He says he has vivid memories of being terrified by the clown. He was so scared his mother had to take him home. Same party, same clown, different experiences, different memories! Let's fast-forward Eloise and Joe 26 years on. They now work for the same social media giant. They've just come out of a marketing meeting and are comparing notes. Joe says, 'I don't know how we're going to hit the new deadline management has set.' Eloise says, 'What new deadline? I didn't hear anything about a new deadline.'

Same meeting, same people, different focus, different memories!

The faintest ink

There is a Chinese proverb: the faintest ink is more powerful than the strongest memory. It is why a contemporaneous record of events carries so much more weight in a court than a memory that lacks a written record.

The retrieval of a memory is not like pushing the replay button on a recording device, digital or otherwise. As we remember someone or something, our brain engages in a process of reconstruction and renovation (Fernyhough, 2012). Inaccuracies can result in misunderstandings, mis-attributions and faulty accusations – sometimes with dire consequences. With the introduction by judicial systems of DNA evidence people who have been wrongfully accused and convicted of crimes based on faulty eyewitness accounts are having convictions overturned, sometimes many years after the fact. The Innocence Project was founded in 1992 to assist prisoners who could be proven innocent through DNA testing. More than 300 people have been released from prison to date and they believe many more will be identified and released (Innocence Project, 2014).

So many different elements affect memory that our memories are fallible. We encode and store only bits and pieces of the entire story and they are stored in different parts of the brain. In reconstructing an event, person, place or thing the picture brought to mind may contain gaps and imperfections. The brain fills in the missing pieces based on inference, speculation and information gained after the event (Innocence Project, 2014).

Familiarity primes the memories we form. 'The experience of familiarity has a simple but powerful quality of 'pastness' that seems to indicate that it is a direct reflection of prior experience' (Jacoby *et al*, 1989 cited by Kahneman, 2011). The illusion of the familiar can have an effect on decision-making at work.

Eloise and Joe were asked to create a shortlist of prospective candidates for the junior position of editorial assistant. They had appointments with Ellen, Lisa, Robert and Anthony. You wouldn't think it, and Eloise and Joe were not aware of it, but the names of the candidates had an impact on their decisions as to who to put forward. Ellen was the name of Eloise's best friend; an hour before the interviews Joe's manager called him about a problem he was having with the head of IT who happened to be named Anthony. All the candidates they interviewed were qualified for the job. Eloise favoured Ellen; Joe made it clear that he was just not comfortable with Anthony.

We may not be able to control these undercover memories that influence decisions, but it helps to be aware of the role memory plays in choices we make.

It is possible, through an internal series of checks and balances, to bring into awareness personal experiences that may be affecting our thoughts and decisions. As an example, you might ask yourself what in your experience might be guiding current thinking. If you're having a negative response to a person or an idea, you might question what, if anything, from your past is the source of the negativity. If you're feeling very positive about an idea or a person you might ask yourself what in your past experience is informing your judgements.

The eureka effect

I believe in intuitions and inspirations. I sometimes feel I am right. I do not know that I am... I am enough of the artist to draw freely upon my imagination. Imagination is more important than knowledge. Knowledge is limited. Imagination encircles the world.

Albert Einstein, quoted by Viereck (1929)

Given that all mental processes are biological, memories reside *in* and arise *from* the brain. The things that come easily to mind, that we are conscious of, are called short-term, or explicit, memories. The things we know but don't know we know, things that reside in the non-conscious, are called long-term, or implicit, memories. Explicit memories include people, objects, places, facts and events. Implicit memories include skills, habits and conditioning. Explicit memories and implicit memories are stored in different regions in the brain (Kandel, 2006).

While we can easily call upon explicit memories, implicit memories are often automatic and just pop up into awareness. Concurrent with memories popping into our thoughts, there is a whole wealth of neuronal activity in the brain. Neurons are firing and connecting and forming new connections and passing information down systems which link to other systems which are wiring and firing and triggering other systems and on and on it goes.

In the incredibly busy milieu of the brain, memories are triggered that are related to, but not obviously relevant to, what is happening now. Beneath awareness the brain is making subtle connections between things that may, on the conscious surface, not appear to be connected at all. And it is the non-conscious that then controls our behaviour.

Inspirational moments of creativity and invention are the happy result of this neuronal magic.

One day at work in November, 1907, Einstein had what he called 'the happiest thought in my life'.

'I was sitting on a chair in my patent office in Berne. Suddenly a thought struck me: if a man falls freely, he would not feel his weight. I was taken aback. This simple thought experiment made a deep impression on me. It was what led me to the theory of gravity.'

Anon (1907)

FIGURE 3.1 The death of a eureka moment

It's not just great scientists who rely on 'aha' moments. All seemingly spontaneous ideas or acts of creativity involve neural firing that connects current thought to past experience resulting in – eureka!

Cartoonist Gray Jolliffe shares his thoughts and a cartoon on eureka moments:

Even a person of moderate education will tell you that 'eureka' in classical Greek means 'I found it'. Archimedes had a eureka moment in his bath when he hit on the displacement principle. 'Eureka!' he shouted. And he continued to shout it, running naked through the streets of Athens. This didn't go unnoticed, which is why we know it to be true. Now, any sudden inspiration or revelation is known as a eureka moment.

As a cartoonist I rely on them. Some days you may get thousands, other days just a few hundred. When I sit at my desk trying to dream up something funny I realize that one of the best eureka catalysts is money. One minute you can be in catatonic mode, staring at nothing in particular, and the next you're answering a call from your agent. The eureka moment is waving a big fat cheque.

But as this cartoon demonstrates, eureka moments are also vulnerable. They can be murdered by the merest distraction: a banal request from a family member; a proffered toffee; a phone call from someone other than your agent. The idea that was so close and so precious vanishes like a missed bus, leaving you to hope there'll be another one along in a minute.

But what if there isn't? Let's say, right at that eureka moment, Phoebe Archimedes had wandered into the bathroom with a cup of tea and a saucy twinkle. Today we might still be scratching our heads trying to measure the volume of a frozen turkey.

What makes for a good cartoon, or a funny joke, or a great comedy sketch is that it comes from the experiences of the author as well as tapping into a familiar place in the audience. And visualizations tap into brain circuits that words alone do not. Simply *telling* the story that Gray Jolliffe depicts would not trigger the same range of responses as *seeing* it. It may be that one of the problems of mis-communication in many organizations is that there is more telling (words and numbers) than really seeing.

Working under pressure, with increasing demands to come up with the next great idea, is not the ideal environment for an 'aha' moment. The harder we concentrate on coming up with inspirational ideas the more frustrated we are likely to become. An idea emanates from a new network of neurons firing in sync with each other inside your brain. The network is the end product of a culmination of ideas that have been simmering on the brain's back burner, perhaps for quite a long period of time. Trying to pull them together inhibits the flow.

Sometimes a eureka moment can change a person's life in unexpected ways.

Herbert Kretzmer wrote the English lyrics for *Les Misérables*. He talks about how the job of his lifetime came about.

'I was 60 and living in a small flat on Basil Street in London, working for the *Daily Mail*, writing lyrics in my spare time. I didn't think I'd ever leave journalism. I was a newspaper man – that's what I did. But I did like lyrics, and the feeling of lyrics put to music. It always moved me. Not that I thought I'd be a great lyricist then – I was 60 for goodness' sake. Then, one day, everything changed forever.

'It was the mid-80s, and I'd written to Cameron [Mackintosh] to persuade him to get involved in a revival of a 60s musical called *Our Man Crichton*. I'd written the lyrics and thought it was due for a comeback.

Cameron wasn't interested so I was leaving. Out of politeness and small talk he asked me what other songs I'd written. 'I wrote "She" and "Yesterday When I Was Young" for Charles Aznavour,' I explained. Cameron stopped and said, 'My God. Really? You've just named two of my favourite songs.' He looked delighted. But he still didn't want to back a revival of my musical, so I left and went back to the office.

'Six months later, Cameron called me. He'd been struggling to come up with an English lyricist for *Les Misérables* and without the right lyricist it seemed the project was doomed to fail. Cameron said he'd woken up in the middle of the night and thought of me. He remembered the songs I'd written, and that I'd worked with Charles Aznavour... a Frenchman.

'OK, I thought... this sounds strange. He asked me whether I could meet him for lunch at The Ivy. We met and he asked me to write the lyrics for *Les Misérables*. I devoted the next four weeks to reading Victor Hugo's novel, in English, then said yes.'

Harvard Business Review has reported research led by Sophie Ellwood at the University of Sydney indicating that great ideas require a period of incubation (Barkus, 2014). A period of incubation is time out from focusing on trying to be creative and instead doing something mundane and thoughtless. In Ellwood's study 90 students were split into three groups and given a task of listing as many uses for a piece of paper as possible. The first group worked for four minutes without interruption; the second group was interrupted after two minutes, asked to do a creative task, and then given another two minutes to come up with alternative uses for paper; the third group was interrupted after two minutes, and asked to take the Myers–Briggs test, which takes about 40 minutes to complete, and then given two more minutes to get back to listing odd uses for paper.

The third group – the one given the longest time for incubation – hatched the most ideas, an average of 9.8. The second group averaged 7.6 ideas, while the first group came up with an average of only 6.9 ideas. In short, the numbers show an incubation period – even a short one – can increase creativity (DesMarais, 2014).

Taking a break and focusing on something else allows the brain to go about its business of making connections. Concentrating too hard on a problem hijacks the neuronal processes of firing, wiring and connecting; the pressing need to come up with a solution stops ideas in their tracks. The brain's energy is devoted to *making* it happen, not *letting* it happen. Constantly focusing on the same problem takes your thoughts back over and over again to the same solutions you've previously come up with. This is much like when you misplace your keys and keep looking over and over again in the same places. But if you walk away and stop looking you will suddenly remember the telephone call you answered (ah, the keys are next to the phone) or the scarf you put on at the last minute (ah, the keys are on top of the dresser) or the handbag you used last night (ah, that's where the keys are).

One psychologist we know habitually uses sleep time to focus connectivity energy. Sometimes it's for creative purposes, sometimes problem-solving, as when he misplaced a much-treasured fountain pen.

No amount of searching during the day that he had misplaced the pen had found it.

So as he went to sleep he proposed to himself that he dream about it. And his dream provided a perfect account of how during the day he had been climbing on a set of library steps to a top shelf looking for a book with the pen in hand, had needed two hands to balance on the top of the steps and stretch for the book he wanted; and had automatically put the pen down on the edge of the shelf that he was holding on to whilst stretching. Once at floor level the pen was out of sight. But his dream reconstructed the sequence entirely and there in the morning was the pen.

Taking time out can actually reap rewards. If you're having problems coming up with ideas, are unable to write that next paragraph, having difficulty putting together a report, or are stuck on strategic planning, you will probably find it helpful to switch to doing something unrelated to the task at hand. You might focus on something else like clearing out your e-mails, cleaning up your computer desktop, or organizing files – the more mundane the task the better. The key is to trust that your brain is doing the work for you, and doing it more efficiently without interference from you. Sometimes procrastination leads to some really good ideas. Actually it's not so much procrastination as trusting your brain to find the answer by stopping interfering with its creatively connective processes.

Creativity by association

Ideas evoked through association trigger many other ideas in a spreading cascade of activity in your brain. Some ideas trigger into bursts of creativity. But an idea that has associations with fearful memories immediately links into intense feelings and avoidance behaviours.

Kahneman (2011)

It stops you even trusting yourself.

In the early 1960s Sarnoff Mednick, a professor of psychology at the University of Southern California, created a test to support his idea that associative memory is the essence of creativity. His Remote Association Test (RAT) asks subjects to identify a word that links three words. For example, what word links:

- cottage – Swiss – cake? (easy: cheese)
- dive – light – rocket (not so easy: sky)
- dream – ball – book (impossible: there is none)

In recent years studies of RAT by teams of German psychologists have yielded fascinating results. What they're looking at is cognitive ease vs cognitive strain: the ease or difficulty with which words or phrases or slogans are processed. Of key importance is the impact mood has on associative memory and cognitive ease. When we are in a good mood we let our guard down, relax, and are more likely to access associative memories that underpin creativity. When fear dominates our external environment and our internal world, our guard goes up and we become defensive, vigilant and cautious. Fear blocks associative memories, is not conducive to using your imagination, and blocks creativity (Kahneman, 2011).

Herbert Kretzmer talks about how associative memories play an important part in the inspirations beneath his lyrics:

> I was writing late into the night working on 'I Dreamed a Dream'. I remember the thought of tigers coming into my head and I couldn't get rid of it. It's about dark forces that can creep up and destroy lives. It's about the influences in my childhood – growing up in a small town in South Africa. And – undoubtedly – William Blake's poem as well: 'Tyger Tyger, burning bright...' That must have been another reason why I chose the image.

I remember it well

We are living in an age of information overload. A high value is placed on the accumulation of knowledge but interference comes at us from all directions. Keeping up with e-mails is quite a feat, returning phone messages is time-consuming when time is at a premium. What with keeping track, staying on top of things, filling in forms, and participating in training, there is barely time to think, to register, to learn, never mind to get work done. And then there are meetings – endless meetings. In many organizations not a decision can be made without calling a meeting. Fear of making a mistake trumps the willingness to take risks. And without some risk-taking there is little chance of creating an exciting future. So rather than risking a decision, leaders and managers have meetings.

Meetings are often a muddle with a minority of people in positions of power doing most of the talking and looking for support for whatever proposal they are pushing forward. The talkers interrupt, ideas get lost in the noise, and people get bored, frustrated, angry and tired. Agendas get thrown to the winds. And as often as not people come away from meetings with completely different ideas about what has been discussed, dissected or decided.

Imagine coming out of a meeting feeling energized, excited, invigorated, motivated and full of new ideas. Nancy Kline (Kline, 2009) has her 'thinking environment' meetings fear-free. They are productive, focused, short and enjoyable. Agendas are clear and constructed to contain only essential item. Agenda items are written as questions that drive for a clearly articulated outcome. Interactions are enlightening, respectful and engaging. All attendees are given equal time to contribute. Interruptions are forbidden because nothing destroys an idea faster than an interruption.

As memory is coloured by each individual's personal history people may come out of a meeting with entirely different understandings of what was discussed, agreed, and set for action. At Atlantic Crossing the CEO was concerned about lack of common understandings and goals that employees were taking away from meetings. He thought he'd come up with the perfect solution to combat faulty memories and consequent misunderstandings. So he decided he'd have the meetings filmed:

> Andrew reported that the CEO also took the decision to have everyone in attendance make notes on their iPads in real time throughout each meeting. Then after a meeting, and in pursuit of 'the truth', he had everyone rate each person present at the meeting. We were rated on participation, enthusiasm, contribution made etc. Andrew said, 'I was subject to constant criticism. My meeting performance was typically below 5 – this was out of 10. I'd get a meeting performance review that was circulated to everyone on my team. Comparisons were made and we were all competing with each other. Not very conducive to team building and teamwork. I felt humiliated, embarrassed, and I found it difficult to make any contribution for fear of making a fool of myself. Which just made things worse. At some point I just ceased to care. That's when my ratings started to go up.'

Because you can't DVD emotions and memories, there appears to be little value in filming meetings as a way of creating an accurate record. What happens beneath the surface and what people take away from meetings are pictures not available for public viewing – internal images triggered by and suffused with emotions that have tapped into personal experience.

The pursuit of truth is an important aspect of the organizational culture of Atlantic Crossing. It is integral to the mission statement and drives a large part of the way things are done in the organization.

At the time of writing, the growing problems at Atlantic Crossing are about a lack of understanding of how to tap into the creativity of its employees. Fear has overtaken truth seeking. Learning and the gathering of knowledge are increasingly put on the back burner because people are far too busy managing fear in themselves and their colleagues.

Different people hear organizational information in differing ways and with differing understandings. It is the job of leadership to communicate clearly and to ensure that everyone understands what is being said and agreed upon.

> Miranda is managing director of a large PR agency specializing in risk management. She's incredibly good at working with clients but not terribly good at the internal stuff – like running meetings. Miranda knows what she wants to say but seems to have trouble staying on topic. At the beginning of every meeting she hands out an agenda and then proceeds to start somewhere in the middle. This takes people off guard. Then someone will jump in and bring up a subject not on the agenda. The interrupters with the loudest voices get heard, the thinkers withdraw into themselves, the quiet ones have difficulty finding a way to contribute, the creative people doodle and laugh to themselves. It's all rather knee-jerk chaos. People come from these meetings feeling very confused and with little clarity about what was discussed and with little sense of an action plan.

It is equally the job of leadership to ensure that the right people are invited to attend the meeting for the right reasons.

A US under-secretary of state ran a meeting that was attended by 60 potential suppliers. Nonplussed, she invited the participants to form a circle, state their names, and explain their purpose for being there. After the first few people identified themselves she thanked them and asked them to please excuse themselves as their presence was not necessary. The end of the process left 12 people in the room – a productive meeting followed (Mankins, 2014).

Meetings are useful forums for communicating, for gathering information and for giving people a say. But meetings take time.

> Most executives are spending 20 hours or more every week in meetings. And one meeting usually spawns many more. For example, my colleagues and I found that a single weekly executive committee meeting at a large company generated about 300,000 hours of preparation time each year (the equivalent of nearly 150 full-time-equivalent employees).
>
> Mankins (2014)

Here are some tips for running meetings that might help to make them more productive, enjoyable and relevant and, most importantly, fear-free:

- clarify the purpose of the meeting;
- include only those critical to the meeting;
- ask for ideas ahead of time;
- send out a pre-meeting agenda: make clear what won't be discussed as well as what will;

- keep the focus on solutions vs problems;
- don't let people interrupt;
- set time limits for speaking;
- give all participants a specific slot on the agenda;
- end the meeting with a bullet point list of next steps, who's responsible for each point, and what is the time frame;
- create a decision log that captures all the decisions made in the meeting;
- send a follow-up e-mail ensuring everyone is clear and accountable.

What lies beneath

There are deeper forces at play in considering the impact of learning and memory on the culture of families, organizations and societies.

As we have observed, calling memories to mind can be a rather hit-or-miss affair. But at the neurobiological level experience, memory and learning have a lasting impact on brain development throughout the entirety of life.

Eric Kandel, a US neuropsychiatrist, shared the 2000 Nobel Prize in Physiology or Medicine for his research on the physiological basis of memory storage in neurons. He demonstrated that when people learn something it changes the wiring in their brains and that these physical changes are happening concurrently with learning. Memory is not like a filing cabinet we can dip into and pull up a historical record. It is a dynamic process, continuously recreated. So the learning brain is constantly rewiring itself. Learning involves alterations in how nerve cells communicate with each other. Short-term memory involves transient changes of the connections between the cells whilst long-term memory involves anatomical changes that are enduring resulting from the growth of new synaptic connections (Kandel, cited by Dreyfus, 2012). Studies cited by Kandel (2006) support the idea that 'learning is conserved through evolution because it is essential for survival'.

> For me learning and memory... address one of the fundamental features of human activity: our ability to acquire new ideas from experience and to retain these ideas in memory. In fact, most of the ideas we have about the world and our civilization we have learned so that we are who we are in good measure because of what we have learned and what we remember.
>
> Kandel (2000)

Kandel did his research on the neural system of *Aplysia Californica*, a simple sea slug with a very large nerve cell. *Aplysia California* is capable of simple learning and learns at a neural level in the same way as humans do (Medina, 2008).

A psychiatrist and psychoanalyst, Kandel believed that soft psychological explanations of learning and memory needed to be grounded in the hard science of neurobiology. Kandel understood that the cellular mechanisms of learning and memory reside in the connections a neuron makes and receives with other neurones, (Kandel, 2006). This research takes learning to a deeper level than Hebbian Plasticity (see Chapter 2), which is concerned with synapses.

Kandel's understanding that knowledge of the past is transmitted down through the generations is one of the cornerstones of the new science of epigenetics.

Epigenesis

> Epigenesis (Res): The process in which experience alters the regulation of gene expression by way of changing the various molecules (histones and methyl groups) on the chromosome.
>
> Siegel (2012)

Human history is built on learning and memory. From the earliest cave paintings, through storytelling, folk tales, songs, fairy tales, written records, photographs and film, human beings have recorded events and their consequences. The examination of fossils and artefacts allows scientists, biologists and archaeologists to place the evolution of species, and the human race in particular, in the context of place and time.

Within each of us 'is a massive library of DNA, three billion base pairs that have been passed down to us' (Kenneally, 2014). There is growing evidence that societies shape DNA and that the operation of genes also shapes history. For example it is believed the avoidance of dangerous plants and animals, crucial to survival, is embedded in our DNA; the methods employed in the planting of crops and the taming and domestication of animals has completely changed their biology (Kenneally, 2014).

Scientists now know that genes are not the only authors of inheritance, (Rogers, 2012). It has been discovered that there are biochemical entities that can affect gene expression.

Epigenetics is the study of changes in the way genes express themselves and which are caused by external factors (Swaab, 2014). 'It refers to anything that changes a gene's effect without changing the actual DNA sequence... The idea that experience can echo in our genes is certainly a powerful one' (Dobbs, 2013). Studies of the effects of famine among expectant mothers in the Netherlands during World War II reveal the effects on gene expression and behaviours in their children. Culture, by influencing the expression of genes, can shape lasting differences in human values and behaviour.

In March 2104 Virginia Hughes reported in *Nature* the work of epigeneticist Brian Dias on how fearful experiences can be passed down the generations.

Dias had been exposing male mice to acetophenone – a chemical with a sweet, almond-like smell – and then giving them a mild foot shock. After being exposed to this treatment five times a day for three days, the mice became reliably fearful, freezing in the presence of acetophenone even when they received no shock.

Ten days later, Dias allowed the mice to mate with unexposed females. When their young grew up, many of the animals were more sensitive to acetophenone than to other odours, and more likely to be startled by an unexpected noise during exposure to the smell. Their offspring – the 'grandchildren' of the mice trained to fear the smell – were also jumpier in the presence of acetophenone. What's more, all three generations had larger-than-normal M71 glomeruli, structures where acetophenone-sensitive neurons in the nose connect with neurons in the olfactory bulb. In the January issue of *Nature Neuroscience*, Dias and Ressler (2014) suggested that this hereditary transmission of environmental information was the result of epigenetics – chemical changes to the genome that affect how DNA is packaged and expressed without altering its sequence.

Hughes (2014)

It has now become well established that the grandchildren of holocaust survivors suffer lasting effects of the horrors that had been endured by their grandparents in that they experience high levels of anxiety and engage in risk-averse behaviours. These effects used to be attributed to social causes such as the passing on of memories through storytelling or by over-protective parents and grandparents (Haaretz, 2015). But it now appears that the experience might have been encoded.

Epigenetics is therefore demonstrating that experience gets transmitted not by altering the fundamental DNA, but in the way that genes express themselves as a result of the way the biochemistry of experience gets transmitted down the generations.

So 'culture', organizationally, may have a transmitted factor in it that is very powerful. A managing director of one of the international subsidiaries of a great airplane engine manufacturer described recently in conversation how his 39 years with the company were preceded by his father's 42 years with the same company and his grandfather's 37. He himself had gone straight from school at 16 to become a bench engineer, learning his trade and breathing in the company's internationally known standards of perfection in the old craft manner. No destruction of youthful skills there by a university education. But perhaps some of his essential values came to him epigenetically too as he himself transmits the cultural values of the company socially.

Organizational culture

History is important. If you don't know history, it is as if you were born yesterday. And if you were born yesterday, anybody up there in a position of power can tell you anything, and you have no way of checking up on it.

Zinn, cited by Kenneally (2014)

Organizations have memories too. Organizational culture contains all the history, learning and knowledge that have accrued from the establishment of the organization.

Edgar Schein is the Society of Sloan Fellows Professor of Management Emeritus and a professor emeritus at the MIT Sloan School of Management. He has done extensive research on how organizational performance is influenced by culture in organizations, institutions, governments and occupations. Schein believes that 'the only thing of real importance that leaders do is to create and manage culture' (Schein, 1992). Schein's work enables people who work in organizations and 'experts' who study organizations to have a template from which to understand what is meant by organizational culture.

Culture stems from the original beliefs of the organization's founder(s). As a venture develops and grows a common history begins to be built.

Founders usually have a major impact on how the group initially defines and solves its external adaptation and internal integration problems... Because they had the original idea, they will typically have their own notion, based on their own cultural history and personality of how to fulfil the idea.

Schein (1992)

The basic underlying assumptions that underpin the successful early decisions of the founder become accepted as the way business gets done and decisions are made. As the business moves forward in time the basic assumptions become givens – part of the memories of the organization that guide behaviours, perceptions, thoughts, feelings. These memories are often implicit (Argyris, 1976; Schein, 1992).

Culture is neither tangible nor visible yet it is strongly felt. Culture implies the existence of a coherent whole that has stability, depth and breadth. Culture derives from a human need to make sense of things and to create order (Schein, 1992).

Edgar Schein's definitions of culture include:

- Group norms: implicit standards and values.

- Espoused values: what is stated to be the way things are done around here; what is claimed to be of importance.

- Formal philosophy: publicly articulated principles guiding a group's actions.

- Rules of the game: implicit and unwritten. The way we do things around here; the ropes; what really matters.

- How it feels: feelings conveyed by the kinds of people employed, the physical layout, the look of the organization, the way people interact.

- Embedded skills: the competencies necessary to accomplish tasks. These are passed down through the generations without having to be put in writing.

- Habits of thinking, mental models, and linguistic paradigms: the shared thinking that guides perceptions, thought and language.

- Shared meanings: what group members understand as they interact.

- Root metaphors: the emotional response of group members to the organization; how groups characterize themselves.

- Formal rituals and celebrations: how key events are celebrated.

Stephen was born between the wars within the sound of Bow Bells (in the East End of London). His father was rather kind and ineffectual – his children described him as henpecked. His mother was made of stern stuff and was thought of as having a backbone of steel. Stephen was one of five children, three brothers and one sister. Life was tough, money was scarce, and family was everything. What mattered in the family was loyalty and putting your nose to the grindstone. Illness was not tolerated; negative thinking was not abided. The rules as set down by Stephen's mother were clear, tough and fair. She adored her children but was very quick to enforce punishment if boundaries were crossed. Stephen was the bright one, the one with the most promise – but he had to leave school at 14 to earn his keep. He got a job as an apprentice in a tailor's shop, showed real talent and over the next decade developed his own following. One of Stephen's clients offered to back him in a new venture.

Within five years Stephen built a thriving clothing manufacturing business. As his business developed and grew he employed men who were kind, nice, unthreatening and rather ineffectual. The women tended to have strong natures. He appointed as his CEO a woman who ruled with an iron fist. In his employees Stephen valued loyalty and hard work. He treated his employees with 'unconditional love' and people generally worked for him for many years.

The family values that Stephen learned in childhood went on to permeate his business culture. Thirty years later Stephen remains at the helm of the business. Much has changed but the underlying values and guiding principles remain the same.

> Culture formally defined... a pattern of shared basic assumptions that was learned by a group as it solved its problems of external adaptation and internal integration, that has worked well enough to be considered valid and, therefore, to be taught to new members as the correct way to perceive, think, and feel in relation to those problems.
>
> Schein (1992)

References

Anon (1907) Albert Einstein, 9 aha! moments that blow Oprah off the screen, available at http://www.soulscode.com/aha-moments-that-blow-oprah-off-the-screen/?nggpage-name=1907-albert-einstein [accessed 11 October 2014]

Argyris, C (1976) *Increasing Leadership Effectiveness*, Wiley-Interscience, New York

Aristotle, The Internet Classics Archive, *On Memory and Reminiscence*, Aristotle, available at http://classics.mit.edu/Aristotle/memory.html [accessed 27 September 2014]

Barkus, D (2014) How to have a eureka moment, *Harvard Business Review*, available at http://blogs.hbr.org/2014/03/how-to-have-a-eureka-moment/ [accessed 12 October 2014]

Churchland, PM (2012) *Plato's Camera: How the physical brain captures a landscape of abstract universals*, MIT Press, Cambridge, MA; London, UK

DesMarais, C (2014) Simple trick for better brainstorming sessions – Yahoo Small Business Advisor, available at https://smallbusiness.yahoo.com/advisor/simple-trick-better-brainstorming-sessions-140000367.html [accessed 25 October 2014]

Dias, BG and Ressler, KJ (2014) Parental olfactory experience influences behavior and neural structure in subsequent generations, *Nature Neuroscience*, **17**(1), pp 89–96, doi:10.1038/nn.3594

Dobbs, D (2013) The social life of genes: Shaping your molecular composition, *Pacific Standard*, available at http://www.psmag.com/navigation/health-and-behavior/the-social-life-of-genes-64616/ [accessed 19 October 2014]

Dreyfus, C (2012) A quest to understand how memory works, *New York Times*, available at http://www.nytimes.com/2012/03/06/science/a-quest-to-understand-how-memory-works.html? [accessed 15 April 2014]

Evans, D (2015) New Israel: Study finds signs of trauma in grandchildren of Holocaust Survivors, *Haaretz*, http://www.haaretz.com/news/national/new-israeli-study-finds-signs-of-trauma-in-grandchildren-of-holocaust-survivors-1.424480

Fernyhough, C (2012) The story of the self, *The Guardian*, available at http://www.theguardian.com/lifeandstyle/2012/jan/13/our-memories-tell-our-story [accessed 4 October 2014]

Hughes, V (2014) Epigenetics: The sins of the father, *Nature*, **507**(7490), pp 22–24, available at http://www.nature.com/news/epigenetics-the-sins-of-the-father-1.14816 [accessed 20 November 2014]

Innocence Project (2014) Understand the causes: Eyewitness misidentification, The Innocence Project, available at http://www.innocenceproject.org/understand/Eyewitness-Misidentification.php [accessed 5 October 2014]

Jacoby, LL, Kelly, C, Brown, J and Jasechko, J (1989) Becoming famous overnight: Limits on the ability to avoid unconscious influences of the past, *Journal of Personality and Social Psychology*, **56** (3), pp 326–28

Kahneman, D (2011) *Thinking, Fast and Slow*, Farrar, Straus and Giroux, New York

Kandel, E (2000) Eric R Kandel, Nobel Lecture, available at http://www.nobelprize.org/nobel_prizes/medicine/laureates/2000/kandel-lecture.pdf [accessed 19 October 2014]

Kandel, E (2006) *In Search of Memory: The emergence of a new science of mind*, WW Norton and Company, New York

Kenneally, C (2014) *The Invisible History of the Human Race*, Viking, New York

Kline, N (2009) *More Time to Think*, Fisher King Publishing, Pool-in-Wharfedale, England

Mankins, MC (2014) Yes, you can make meetings more productive, *Harvard Business Review*, available at http://blogs.hbr.org/2014/06/yes-you-can-make-meetings-more-productive/ [accessed 27 October 2014]

Medina, J (2008) *Brain Rules*, Pear Press, Seattle, WA

Rogers, K (2012) Epigenetics: A turning point in our understanding of heredity, Guest Blog, *Scientific American*, available at: http://blogs.scientificamerican.com/guest-blog/2012/01/16/epigenetics-a-turning-point-in-our-understanding-of-heredity/ [accessed 19 October 2014]

Schein, EH (1992) *Organizational Culture and Leadership*, 2nd edn, Jossey-Bass, San Francisco, CA

Siegel, DJ (2012) *Pocket Guide to Interpersonal Neurobiology; An integrative handbook fo the mind*, WW Norton and Company, New York

Snopes.com (nd) 'Fargo': A true story? available at http://www.snopes.com/movies/films/fargo.asp [accessed 9 September 2014]

Swaab, R (2014) *We Are Our Brains; From the womb to Alzheimer's*, Penguin Books, London

Viereck, GS (1929) What life means to Einstein, *Saturday Evening Post*, available at http://www.saturdayeveningpost.com/wp-content/uploads/satevepost/what_life_means_to_einstein.pdf [accessed 11 October 2014]

Relationships

04

Introduction

One day Ken Hyman, a successful movie producer, found himself catapulted into a key role at a Hollywood movie studio. He told us the following story.

'I'd just finished filming *The Dirty Dozen*. My Dad called: "I've just bought Warner Brothers; come back and run the studio."

'I took the job. Jack Warner ran the studio with a rod of iron. He was a demi-god and people were terrified of him. And there I was, the new Jack Warner. The first thing I did was to call all the department heads. I said, "Happily, I'm not just an executive; I'm a picture maker. I appreciate all you do. But I'm not a mind reader. Let's work together. You got any gripes – call me. Let's work together – we should be a happy family."

'I met Sam Peckinpah in 1962 at the Cannes Film Festival. He'd just done *Ride the High Country*. I said to his publicist, "Get me that bastard's number." Peckinpah had a bad reputation and nobody would hire him. But we were both marines and we felt connected. I trusted him. He brought me a 10-page treatment for *The Wild Bunch*. The rest is history. For me it was all about relationships. Most of the studio hierarchy didn't have relationships. I found if you respect who you're dealing with then you get the best.'

Throughout life we are dependent upon the quality of relationships in which we find ourselves. In early life relationships are vital for provoking physical structures in the developing architecture of the brain. As adults, relationships at work profoundly affect the well-being of the individuals, and so the well-being of the company.

This chapter explores the significance of these observations for organizational effectiveness; considers what happens when relationships break down; and what the optimum conditions are for effective working relationships anywhere.

Think again

If you think that when we are born our minds are a blank slate then think again. If you think that everything is down to inheritance and genes then think again. If you think that nurture determines character and abilities then think again. Nature vs nurture has been the subject of debate through history. With the coming together of knowledge from the sciences of mind, brain, genes and evolution the debate has been transformed. There is no longer dispute within the scientific community about the psycho-biological influences of genetics, inheritance and early experience. Scientists now widely agree that biology is not destiny, but it has a huge influence; and also that there is no such thing as a blank slate coming into the world. The infant on day one has a brain already working and ready to deal with the world it was expecting.

Discoveries from evolutionary psychology, behavioural genetics and neuro-science have meant a reframing of the understandings about nature and nurture. Evolutionary psychology has identified 'hundreds of universals that cut across the world's cultures'. Behavioural genetics 'has shown that temperament emerges early in life' and continues throughout life; that variations within cultures come from genetic differences. 'Neuroscience has shown that the genome contains a rich toolkit of growth factors, axon guidance molecules, and cell adhesion molecules that help structure the brain during development, as well as mechanisms of plasticity that make learning possible' (Pinker, 2004).

Make or break

Relationships are the making of us. Our brains develop and evolve in the context of relationships. This is as true for the developing foetus as it is for the newborn, the baby, the child, the adolescent, the young adult and the adult. And it holds true across all cultures. Our sense of self begins to be established in the earliest days of life. Across cultures sense of self is built on the emotions that define the interpersonal environment.

From the earliest bonds of attachment, and given a biologically normal course of development, we have evolved to connect and to be social. The socio-emotional interactions between care-giving adults and an infant indelibly shape the developing brain and the ongoing ability of the growing child to regulate his or her emotions (Schore, 1994).

Love, human kindness, and care are the currency of emotional stability, well-being, self-confidence and self-belief. Just as love and joy are the magic of childhood so extremes of fear, anger, disgust, sorrow and shame cast a dark spell over the growing years.

Being and nothingness

In order to provide protection and security, primitive humans survived and prospered by banding together in couples, in family units, in tribal communities. We humans have evolved with mechanisms to ensure we are motivated to stay connected (Eisenberger and Cole, 2012). Studies show that these motivations are so powerful that an infant will form bonds to a caregiver regardless of the quality of the care; that in the face of imprisonment or abduction people will forge attachment bonds with their jailers or abductors (Sapolsky, 2009).

When relationships are disrupted or broken the brain may process these events in the same way as threats of physical harm. The effects of social isolation are such that the immunological system may be compromised.

> The causal role of loneliness on neural and neuroendocrine mechanisms is difficult to test conclusively in humans. Mechanistic animal studies provide a lens through which to evaluate the neurological effects of a member of a social species living chronically on the social perimeter. Experimental studies show that social isolation produces significant changes in brain structures and processes in adult social animals.
>
> Cacioppo (2014)

> Relative to socially isolated individuals, socially connected individuals live longer and show increased resistance to a variety of somatic diseases ranging from heart disease to cancer.
>
> Eisenberger and Cole (2012)

In a neuroimaging study the neural underpinnings of social exclusion were examined. The results showed the similarities between the brain bases of social pain and those of physical pain. In the first study participants were placed in a scanner and told that they could watch two other people (also in scanners) play a game of ball, but because of a computer glitch they would not be able to participate (implicit social exclusion, or ISE). In fact there were no other players and the ball-tossing game was a pre-set computer game. In the second study participants perceived they were participating fully in the game with two other players (inclusion, I). In the third study participants were 'thrown' seven balls but then the game continued on without them being thrown the ball (explicit social exclusion, or ESE).

Questionnaires filled out by participants after the fMRI studies showed that people felt distressed, ignored and left out under the first and third conditions. The study's neural correlates of ESE and ISE showed activations similar to those seen in fMRI studies of physical pain. Interestingly, the results also indicated that when participants believed they were excluded through the computer glitch and not through the deliberate actions of the other players, they were by and large able to successfully regulate their feelings of distress. Physical and social pain seem to be affected by both social support and underlying neurochemicals. From a bio-psycho-social perspective it really does 'hurt' to lose someone we love (Eisenberger *et al*, 2003).

Cooperation and collaboration

> When dealing with people, remember you are not dealing with creatures of logic, but creatures of emotion.
>
> Dale Carnegie (1937)

Great leaders seem to have an intuitive understanding of the significance of relationships. On 5 March 1946 Winston Churchill stood to address an audience at Westminster College in Fulton, Missouri. In the audience, just a month before he died, was the president of the United States, Franklin Delano Roosevelt. World War II had come to an end six months before, leaving vast parts of Europe in ruins and trying to pick up the pieces. Churchill's speech defined what he called 'a special relationship between the British Commonwealth and Empire and the United States'. Churchill saw this as essential to safeguard the world from a return to the tyranny of war, a return to the Dark Ages in which the dark uses of scientific knowledge might bring about the total destruction of mankind (Churchill, 1946).

> I spoke earlier of the Temple of Peace. Workmen from all countries must build that temple. If two of the workmen know each other particularly well and are old friends, if their families are inter-mingled, and if they have 'faith in each other's purpose, hope in each other's future and charity towards each other's shortcomings' – to quote some good words I read here the other day – why cannot they work together at the common task as friends and partners? Why cannot they share their tools and thus increase each other's working powers? Indeed they must do so or else the temple may not be built, or, being built, it may collapse, and we shall all be proved again un-teachable and have to go and try to learn again for a third time in a school of war, incomparably more rigorous than that from which we have just been released. The Dark Ages may return, the Stone Age may return on the gleaming wings of science, and what might now shower immeasurable material blessings upon mankind, may even bring about its total destruction.
>
> Churchill (1946)

As world governments now tackle global problems, cooperative initiatives are becoming the norm. Governments form and break alliances and form them again based upon practical survival needs. Modern business is global business. Organizations learn how to operate, cooperate and do business across cultures.

Throughout history it has been demonstrated that cooperation is mutually beneficial, pays rewards to everyone involved, and benefits others whose connections are more tenuous. In organizations individuals may be conflicted about individual vs group interests. One of the roles for leaders is to ensure that, whilst individuals are encouraged to think out of the box and to pursue creative solutions, the eye is kept on the ball – the greater good. Relationships develop based upon internal common goals as well as upon the perceptions of external common enemies (the competition). The bottom line is that when relationships work, everyone's a winner.

Good leaders are good at relationships. It's a tricky business because, as we've seen, relationships involve intimate brain-to-brain connections. As mind, brain and body are intricately linked together, every personal interaction creates changes in our neural wiring and neurochemistry. 'To a surprising extent, then, our relationships mould not just our experience, but our biology' (Goleman, 2007). Simply put, good relationships make us feel good. They also support our physical systems at all levels. Dysfunctional, disordered and toxic relationships bring us down and they massively compromise the immune system. How exciting to know that while you are working with colleagues on an interesting and engaging project your brain is being tickled and tantalized by the experience. How sad to think that a withering look or an ill-thought phrase can tap down into feelings of despair.

Relationships at work matter very much indeed. They matter so much that studies show that performance-related pay is not the be-all and end-all to motivation; and pay rises do not equate with people being more productive. Bosses seem to be motivated by self-interests such as being the most successful, beating the competition, and making the most money. It is not surprising then that employers would ascribe those same motivations to their employees. In fact studies show over and over that people value strong reciprocity and have 'a predisposition to cooperate with others and to punish those who violate the norms of cooperation, at personal cost, even when it is implausible to expect that these costs will be repaid' (Gintis *et al*, 2002).

The fMRI studies show that when people perceive themselves or others as being treated fairly the reward system in the brain is activated. Praise and positive social regard are more powerful in triggering the brain's reward system than monetary gains. Bearing in mind that one person's pain may be another's pleasure, research demonstrates that people place a higher value on feeling fulfilled than they do on purely monetary gains (Kahneman and Tversky, 1981).

The business of relationships

Relationship building is good business practice. But oddly, as a modern management truism, 'relationship' seems to be focused outwards, to customers. It is unfortunate that many organizations don't understand the economic benefits of creating robust social environments *internally*. 'Growing and leveraging strong relationships is key for anyone looking to increase their net worth or influence' (Corcoran, 2014).

Daniel Goleman's book *Emotional Intelligence* (1995) took the world by storm. In it he introduced cutting-edge neuroscientific research from the lab of Joseph LeDoux; research that brought to worldwide general attention for the first time the evolution of the emotional (limbic) system as being part of the hard-wiring of the brains of mammals (see Chapters 1 and 2). His work defined what he called emotional intelligence (EQ) as an essential aspect of effective social behaviour; that EQ is every bit as, and perhaps even more important, than IQ. Over the ensuing years since the publication of *Emotional Intelligence*, the spotlight has turned on the new science of social intelligence. Successful models for developing managers and leaders with EQ are being used in emotionally smart organizations throughout the world.

To date *Emotional Intelligence* has sold over 5,000,000 copies. The road to success is paved with emotional intelligence.

> Brilliance alone will not propel a scientist to the top unless she also has the ability to influence and persuade others, and the inner discipline to strive for challenging goals. A lazy or reticent genius may have all the answers in his head, but they amount to little if no one knows or cares.
>
> Goleman (1998)

Goleman's emotional competence framework describes two dimensions: Personal Competence – how we manage ourselves; and Social Competence – how we manage others.

Personal competence

- Self-awareness: knowing your internal states, preferences, resources and intuitions:
  - emotional awareness;
  - accurate self-assessment;
  - self-confidence.
- Self-regulation: managing your internal states, impulses and resources:
  - self-control;

- trustworthiness;
- conscientiousness;
- adaptability;
- innovation.

- Motivation: emotional tendencies that guide or facilitate reaching goals:
  - achievement drive;
  - commitment;
  - initiative;
  - optimism.

Social competence

- Empathy: awareness of feelings, needs and concerns of others:
  - understanding others;
  - developing others;
  - service orientation;
  - leveraging diversity;
  - political awareness.
- Social skills: adeptness at inducing desirable responses in others:
  - influence;
  - communication;
  - conflict management;
  - leadership;
  - change catalyst;
  - building bonds;
  - collaboration and cooperation;
  - team capabilities.

David Rock, who runs the Neuroleadership Institute, believes that social skills are as fundamentally important to organizational success as work-related skills. Rock cites a study by the Management Research Group that collected data from 60,000 managers over 10 years across four continents. The data determined what percentage of managers could be considered among the top 33 per cent of performers as measured by their ability to focus both on work goals as well as the needs of other people. Less than 1 per cent of leaders and managers were perceived to be strong in both areas (Rock, 2013). Rock has developed a model for business he calls SCARF. It is based on the five primary rewards or threats that tap into the brain's emotional system. Rock believes that business environments benefit when individuals have:

- **S**tatus: which is about knowing where one is in any hierarchy.
- **C**ertainty: concerns being able to predict the future.
- **A**utonomy: provides a sense of control over events.
- **R**elatedness: is a sense of safety with others.
- **F**airness: is a perception of fair exchanges between people.

    (Lieberman, 2013)

The SCARF model helps individuals to understand the five domains of social experience that the brain is always monitoring. Table 4.1 (Cecil, 2013) summarizes how the SCARF model links to the brain, minimizing threats and maximizing rewards in organizational settings.

Nancy Kline believes that changing the way we treat each other creates an organizational environment where people practise values of inclusiveness, respect, collaboration, integrity and innovation. She has identified 12 key enablers to improve thinking and generate time to think (Kline, 2009):

- attention: listening with palpable respect and without interruption;
- equality: ensuring equal turns to think and speak;
- ease: offering freedom from internal urgency;
- incisive questions;
- finding and removing untrue assumptions that distort thinking;
- information;
- supplying the facts; dismantling denial;
- diversity: encouraging divergent thinking and diverse group identities;
- encouragement: giving courage for cutting-edge thinking by removing internal competition;
- feelings: allowing sufficient emotional release to restore thinking;
- appreciation: practising a 5:1 ratio of appreciation to criticism;
- place: creating a physical environment that says to people, 'you matter'.

TABLE 4.1 SCARF model application

Domain	Description	Brain part	Threat	Reward
Status	Relative importance to others	• Reduction in status from being left out activate same regions as physical pain	• Do you need advice? • Annual performance review	• Pay attention to work done and improvements • Positive feedback and public acknowledgement • Allow people to provide feedback on their own work
Certainty	Ability to predict the future – without prediction, the brain must use more resources, involving more energy	• Uncertainty generates 'error' in the orbital frontal cortex – it takes attention away from goal	• Change • Not knowing people's expectations	• Vision, strategies, maps, plans (even if we know things won't be as planned) • Turning implicit into explicit • If unable to tell now, give date when you'll be able to tell
Autonomy	Perception of exerting control over events	• Strong correlation between sense of autonomy and health outcomes	• Inescapable stress can be highly destructive • Working in teams reduces autonomy	• A choice between two options: which one do you prefer? • Enable individual point of need decision making without intervention of managers • Hard-wire autonomy in organization processes

TABLE 4.1 *continued*

Domain	Description	Brain part	Threat	Reward
Relatedness	Sense of safety with others	• Need for safe human contact is primary driver like need for food • Thoughts from people like us use same circuitry as our own thoughts	• Meeting someone unknown • Feeling let down, not involved	• Shaking hand, swapping names, discussing something in common • Share personal information with team mates • Mentoring, coaching
Fairness	Perception of fair exchanges between people	• Insular (involves intense emotions, eg disgust)		• Increase transparency and level of communication • Establish clear expectations • Groups creating their own rules • Help people see situations from other perspectives

SOURCE: Cecil (2013)

Emotional radar

Doctors have long understood that emotions can get in the way of objectivity and good judgement and that it's not a good idea to diagnose and treat the ones you love. The code of ethics of the American Medical Association (AMA) sets forth that physicians are not to treat close family members or themselves. Professional objectivity is likely to be compromised, feelings may unduly influence medical judgement, patients may feel uncomfortable, professional limits may be misjudged and tensions may ensue (AMA, 1993). This seems like good practice. But in the real world, staying objective when making decisions and forming judgements is difficult to achieve. And actually may not always be in our best interests.

Our emotional radar is perpetually scanning the external world for danger. Relationships are made or broken based on signals from our emotional system. These messages might be in conflict with trying to maintain an objective stance and with decision-making based on pure logic.

Chen was interviewing for a new assistant. She was taking on more responsibilities and needed somebody she could really count on. Although an entry-level job it had huge future possibilities; this consulting partnership liked to grow people from within. Chen's last assistant was okay and Chen liked her but she had not kept up with the more mundane tasks of the job. Chen wanted to hire someone with ambition but also the interest in doing the day-to-day stuff to the best of his or her abilities. Chen had short-listed two final candidates and she was struggling to make a decision. The candidate who showed the most ambition felt threatening to Chen. She perceived that junior colleagues often outshone her, highlighted her weaknesses, and were after her job. The other candidate was very talented and Chen felt he was a kindred spirit. But Chen felt he lacked the competitive edge. In the end Chen went for candidate 2; she reasoned that he would fit in better with people at the office and people would like him.

Chen's decision was based on gut feeling. Gut feeling arises from neural signals emanating from two structures: the amygdala and the insula. Neuroscientist Antonio Damasio calls these messages 'somatic markers' (Damasio, 2010; Goleman, 2013). Somatic markers are there to help guide decisions by telling you if something or someone feels right or wrong (Goleman, 2013). These messages may not always be reliable but, when you're weighing things up that appear to be equal, gut feelings are probably a better source of information than the toss of a coin. It is likely Chen's decision had more to do with her own perceptions of safety vs survival than with who she believed was going to do the best job. But the source of an emotion and the world of relationships cannot be separated. Our social interactions drive our emotions (Goleman, 2007) and are driven by them.

Robin's manager was promoted up and she had a new boss. 'I'd been with the company 12 years when my new director arrived. From day one she just didn't like me. It started with her trying to win over people's regard by embarrassing me at meetings. In front of my colleagues she'd say, "I have a problem with you, I can't rely on you"; I began to hear of meetings that I wasn't asked to attend. E-mails relating to my work were circulated to everyone but me. Lame excuses were given. She began to pile irrelevant work on my desk; the deadlines were impossible to meet.

'I did everything to please her, but nothing was good enough. She criticized my manner, appearance, and management of others; in fact everything I did. Worst of all, she presented my ideas as her own. I felt helpless, inadequate, confused, and anxious.'

Luckily for Robin the members of her team saw what was going on and the injustice of the way she was being treated. They mobilized themselves, rallied round her and helped her come up with strategies to manage the situation and hopefully turn things around.

They helped Robin gather information. They'd heard rumours through the grapevine. There was takeover talk in the air. They suspected the new director had been brought in as an agent of change. With the support of her colleagues Robin became proactive: she kept a diary; she wrote a memorandum to her new boss setting out the criticisms concisely, coldly and clearly; she requested an immediate and detailed response; she sent a copy to the HR department and to relevant directors. 'It was a difficult time but it meant more to me than I can say to be supported by my team. They turned a negative into a positive and I'll never forget it.'

When it comes to relationships at work, it's a good idea to be clear about their limitations and your expectations. Work-related relationships have a different set of boundaries than friendships.

Friendships have strong emotional ties that are not present in professional relationships. Friends are attuned to each other's inner worlds. Friendship implies a bond between two people that neither time nor distance can diminish nor break. It is a relationship that does not rely on the fulfilment of expectations – it is an end in itself.

In a friendship the two people become greater than the whole of the sum of their parts.

Whilst professional relationships might develop into friendships they begin with the promise that something will be delivered. It might be goods or services or work or productivity. But when the ability to deliver is not met, or is unable to be fulfilled, then the relationship is likely to end.

Ken Hyman recalls the day he sealed the deal to sell Warner Brothers:

I turned to my personal assistant. 'Today I have 5,000 intimate friends. The phone never stops ringing. When the word gets out it's going to get very quiet around here. These are the eight people who I'm going to hear from next week.' I'm a realist and I knew without question who my real friends were – the people I could talk to. Those people stayed in my life and the others fell away.

References

AMA (1993) Opinion 8.19: Self-treatment or treatment of immediate family members, available at http://www.ama-assn.org/ama/pub/physician-resources/medical-ethics/code-medical-ethics/opinion819.page? [accessed on 13 November 2014]

Cacioppo, J (2014) Social brain, available at http://www.johncacioppo.com/social-brain/ [accessed on 9 November 2014]

Carnegie, D (1937) How to Win Friends and Influence People, reissued edn, Simon and Schuster, New York, London, Toronto, Sydney

Cecil, poster at the blog Hypertextual (2013) Social neuroscience, SCARF model and change management, available at http://thehypertextual.com/2013/04/23/social-neuroscience-scarf-model-and-change-management/

Churchill, W (1946) The sinews of peace, available at http://www.winstonchurchill.org/learn/speeches/speeches-of-winston-churchill/120-the-sinews-of-peace [accessed on 1 November 2014]

Corcoran, J (2014b) Lewis Howes: How a former pro athlete turned entrepreneur builds relationships, Forbes, available at http://www.forbes.com/sites/johncorcoran/2014/11/06/lewis-howes-how-a-former-pro-athlete-turned-entrepreneur-builds-relationships/2/ [accessed on 8 November 2014]

Damasio, A (2010) Self Comes to Mind: Constructing the conscious brain, Pantheon Books, New York

Eisenberger, NI and Cole, SW (2012) Social neuroscience and health: Neurophysiological mechanisms linking social ties with physical health, *Nature Neuroscience*, **15** (5), pp 669–74, doi:10.1038/nn.3086

Eisenberger, NI, Lieberman, MD and Williams, KD (2003) Does rejection hurt? An fMRI study of social exclusion, *Science*, available at http://dtserv2.compsy.uni-jena.de/ss2010/sozpsy_uj/17512154/content.nsf/Pages/4ECAB2CDBFA73BDDC1257706003665A8/$FILE/Eisenberger Lieberman Williams 2002.pdf [accessed on 9 November 2014]

Gintis, H, Bowles, S, Boyd, R and Fehr, E (2002) Explaining altruistic behaviour in humans, *Evolution and Social Behavior*, **24**, pp 153–72, available at http://tuvalu.santafe.edu/~bowles/2003E&HB.pdf [accessed on 14 November 2014]

Goleman, D (1995) *Emotional Intelligence*, Bantam Books, New York, Toronto, London, Sydney, Auckland

Goleman, D (1998) *Working with Emotional Intelligence*, Bloomsbury, London

Goleman, D (2007) *Social Intelligence: The new science of human relationships*, Bantam Dell, New York

Goleman, D (2013) The focused leader, *Harvard Business Review*, available at https://hbr.org/2013/12/the-focused-leader [accessed on 13 November 2014]

Kahneman, D and Tversky, A (1981) The psychology of preferences, *Scientific American*, pp 160–73, available at http://www.scientificamerican.com/article/the-psychology-of-preferences/ [accessed on 13 November 2014]

Kline, N (2009) *More Time to Think*, Fisher King Publishing, Pool-in-Wharfedale, England

Lieberman, MD (2013) *Social: Why our brains are wired to connect*, Crown Publishers, New York

Pinker, S (2004) Why nature and nurture won't go away, available at http://pinker.wjh.harvard.edu/articles/papers/nature_nurture.pdf [accessed on 7 November 2014]

Rock, D (2013) Why organizations fail, *Fortune Magazine*, available at http://fortune.com/2013/10/23/why-organizations-fail/ [accessed on 15 November 2014]

Sapolsky, R (2009) Any kind of mother in a storm, *Nature Neuroscience*, **12** (11), 1355–56, doi:10.1038/nn1109-1355

Schore, AN (1994) *Affect Regulation and the Origin of the Self: The neurobiology of emotional development*, Lawrence Erlbaum Associates, Hills Dale, NJ

Trust

05

Introduction

'Ginny!' said Mr Weasley, flabbergasted. 'Haven't I taught you *anything*? What have I always told you? Never trust anything that can think for itself *if you can't see where it keeps its brain*.'

JK Rowling (1998)

SARAH CONNOR (Linda Hamilton)   What's he like?
KYLE REESE (Michael Biehn)   You trust him. He's got a strength. I'd die for John Connor.

Dialogue from *The Terminator*, directed by James Cameron (1984)

One of the main drivers of relationships is trust. Trust is essential to cooperation and working towards common goals. Blind trust can lead us into unreliable relationships where false promises may have disastrous consequences. Broken trust can produce feelings of betrayal and anger; loss of faith in others and loss of faith in one's own ability to make good judgements. In the presence of fear trust quickly breaks down.

Trust begins with trust in one's self. Our emotional system evolved to help ensure survival. Of all the eight basic emotions, fear is the one that warns us of danger and helps us keep out of harm's way. But all too often we brush fear aside without taking heed of the messages emanating from within.

Attachment: The foundation of trust

Although food and sex sometimes play important roles in attachment relationships, the relationship exists in its own right and has a key survival function of its own, namely protection. Initially the only means of communication between infant and mother is through emotional expression and its accompanying behaviour. Although supplemented later by speech, emotionally mediated communication nonetheless persists as a principal feature of intimate relationships throughout life.

Bowlby (1988)

Trust is a basic experience that is either met, or not met, or inconsistently and variably met, early in life. The basis of trust begins at the beginning in the context of early nurturing relationships that are crucial for survival. Robust newborns may survive for a surprisingly long time without food or succour, but will eventually succumb to the elements unless someone appears to provide the basic needs. John Bowlby called the relationships that form in the early months of life 'attachment relationships' (Bowlby, 1988). Bowlby was a British psychiatrist and psychoanalyst. He studied the psychological and physical effects on infants and babies of separation from their primary caregiver – in most cases, but not necessarily, mother. He drew on ethological theory to hypothesize that all mammals engage in 'attachment behaviours' (ie crying and seeking) when separated from their caregiver. Attachment behaviours are biologically-based adaptive responses to separation. Survival is dependent upon the close attachment of maternal figure and baby (Fraley, 2010).

When babies and children are removed from the maternal/parental sphere the known and trusted world vanishes and the emotional stage is set for mistrust. Up until the mid-1960s hospital visits for parents of ill babies and children were strictly controlled, with visits often limited to one hour per week. In 1946 Bowlby and social worker James Robertson collaborated on a study about the impact of hospital stays on babies and children. They concluded that young patients suffered emotional damage from hospital stays. But many were still not convinced about the:

> … extreme emotional trauma endured by children during hospital stays. In response, Robertson prepared a documentary film depicting a young child's distressing hospital experience. *A Two-Year-Old Goes to Hospital* was initially met with outrage from healthcare professionals; but eventually, hospital policy did change to allow caregivers unlimited visiting rights.

> AboutKidsHealth (2010)

Bowlby formulated attachment theory to explain certain patterns of behaviour that persist throughout the lifespan. The influence of childhood separations and broken trust can reverberate down the years.

Graham, 38, was employed by MI5 in the IT department. He was undergoing a period of extreme work-related stress connected to being assigned to Denise, a new female manager. He found this new relationship very stressful. Graham could not relate to her. Denise was not giving him direction, was very dismissive, did not respond to Graham's requests for guidelines, failed to inform him of new policies she was implementing and in consequence Graham didn't know what was expected of him. The stress was tapping into deep-rooted anxieties and he was suffering frequent panic attacks. (See Chapter 6 for a definition of the differences between stress and anxiety.)

Graham had a history of panic attacks but had not had one in many years. Graham was unable to cope with his work and was seconded to a less demanding department. MI5 had to keep his original job open and, as part of Graham's rehabilitation, MI5 agreed to fund professional help with a clinical psychologist. During the course of these sessions it emerged that as a child Graham had undergone a series of operations to correct a heart defect. It meant long hospital stays over several years. He only had his mother, and as she was the breadwinner was rarely able to visit him. Her absences got overlaid in his memory. He said he remembered his hospital stays as very pleasant with doctors and nurses being very caring and kind. He did report that other children on the ward were very distressed and spent a lot of time crying and pining for their parents; but not Graham.

The procedures were successful and Graham returned to home and school. He excelled at maths and sciences and went on to a top university; but he did not do so well socially.

Graham reported that as a young man he had a difficult time forming intimate relationships, particularly with women. He would get involved and then something would happen to break his trust. He had an especially difficult time working with women managers. He felt men were fairer and more trustworthy. With good psychological support, Graham's panic attacks eventually receded and he was able to return to his old job. Happily for Graham, a man was now managing his team.

Bowlby's attachment theory (Bowlby, 1988) is based on:

1 The propensity to make intimate emotional bonds as a basic component of human nature that continues through the lifespan.

2 The neurobiological connections formed through attachment bonds that are part and parcel of intimate relationships.

3 The powerful influence of parental treatment to the child's development.

4 The fluidity of infant and childhood development that is neither rigid nor fixed.

Broken trust

Mixing a business relationship with friendship, romance or sex can lead to a very messy situation, especially when trust is broken and the relationship fails.

J wanted to tell us her story. This is what she said.

It was 1970. He was 33 and I was 24. I was a young executive with big ambitions. I was working in London for a top talent agency. He was on his way to becoming one of the leading TV writers in New York. He had a contract on a hugely popular late-night talk show and was being wooed by the top studios. The attraction was immediate. He asked me to come to New York and manage his career. I didn't know what to do. I went to my mother for advice. She said, 'He clearly trusts you. I think you should take the risk. You're young and if it doesn't work out you've lost nothing.' Talk about famous last words. We became an item and I was on a real high. I insisted on a contract – I wasn't entirely naïve. I told him I needed authority, security. But he managed to wriggle out of that.'

J continues: 'I went to New York and moved in with him. But we didn't stay a couple for long. His career was taking off big time and I negotiated all his deals. The business side of things worked beautifully for both of us. We remained very close and there was still a lot of trust between us. He bought me an apartment in Greenwich Village. But there was a price to pay – he took prisoners.

'He never wanted me to know what he was up to. It was clear he was heavily into drugs, alcohol; his spending was out of control. I wanted out but I felt responsible for him. I stayed out of loyalty. Twenty-five years rolled by. By this time I was in a solid personal relationship with L that didn't interfere with the business side of things. I met L 18 years ago and we're still together. I'm a pretty loyal person.

'We decided to move back to London and base operations from here. Then everything changed. He met Richard, the person who he thought he wanted to spend the rest of his life with. He immediately involved Richard in all key decisions. I'd walk into a room and they'd go silent. He received a big industry award and I wasn't invited. He and Richard went on the attack. To keep the peace I offered to take a reduction in commissions. They came up with a spurious lawsuit. Instead of suing me they went after the accounting firm. I was the principal witness. He lost the lawsuit but I lost my reputation. He and Richard made it seem like I was the one who'd been sued and he didn't do anything to dispute that. He wouldn't see me, he wouldn't talk to me.'

J continues: 'I was gutted. I didn't think it would happen to me. I was a mess for two years. My mother died and shortly thereafter my father. I started having panic attacks. My life crumbled. There was a fatwa around London against me. People wouldn't take my calls. My world imploded. Today I'm very cautious about business relationships. I see the end of a relationship before I go into it. I will never personally represent anyone again. I will only undertake projects that don't require an emotional commitment.'

The effects of broken trust can lead to disorganization at work, lowered self-esteem, and depression; feelings of helplessness, inadequacy, confusion and anxiety. It takes time and energy to build a relationship. Betrayal can tear everything down in a moment.

The gift of fear

Gavin de Becker has a very personal reason for dedicating his life to teaching people about trust and fear. (De Becker designs security systems to screen threats to justices of the US Supreme Court, CIA officials, members of Congress and governors of 12 US states.)

'The woman was now backing away from her husband. To someone else, this may have looked like a retreat, but I intuitively knew it was the final pre-incident indicator before the pulling of the trigger. Because guns are not intimate weapons, her desire for some distance from the person she was about to shoot was the element that completed my prediction, and I quickly acted.'

A young girl was napping in a small bedroom nearby.

'As I crossed the room to wake the child, I heard the gunshot that I had predicted just a moment before. I was startled, but not surprised. The silence that followed, however, did concern me... It wasn't the first time I'd heard that gun go off in the house; my mother had accidentally fired it toward me a few months earlier, the bullet passing so close to my ear that I felt it buzz in the air before striking the wall.'

de Becker (1997)

De Becker's stepfather survived. His mother was in and out of mental institutions through de Becker's childhood. Growing up in a volatile and dangerous atmosphere taught de Becker to attend to the warnings from his emotional system. He believes that in order to protect ourselves we need to learn to trust and act on our gut instincts. For de Becker fear is a gift that will help you identify and avoid dangerous people, situations and places. He thinks we can see trouble coming but tend to brush aside these warning signals as distractions and petty annoyances.

Organizations pay a very high price when they unwittingly hire unreliable, untrustworthy people. Even with all the checks and balances in place human nature is such that mistakes are inevitably made. Sometimes these mistakes are very expensive indeed; the costs of internal fraudulent activities to financial services organizations have been in the hundreds of billions of dollars. Somewhere along the line the decision-making processes about who to hire get compromised. Decisions can be driven solely by bottom-line delivery goals ('do whatever is necessary to generate income') rather than by aligning organizational values with individual values ('do the right thing'). These conflicting messages and goals might be explicit or implicit.

> It is difficult to get a man to understand something, when his salary depends upon his not understanding it.
>
> Sinclair (1935)

With all the will in the world, organizations hire people who prove to be quite destructive. Although only a small percentage of people will fail to live up to promises and expectations, the ones that break trust and let the side down can do untold damage. They are like a virus in the system. When things go wrong management often engages in defensive behaviours. Those in an organization who try and bring wrongdoing to the attention of management risk being perceived as pessimistic and trouble-makers for over-reacting and wrong for not being able to manage the situation themselves (de Becker, 1997). Things can spiral dangerously out of control and become endemic throughout large areas of an organization. Whistle-blowers get ostracized and find themselves at the wrong end of justice. Sometimes the cost is in human lives.

Between January 2005 and March 2009 at Stafford Hospital, it is estimated that between 400 and 1,200 patients died as a result of poor care. The evidence was horrifying and in 2009 was described by Sir Ian Kennedy, the chairman of the Healthcare Commission, as the most shocking scandal he had investigated. There were warning signals as early as 2007 when it was noted that Stafford seemed to have unusually high death rates. The hospital put the problems down to 'coding errors' (Campbell, 2013).

In 2006 Terry Deighton, a member of a local patients' group, carried out an inspection of the hygiene standards at Stafford Hospital. He found A&E to be in a shocking state. His report was ignored. Nurse Helene Donnelly also made complaints and was told to 'fill out an incident form' if she had a concern. During her six years in A&E she submitted nearly 100 forms. 'I had no indication these were read; managers were just not listening and didn't want to know' (BBC News, 2013).

In 2007 Stafford Hospital management finally came up against a whistleblower they couldn't silence. Julie Bailey, whose mother had died as a result of the appalling neglect at the hospital, started a campaign called CURE to demand change. The response from the public was overwhelming. In December 2010 Prime Minister David Cameron launched the first public inquiry into Stafford Hospital.

On 14 October 2014 the BBC reported that a new trust is being set up to run the hospital, which is being renamed County Hospital.

As for Julie Bailey, despite receiving an OBE, she was the subject of an intensive and extensive hate campaign and 'run out of town'.

Why are they hounding her? She has helped prevent her neighbours' suffering, and maybe saved lives. A short answer is that Bailey took on powerful interests: the NHS, the borough and county council, which were both criticized by the inquiry, and the Labour Party, which cannot face what happened in the hospital on its watch. But there is more to it than the powerful turning on a woman who challenged them.

... People don't want to know about abuse at the hands of doctors and nurses. They will read about the incompetence of managers, certainly, and the danger of cuts to hospital budgets. But they do not like news that the people who care for them – before whom they lie powerless and vulnerable – are not always the angels of hospital dramas. Or as Bailey puts it, 'the public doesn't want to believe that the NHS is unsafe, even though small general hospitals, which are jacks of all trades and masters of none, are dangerous.'

Cohen (2013)

The neurobiology of trust

The story of three ducklings and a cat.

Ronan and Emma Lalley bought a farm in Northern Ireland. They wanted some ducks and got in some fertilized eggs. On the day the ducklings hatched the Lalleys went to check on them but the ducklings were nowhere to be found. They eventually found the ducklings. But their cat had got there first. It looked like the ducklings were going to be dinner. And then an amazing thing happened. The cat lay down on her side and the three little ducklings waddled straight under her for warmth and comfort. The Lalleys were 'blown away'. Then they noticed that there were also newborn kittens suckling as well. Mothering hormones – oxytocin – had been coursing through the cat's body causing her to love and nurture any small warm furry creature she found next to her. The ducklings and the cat formed an unbreakable bond. As the ducklings grew they continued to have an attachment to their surrogate mum.

https://www.youtube.com/watch?v=YlqTHhdCQko

Paul Zak, a neuroeconomist, has done extensive research on the neurobiology of trust. Neuroeconomics is a relatively new multi-disciplinary field bridging neuroscience, psychology and economics. Neuroeconomists consider the neural mechanics of decision-making and how economic decision-making actually happens inside the brain (Cohen, 2010). As economic decisions are fundamentally predictions about the future, there is a high degree of trust involved in deciding what to invest in.

In 1998 Zak and his colleague Stephen Knack of the World Bank's Development Research Group were engaged in a research project focused on neural mechanisms of trust.

I began trying to find out why trust among people varies dramatically across different countries. As part of this effort, we constructed a mathematical model that described the kinds of social, legal and economic environments that might be expected to produce high and low levels of trust. In the course of the study, we discovered that trust is among the strongest known predictors of a country's wealth; nations with low levels tend to be poor. Our model showed that societies with low levels are poor because the inhabitants undertake too few of the long-term investments that create jobs and raise incomes. Such investments depend on mutual trust that both sides will fulfil their contractual obligations.

Zak (2008)

In further research into the neural underpinnings of trust, Zak introduced oxytocin to human subjects via inter-nasal sprays. The results indicated a substantial increase in trust, which greatly increased the benefits arising from social financial interactions.

- Oxytocin is produced by the hypothalamus and secreted by the pituitary gland. It acts as both a neurotransmitter in the brain and a hormone when it slips into the bloodstream.

- Oxytocin induces labour in expectant mothers and also stimulates milk flow in nursing women.

- Oxytocin has been found to strengthen the bond between partners during and after sex. Many types of touching such as kissing and cuddling can trigger higher production levels.

- Oxytocin is controlled by a positive feedback mechanism where release of the hormone causes an action that stimulates more of its own release. The release of oxytocin is continually increased until the stimulus is stopped. It creates cow-eyed courting couples.

A study published in 2014 indicates that the presence of oxytocin is able to inhibit the fear centre in the brain and allow fearful feelings to subside more easily (*Medical News Today*, 2014).

The trust game

We're paying the highest tribute you can pay a man. We trust him to do right. It's that simple.

Harper Lee (1960)

Intuition usually does very well in guiding our decisions. But this is not always the case. Daniel Kahneman (2011) believes that intuition does not help guide us when we are placing our financial decisions in the hands of financial advisers and stock traders – people who have much to gain by treating our money like chips at their poker tables.

By and large, whenever individual investors buy or sell a stock they buy and sell the wrong stocks and financial institutions benefit from these mistakes. The cost of having an 'idea' is nearly 4 per cent for an individual investor. There is research showing that men have more of these 'ideas' than women do, so women are more successful investors than men (on average) because they churn their portfolios less. As Odean and Barber have observed, individual trading is hazardous to people's wealth.

The Economist (2012)

Based on Swiss researcher Ernst Fehr's 'The Trust Game', invented in the 1990s to measure psychological motives for revenge, Paul Zak and his colleagues developed a version of the game to measure degrees of trust between two strangers (Zak, 2008). During the game the participants' brains were being scanned by PET to examine the neurobiological underpinnings of punishment. When participants were given the opportunity to punish the other person who had betrayed their trust, the reward areas of the brain were activated indicating that the decision to punish is related to feelings of pleasure (Ariely, 2008).

Participants were each given $10 and were then divided into pairs and placed in separate rooms so as to maintain anonymity. In each pair Subject 1, prompted by a computer, decides whether to send some of the money to Subject 2. If Subject 1 decides to send money then the amount received by Subject 2 is tripled and added to the original sum (ie if Subject 1 sends $6 then Subject 2 ends up with 3 × $6 + $10 = $28, whilst Subject 1 is left with $4). In the next step Subject 2 can, but need not, return some of the money to Subject 1. Immediately after the money transfer decisions had been made participants provided blood samples so as to measure oxytocin levels.

It is experimentally proposed that the initial transfer of funds measures trust while the return transfer measures trustworthiness. The results of the studies show that 85 per cent of Subject 1 participants transferred some money and 98 per cent of Subject 2 participants returned some of the money they received. The results indicate that when participants received money they felt trusted, and had raised levels of oxytocin. Subject 2 participants with high levels of oxytocin were more trusting (seeing the sender as trustworthy) in that they sent more money back to Subject 1 participants. 'Receiving a signal of trust appears to make people feel positive about strangers who have trusted them' (Zak, 2008).

The results of the trust game have important implications for the amount of trust displayed by leaders and managers in organizations. Trust feeds into positive reciprocal feelings of 'trustingness' (assigning trustworthiness to others) that in turn have positive emotional impacts on people as well as bottom-line pay-offs. In the presence of oxytocin a positive feedback loop is established. This is a win–win for organizations.

In virtual reality we trust

With the advent of our society's love affair with technology, especially in the younger generations, my wish is that those generations understand that communication screen-to-screen is not the same – by a factor of 1,000 – as communication face-to-face. That goes for the classroom, the living room, and the bedroom.

Anon (2013)

When it comes to forming bonds, technology is a double-edged sword. On the one hand, it's now easier to get connected – and stay connected – with other people using high-speed communication devices. On the other hand, the very devices that bring us together also drive us apart. There's still no substitute for the trust and rapport that can form through face-to-face interactions.

Adam Grant quoted by Schwabel (2013)

The global workplace has changed in ways that were unimaginable to most people 50 years ago. For better or worse, today's world of work depends upon interconnectivity in virtual reality. Technology has brought about a myriad of changes in the ways we communicate, read, write, work and learn.

Nicholas Negroponte, born in 1943, is the founder and Chairman Emeritus of MIT's Media Lab and founder of One Laptop per Child. Unlike many of his generation, Negroponte has always held the optimistic view that computers would improve the quality of life for everyone. He believes the digital age has four very powerful qualities: decentralizing, globalizing, harmonizing and empowering (Negroponte, 1995).

Negroponte is making some fantastic predictions about nanotechnology of the future. He believes that 30 years from now we will ingest information through the bloodstream. If we want to learn something, like a new language for example, all we will have to do is swallow a pill containing the information we want. The information will enter the bloodstream and travel to the brain where it will be deposited (Negroponte, 2014).

For some the digital age has left them in its wake. At first it was low-skilled workers, secretaries, assembly-line workers and cashiers who had the rug pulled out from under them. In the last decade there has been an enormous shift – and not always for the better – for writers, journalists, editors, publishers, broadcasters and cameramen, to name but a few. For a 55-year-old newspaper journalist almost everything he or she took for granted about work no longer holds true.

Through the 1980s and 1990s D was one of the United States' top journalists. His byline appeared in newspapers all over the US. His fees were considerable. Then everything changed. In April 1995 *USA Today* launched an internet edition followed by CNN in August 1995. Then in January 1996 *The New York Times* went online offering free access to news stories. Advertisers followed readers from print media to the internet, newspaper revenues shrank and journalists' salaries were slashed. *The Huffington Post*, launched in 2005, provided a platform for journalists but they paid little, if anything at all, for content.

There are negative and potentially life-changing implications for people like D who did not grow up in the digital world. Adding to the anxieties accompanying a drop in, or loss of, income (and for some a total loss of gainful employment) are the difficulties of having to learn, become adept in, understand and be able to operate all the working implications of new technologies. For some coming to grips with the basics of a smartphone is challenging. Learning how to use e-mail can be a daunting proposition. *The Wall Street Journal* (Shellenbarger, 2014) reports that there is a growing digital divide in organizations between young employees operating completely in their comfort zone and older managers who struggle with new technologically driven communications; people communicate through e-mails and text messages; via chat forums, Twitter, and social media such as Instagram and Facebook. Meetings are held in virtual reality. Conference calls happen over Skype. Companies use Google Hangout to interact with their customers. For senior executives who entered the workplace in the *Mad Men* era, it can be quite disabling.

To help bridge the divide, some organizations have introduced reverse mentoring, pairing younger employees with older colleagues to help teach tech skills. These relationships can be tricky as senior colleagues are not eager to expose their ignorance and younger people feel intimated and awkward. But it's good to persevere; substantial benefits accrue to everyone including the organization. Relationships are built across the generations; mentors get a chance to tap into founts of wisdom; those being mentored benefit from a younger perspective, and to tap into their digital knowledge. It's win–win again all around.

For many the internet has enriched their social lives, created new ways to connect and build new relationships and rediscover friends from the past. For others the negatives may outweigh the benefits.

JC is 32 and creative director at a London-based international marketing and branding agency. Her social world and business life are both highly dependent on using e-mail, texting, social media and Skype.

'I'm constantly bombarded with texts and e-mails. There are too many ways of having your concentration broken and privacy interrupted. Communication becomes meaningless. You can't trust what people say in a text or e-mail. You really have to be careful how you phrase things. In a rush to answer so many communications, you can come across as cold. I think trust is more easily broken. People check on where you've been, who you're with and when you've been there. People can portray themselves as living a certain lifestyle that is not at all how they really live. I actually find talking on the telephone less time-consuming. I prefer face-to-face. There's a lot I can tell by how someone talks, how they express themselves; their personality comes through.'

JC continues: 'Doing business digitally you don't get to build a trusting relationship. You form an opinion about the other person; then when you meet them they are completely the opposite of what you expected. You don't get to build intimacy. You can build resentment for no reason. Someone might be busy and send you a quick snappy e-mail, which gets misread as coldness. You wind up building up stories about people based on how you communicate with them. At the office people are always checking their phones and their e-mail. They experience things through the lens of their iPhone and are never fully in the moment.

'Trust between consumers and business can be quickly broken via social media. Customers expect instant answers. People can feel very let down and post unpleasant opinions about your organization, which has a bad effect on your business. The organization can feel very exposed. It feeds into stress and paranoia at work. People are always able to be in touch and you feel like you always have to respond immediately. On social media it's out there for all to see and you can spend a lot of time fighting fires.

'I think video-conferencing is a good thing. It's great to be able to have meetings with colleagues around the world. That's one real plus.'

Trust me...

For 10 years, between 1998 and 2008, Kirn was friends with a man he thought was Clark Rockefeller, a high-finance mogul and modern art collector from one of the richest, most powerful families in the United States. 'Clark', as Kirn still calls him, turned out to be Christian Gerhartsreiter, a serial imposter from a village in Bavaria, and a psychopathic murderer.

'When I found out who he really was, the whole structure of rationalization and denial that I'd built up just fell away,' Kirn says. 'It was an incredibly de-stabilizing moment. My pride, my instincts, my sense of what was real, were now totally unjustified. It was like walking into your house, and everything has been stolen, and the drawers are turned upside-down on the floor: oh my God, I'm vulnerable. This could happen at any time. For a long time afterwards, I found it very difficult to trust anyone.'

Grant (2014)

It is extraordinary how easily unscrupulous characters can write a narrative of their life that has absolutely no basis in reality. People who have been taken in by con artists say they never saw it coming. We read with increasing frequency about people who have misused positions of power and influence, to deceive others for personal gain. The results can be ruinous; their victims may never recover the losses incurred both financially and emotionally.

Bernie Madoff was arrested on 11 December 2008 for running a $60 billion Ponzi scheme. For almost 50 years Madoff operated a fraudulent hedge fund while being perceived as one of the leading lights in the financial services industry. People trusted him because he set himself up as one of the pillars of his community. He hid under the cloak of respectability. They also trusted him because he appeared to be making the rich richer. And his very clever seduction was to make it incredibly difficult for people to join his 'club', so of course everyone wanted to be a member. To join his fund you had to prove your wealth and your worth, socially and financially. Madoff had access to everyone and everywhere.

In December 2008, with the global economy on the verge of ruin Madoff's house of cards collapsed. Shopped by his own sons Andrew and Mark, Madoff took a lot of people down with him. And not just people: investors included pension funds, hedge funds, capital management funds, private banks, asset managers, money managers, philanthropists, insurance companies, healthcare systems, charitable foundations, country clubs and education institutions.

Bernie Madoff was sentenced to 150 years' imprisonment. He is held in a US federal lockup in North Carolina. His wife Ruth lives quietly in Connecticut. 'I feel the shame,' Ruth, who has insisted she had no knowledge of the scheme, complained on *60 Minutes* in 2011. 'I can barely walk down the street without worrying about people recognizing me.' That just about says it all – it's all about 'me'.

Exactly two years to the day of his father's arrest Mark Madoff committed suicide. His brother Andrew Madoff died of cancer in September 2014.

The power of trust

It is reassuring that most people start from a position of trust and with the belief that others operate from a similar value system.

When we are drawn into a deceitful relationship our faith is eroded and we tend to create self-protective barriers. Organizations typically find themselves having to create increasing numbers of rules and regulations, the mix resulting in more red tape and bureaucratic systems.

Removing the layers of bureaucracy and red tape involves creating an organizational culture that places trust at the top of the agenda.

In an interview in *The Wall Street Journal* Linkedin CEO Jeff Weiner said that he believed leadership is about the ability to inspire others to achieve shared objectives (Rosenbush, 2014). 'The important word there is *inspire*. The key difference between managers and leaders is that managers tell people what to do, while leaders inspire them to do it. Inspiration comes from three things: clarity of one's vision, courage of their conviction and the ability to effectively communicate both of those things.'

Traditionally leaders keep themselves a bit distant and aloof, possibly believing displays of warmth and kindness show signs of weakness. Harvard Business School's Amy Cuddy has led research that shows that leading with kindness builds trust. People are more likely to trust in leadership if leadership trusts in them (Rosenbush, 2014).

Adam Grant is a professor of management and psychology at the Wharton School at the University of Pennsylvania and the author of *Give and Take: Why helping others drives our success*.

Organizational psychology has long concerned itself with how to design work so that people will enjoy it and want to keep doing it. Traditionally the thinking has been that employers should appeal to workers' more obvious forms of self-interest: financial incentives, yes, but also work that is inherently interesting or offers the possibility for career advancement. Grant's research... starts with a premise that turns the thinking behind those theories on its head. The greatest untapped source of motivation, he argues, is a sense of service to others; focusing on the contribution of our work to other people's lives has the potential to make us more productive than thinking about helping ourselves.

Schwabel (2013)

Grant describes three things people at work can do to promote a kinder work environment while, at the same time, adding value:

1 Help others even when the benefits to others outweigh those that accrue to you.

2 Specialize in an area of helping where you can use your knowledge and expertise to add value.

3 Choose an unpopular team task and find a new way to make it challenging and interesting.

References

AboutKidsHealth (2010) Attachment Part Six: Implications of attachment theory: past, present, and future, available at http://www.aboutkidshealth.ca/En/News/Series/Attachment/Pages/Attachment-Part-Six-Implications-of-attachment-theory-past-present-and-future.aspx [accessed 13 November 2014]

Anon (2013) *If I knew then, HBS class of 1963*, retreived 3 April 2015 from http://www.powerovermind.com/reviews/internet/knew-hbs-class-1963-part-iii

Ariely, D (2008) The financial markets and the neurospsychology of trust, *Harvard Business Review*, available at https://hbr.org/2008/12/the-financial-markets-and-the.html [accessed on 23 November 2014]

BBC News (2013) Stafford Hospital neglect examined, available at http://www.bbc.co.uk/news/uk-england-stoke-staffordshire-21228820 [accessed on 19 November 2014]

Bowlby, J (1988) *A Secure Base*, Routledge, London

Campbell, D (2013) Mid-Staffs hospital scandal: The essential guide, *The Guardian*, available at http://www.theguardian.com/society/2013/feb/06/mid-staffs-hospital-scandal-guide [accessed on 19 November 2014]

Cohen, J (2010) What is neuroeconomics? *Yale Insights*, available at http://insights.som.yale.edu/insights/what-neuroeconomics [accessed on 21 November 2014]

Cohen, N (2013) Julie Bailey: Enemy of the people, Spectator Blogs, available at http://blogs.spectator.co.uk/nick-cohen/2013/05/julie-bailey-enemy-of-the-people/ [accessed on 19 November 2014]

de Becker, G (1997) *The Gift of Fear*, Dell, New York

The Economist (2012) Quick study: Daniel Kahneman on economic decision-making: Can we ever trust instinct?, available at http://www.economist.com/blogs/ prospero/2012/02/quick-study-daniel-kahneman-economic-decision-making [accessed on 22 November 2014]

Fraley, RC (2010) A brief overview of adult attachment theory and research, available at http://internal.psychology.illinois.edu/~rcfraley/attachment.htm [accessed on 29 November 2014]

Grant, A (2013) *Why Helping Others Drives Our Success*, Weidenfeld & Nicolson, London

Grant, R (2014) Walter Kirn on being conned by a murderer, *The Telegraph*

Kahneman, D (2011) *Thinking, Fast and Slow*, 1st edn, Farrar, Straus and Giroux, New York

Lee, H (1960) *To Kill a Mockingbird*, JB Lippincott

Medical News Today (2014) The bonding hormone oxytocin inhibits the fear center in the brain, available at http://www.medicalnewstoday.com/ releases/285441.php [accessed on 13 November 2014]

Negroponte, N (1995) *Being Digital*, Alfred A Knopf, New York

Negroponte, N (2014) A 30-year history of the future, *TED.com*, available at http://www.ted.com/talks/nicholas_negroponte_a_30_year_history_of_the_ future#t-11242 [accessed on 28 November 2014]

Rosenbush, S (2014) What your CEO is reading: LinkedIn's Jeff Weiner; Google, Meet GM; Nice Managers: The CIO Report, *Wall Street Journal*, available at http://blogs.wsj.com/cio/2014/11/29/what-your-ceo-is-reading-linkedins-jeff- weiner-google-meet-gm-nice-managers [accessed on 30 November 2014]

Rowling, JK (1998) *Harry Potter and the Chamber of Secrets*, Bloomsbury, London

Schwabel (2013) Adam Grant: Be a giver not a taker to succeed at work, *Forbes*, available at http://www.forbes.com/sites/danschawbel/2013/04/09/adam-grant- be-a-giver-not-a-taker-to-succeed-at-work/ [accessed on 30 November 2014]

Shellenbarger, S (2014) Pairing up with a younger technology mentor, *Wall Street Journal*, available at http://online.wsj.com/articles/SB10001424052702303903304579588122552355480 [accessed on 24 November 2014]

Sinclair, U (1935) I, candidate for Governor: And how I got licked (Repring, 1, p 109), University of California Press

Zak, PJ (2008) The neurobiology of trust, *Scientific American*, **298** (6), pp 88–95, doi:10.1038/scientificamerican0608-88

PART TWO
The organization, energy flow and profit

Fear in the workplace

06

Introduction

No passion so effectually robs the mind of all its powers of acting and reasoning as fear.

Edmund Burke (1756)

Although we try to keep emotions out of it, in fact the experience of work is saturated with feeling.

Ashforth and Humphrey (1995)

In the last five chapters we have been looking at how important fear and its antidote, trust, are in shaping an individual and their behaviours. Fear is one of the key eight basic emotions that determine who we are and how we behave. Fear is crucial in establishing our patterns for survival, and we saw that these patterns can change and adapt depending on our relationships and experience.

We now turn our attention to fear in the workplace – the language we use to define it, and what types of behaviours and attitudes it triggers, not just in individuals but also in organizational cultures. Recognizing that fear is present in the workplace, and then understanding why it is there, are the first steps towards the fear-free organization.

We review different types of leadership styles, illustrating these with stories from organizations about how it feels to be led by each type of leader.

But first, some definitions

Before we can discuss the effect fear has on people and organizations and what it will take to become a fear-free organization, we need to first establish what it is that we mean by the term 'fear'.

Patrick is a calm, thoughtful man, deeply respected, admired and liked in his community. He is a member of several boards and does amazing work with the disadvantaged. He heard that we were writing this book and wanted to tell us his story. This is what he told us.

Patrick worked for the same retail company from the time he left school. The company had a paternalistic, supportive culture, and although the pay wasn't great, he enjoyed the work and did well. Everyone knew everyone else and it was a good place to be. By the time Patrick was in charge of a significant sector of the retail business, news broke that they were to be taken over by another large company, one that had ambitions to grow and had a completely different culture – very macho and arrogant. To make savings, the new company was to be reorganized. Local retail managers were moved into business centres, and retail outlets were consolidated. There were many redundancies, and people became very concerned and fearful. Communication was poor; the new owners wanted the changes to be made quickly. Patrick was asked to carry out a restructuring review. He wanted it to be seen to be fair, but was pushed into cutting corners, which caused much anxiety amongst staff, and was very stressful.

At this critical time, the CEO resigned. A new CEO was swiftly appointed – he had a reputation for being one of the 'macho men' and had a lot of experience in restructuring. Patrick worked directly for the new boss, and got to know him well. He described him to us as 'a maniac, totally dictatorial – he could be cruel and just didn't care that he was unpopular'. Although he was one of the brightest guys Patrick had ever met, he treated his staff with no respect whatsoever. Wherever he went, staff 'just froze'. He set the stakes high and generated a profound fear of failure in his staff, generating great stress. The change process became traumatic for many, and the transition to the new organization was a nightmare. Staff were taken out of their jobs too soon, and junior staff were left with overwhelming responsibility. Fear had gripped the organization, and it would take a long time to recover. Patrick couldn't sleep at night. He would wake at 3 am, worrying about the next day, anxious about what his boss would do. After 34 years of work, during which time he had only been off sick for one week, Patrick was diagnosed with depression and stress and was off sick for six months. He retired early aged 50. Eventually his boss would be poached by a larger retail consortium, and became a CEO whose rather public demise was welcomed in all quarters.

When I spoke to Patrick, these events had taken place 17 years before. Yet he confided in me that he had hardly slept the week before we met: 'Just thinking about it all made me feel as if I was right back there again'.

Stress, anxiety, fear – these are all words we use, as we have done in the story above – to describe our response to a threat or danger at work. But what exactly do we mean by these words? And do we all mean the same thing?

From an evolutionary point of view, stress, anxiety and fear are important, necessary emotions that helped to protect our ancestors from predators and other dangers to their survival. These emotions prepare the body to get ready to act in response to a threat. With the options limited to fight, flight or freeze, the body gets ready by increasing the hormone adrenaline, which raises muscle tension, and increases the heart and breathing rate. Although the brain and physical responses are similar in all three states, according to many experts (eg Sadock *et al*, 2009), there are subtle differences between them.

Stress

Stress is what happens when something *disturbs your equilibrium or causes a change to happen*. The source of stress is called a 'stressor'. This can be something physical in the external world which is causing you to worry, or it could be something emotional generated internally because you sense something bad is going to happen. Stressors may be short lived, or they can last for a long time. Examples of stressors are job uncertainty, bullying at work, or a trauma on the battlefield. Some stressors may not pose a direct threat or danger to you, but they may still cause you to feel stressed – for example, a persistent loud noise, a roller-coaster ride, or too much to do. Stress affects our thinking, feeling and behaviour. Take the stressor away, and in all likelihood, the stress will also disappear.

Stress can be both positive and negative. Increased stress can result in increased motivation, excitement or productivity – but only up to a point, as illustrated in Figure 6.1, which shows the relationship between stress and performance.

At just the right amount of stress for any particular task, performance is optimal: there is a 'comfort zone' in which you are coping well with the stressors you are experiencing. At this point, you feel neither under-worked

FIGURE 6.1   The human function curve

Good stress   Distress

THE HUMP

Fatigue

Exhaustion

Comfort
zone

Ill health

Performance

Health
tension

Breakdown

Arousal stress →

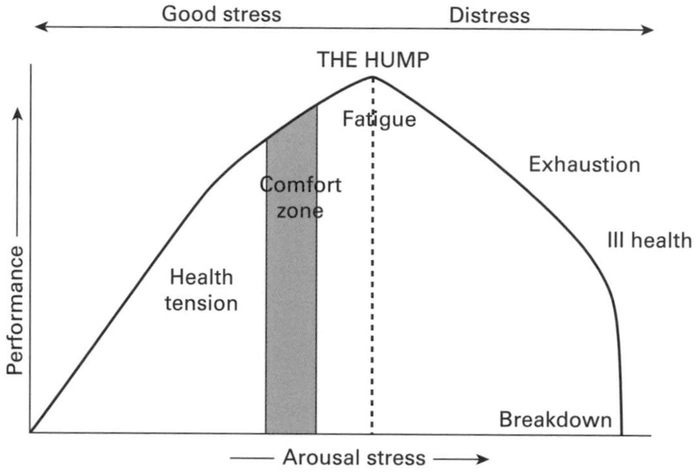

SOURCE: Adapted from Nixon (1982)

nor over-worked. You are alert and responsive. Appropriate stress is positive: it can stop you from making mistakes around dangerous machinery, encourage you to work safely in places like nuclear power plants or offshore platforms, ensure you drive safely at all times, or treat others well.

The 'hump' is the point at which stressors start to have a negative effect; you are no longer coping well and fatigue sets in. This is the start of feeling 'dis-stressed'. Beyond this point, the stress you experience increases, and results in a reduced performance: if allowed to continue it will lead to exhaustion, ill health and eventually breakdown.

Whilst the shape of the human function curve is common to everyone, every individual has his or her own limits for coping with stressors (the 'hump'). In other words, different people respond to the same stressor in different ways, and not everyone will be stressed by the same things. Some people for example thrive in a highly stressful, fast-moving environment, whereas others are not able to cope. Others still feel stressed by repetitive, dull work. It is not the stressor that makes people stressed, but rather how they respond to it, and that is a highly personal thing, as we have seen in the previous section.

At work, stressors such as losing out to the competition, or losing a customer, can lead to better performance, though it depends on the individual. Whilst increasing levels of stress may work in the short term, in the long run it can only result in a deterioration of performance as more staff become stressed and distressed.

Stress is a well-documented issue at work, and has been for many years. Companies report on stress levels in their organizations as work-related sick days, and several government agencies provide national statistics and trends on stress levels and their causes on an annual basis. In 1992, a United Nations report called job stress 'the 20th-century disease' (ILO, 1992) and in 1998 a study by the World Health Organization (WHO, 1998) said it had become a 'worldwide epidemic'.

UK Labour Force Studies (Health and Safety Executive, 2012, 2013) gave the total number of stress cases during 2011–2012 in the UK workplace as 428,000: about 40 per cent of the total of all work-related illnesses. These illnesses resulted in absenteeism, a higher rate of accidents, diminished productivity and higher turnover. Reviewing trends over the past decade, the report concluded that this level of work-related stress had remained broadly flat, meaning that over the first 10 years of the 21st century almost 5 million people had reported ill due to stress at work in the UK. The same study identified the main stressors responsible as work pressure, lack of managerial support and work-related violence and bullying. These stressors are all associated with fear in an organization, as we shall see later.

Another report summarizing the findings from the 2012 Skills and Employment Survey (Gallie *et al*, 2012) also pointed to high levels of fear in the workplace in the UK. The report identified three main causes of fear at work: fear of job loss, job status and unfair treatment at work. The survey results showed significant numbers of people are affected: about a third of employees feared unfair treatment at work, and over half reported a fear about loss of job status. The numbers expressing a fear of job loss rose to a quarter of the workforce following the recession that started in 2008.

In the most recent pan-European poll on occupational health and safety over 16,600 people in 31 countries were questioned (European Agency for Health and Safety at Work, 2013). Over half of all workers interviewed believed that cases of work-related stress were common in their workplaces. The main causes of stress were named as job reorganization or job insecurity (by 72 per cent of respondents), hours worked or workload (66 per cent), being subjected to unacceptable behaviours like bullying or harassment (59 per cent), lack of support from colleagues or supervisors (57 per cent), and lack of clarity on roles and responsibilities (52 per cent). All of these named stressors are also related in some way to fear at work, as we shall see below.

Recent nationwide statistics for the USA are difficult to find, but numerous studies highlighted by the American Institute of Stress (2014) confirm that the most important source of stress for US adults is their job, and that the leading sources of work-related stress are pressures and fears at work. Individual surveys vary due to size, demographics and location, and the results are difficult to compare and summarize, but overall surveys show that between 40 per cent and 80 per cent of workers report that they feel stressed at work.

The 2013 Stress and Wellbeing in Australia Survey carried out by the Australian Psychological Society (Casey, 2013) found that almost half of working Australians rated issues in the workplace as a source of stress, consistent with findings in previous years.

These surveys, and many others in countries all over the world, show that stress at work is significant and widespread, and has a major impact on the bottom line. Most people cannot do their best work when they feel stressed; businesses and economies suffer.

Anxiety

Sadock *et al* (2009) define anxiety as an emotional response to an *imprecise or unknown threat*, for example the perception of possible danger whilst you are walking in the dark on an unfamiliar street, or the sense that the boss at work does not approve of the work you are doing. Anxiety is anticipatory and is usually based on an imagined threat, or a threat that has not yet materialized. *Anxiety causes you to get ready to act and deal with the threat*; it is your attempt to keep safe by foreseeing danger. In the same way that different people have different personal stress limits, the level of anxiety felt for this type of threat is a very personal thing. Responses are physical, and include feeling on edge, heightened senses and muscles tensing getting ready to act on the fight or flight instinct. Being anxious is exhausting too. Depending on the threats perceived, anxiety could become a general state of distress and last a long time. In this case, you may become unable to cope, and the anxiety starts to interfere with daily activities as well as interactions with others.

Fear

Fear is best defined as an emotional response to *a known or definite threat*, for example when an agitated, violent mugger approaches you whilst on a dark street, or the boss tells you he does not like the work you are doing and threatens you with some action. Fear can be triggered by either real or imagined threats – as we have seen, the brain cannot distinguish between the two – but in either case the important thing is that you perceive the threat to be definite. *Fear causes you to act and deal with the threat*, but if no action is taken and the threat is not overcome, the body remains in a state of readiness to act. Fear is your attempt to keep safe by responding to danger; the body's fight or flight response is triggered, with physical changes including rapid breathing, increased heart rate and sweating. Your thinking, feeling and behaviour are all affected, because when you experience fear, you automatically focus on avoiding the threat.

Fear and anxiety are closely inter-related of course, and one can trigger the other. A past fear can trigger an anxiety in the present, as for example in cases of post-traumatic stress disorder (PTSD). The danger is not an actual one, but it is anticipated or expected based on previous experience, and triggers an anxiety that anticipates danger.

Fear in the organization

Fear in an organization is triggered by real or perceived threats. Threats at work are very largely to do with losing something of importance. This sense of loss can be so powerful that it motivates people to take strong actions to avoid it. David Rock's SCARF model (Rock, 2008) is useful to summarize what people at work most fear losing:

- **S**tatus: related to security or position in the workplace, and including the fear of losing power and/or status, of not being promoted or awarded a pay rise, and of losing the job.

- **C**ertainty: related to being able to predict how things will turn out, and including the fear of making a mistake, of not being good enough.

- **A**utonomy: related to having a sense of control over events, and including the fear of doing a job that is hated or demeaning, of working long hours or doing a thankless task with no reward.

- **R**elatedness: to do with a sense of safety with others, and including the fear of being judged, of not being appreciated for the efforts made, of dealing with difficult customers or clients, and of being subjected to violence or bullying.

- **F**airness: related to credibility or reputation and including the fear of being wrong or failing, of not being respected, and of not performing well.

Threats at work may not be very obvious or explicit. Instead, they could be implicit, emerging because people hold the negative assumption that they cannot and do not trust each other. Each side assumes that the other is operating from self-interest at their expense, and so behaves in a self-defensive way to protect themselves from losing something that they value. This in its turn is misinterpreted offensively, reinforcing the original assumption. When people are in a hierarchical relationship – when you as the boss have more power over your staff, or as a subordinate see a boss as having all the power – this is enormously amplified.

Recognizing fear in the workplace is the first important step in doing something about it and starting to build a fear-free organization. In the following story, based on real events but adapted by the approach summarized in Ryan and Oestreich (1998), a lack of trust and poor assumptions created the threats that triggered fear in a team.

Judith was a supervisor in a large multinational company. She had just been appointed to lead a large team of technical experts, who had been doing their jobs for many years and had the reputation of being a difficult bunch to manage.

The team had been set tough targets to deliver this year, which meant that they would have to improve their performance from last year. At stake were everyone's reputations as well as their annual bonuses.

Privately Judith was worried. Her assumptions were that the people in her team didn't really care about their work but were only interested in the money that went with the job, football, cars, and leaving early on a Friday afternoon. They were always looking for excuses when things went wrong, and didn't take accountability for their work. She thought that they didn't understand the bigger picture, and weren't interested in the budget and organizational pressures the team were under. She guessed that they would resist any changes she tried to make, and only concentrate on their entitlements like rights, pay or benefits. She would have to force them to contribute what she wanted them to, and if they didn't like it she was worried that they might be capable of sabotage.

So she decided that the best way to protect herself in this situation would be to micro-manage key members in the team. It would also probably be a good idea if she set up strict policies that ensured the team met clear performance standards, and procedures that dictated how complaints (or suggestions) could be dealt with. In fact it would probably be prudent if she got HR to implement tighter personnel rules all round to keep control of any potential dissent. She thought that Alastair in particular was a troublemaker, and she would look for ways to discipline him, or better still, get rid of him at the first sign of trouble. She decided that she had better limit the communication to the team in case of problems, so would only usually attend meetings with her higher management. When she did meet with the team, she thought she had better be really clear – this would involve coming down hard on people, and telling them without ambiguity or argument about any changes that needed to take place.

The team saw how Judith behaved. They saw Alastair being picked on, and finally transferred to a job he was over-qualified for. Judith was always in meetings with her bosses, and hardly ever met with her team. She never told them anything about what was going on in the company, so they had to rely on the rumours they heard in the corridors. She didn't seem to approve of the team presenting their ideas directly to higher management; it always had to go through her, and she seemed to take the credit for any good work the team had done. She certainly didn't want the team to complain or give any bad news to senior management. There were new HR rules in place that seemed to restrict the team's behaviours and ways of delivering, but no one had explained to them why these rules had been put in place, or what their purpose was. It seemed however that the new rules didn't apply to Judith – she could get away with treating the team unfairly on all manner of issues. Indeed it seemed to them that there were two rules for how things worked now: one for the bosses, and another one for them.

So the team concluded that Judith was a secretive, insensitive and biased boss. They assumed that her main motivators were power and control, and that she was only interested in doing whatever her bosses wanted her to do in order to get herself ahead. She was obviously not interested in doing the right thing technically, but rather in doing whatever was politically correct that would stand her in the best light organizationally. Although she occasionally asked for the team's input, she was rarely influenced by it and did whatever she had already decided to do, often conflicting with their advice. Some people concluded that Judith felt threatened by her competent team, whilst others thought that she considered herself better than they were simply because she held all the power. She was always trying to get the team to work harder, and when they did she never rewarded them for their efforts.

The team decided that they needed to protect themselves from Judith. This involved preventing her from seeing key information or data, and allowing her to make mistakes, especially in front of senior managers. They challenged all of her decisions. They didn't contribute at the meetings she had, and then complained later about how bad the meetings were. Whenever they had performance problems, they blamed others or some difficult circumstance, and never acknowledged their own contribution. When an urgent situation came up, they did not offer to work overtime. They complained about the organization to outsiders like competitors or suppliers, and during any change process did not want to get involved to a significant extent. Some people in the team thought that they should form a workers' union, whose main purpose would be to improve their rights as employees. Others were considering airing their grievances high up in the organization and would even be prepared to file for legal action.

Judith found it tough working with this team. She observed how they weren't cooperating with the suggestions she made, were passively aggressive towards her and spent a lot of time resisting what she thought were very reasonable requests. She saw how they talked a lot amongst themselves, complaining and 'whining', and rarely came up with new or exciting ideas. They worked slowly and delayed progress by asking for special circumstances or additional benefits. Their actions simply reinforced her initial concerns.

We could quite easily have written this story starting with the team's negative perceptions of Judith and their actions to protect themselves from the dangers they felt in working for her. The outcomes would have been very similar. In this story, fear and lack of trust reinforced each other.

The story illustrates typical behaviours in a fear-filled organization: blame, making excuses, being cynical, and restricting the flow of information or participation in important decisions. Also common are the emphasis on processes, procedures, policies and rights, discrediting each other's competence, a general lack of willingness to take accountability, and undermining each other's efforts.

There are numerous studies and reports available describing how to recognize fear in organizations (eg Austin, 2000; Greenleaf, 2014; Jacobs, 2014; Kuppler, 2013; Lennon, 2013; Llopis, 2013; McPherson, 2010; Potter, 2013; Ryan and Oestreich, 1998; Ryan, 2010; Welford, 2013). The following includes our own observations as well.

Individuals can report clear symptoms of fear. Physically, they experience headaches, stomach aches, or can't sleep. They find it hard to balance work with the other parts of their life. They say that they feel angry, intimidated, frustrated or sad *because of their job*, which may also be the cause of problems between them and their close family and friends. They may resort to drinking alcohol or using other addictive substances to cope.

In general, the most easily recognized symptom of fear in an organization is a reluctance to speak up for fear of repercussions. Indeed an interesting question in any organization to assess the fear levels is: 'What can't you talk about around here?'

Other key clues about the organization's culture of fear are how leaders and staff behave, and how the systems and policies operate, especially HR ones. Leaders shape the culture, and HR is often used as an instrument for leaders to implement how they want the culture to be; though sometimes HR can unwittingly create a fear-fuelled exhaustion culture because of the demands it makes for detailed reporting. Compliance also has a very fine line to tread between setting standards and instilling fear that, among competitive men especially, can become a spur to outwitting the system with potentially disastrous results.

We recognize five *leadership* types that generate fear in organizations. Building on the definitions given by Ryan and Oestreich (1998) we call them the Absent, Ambiguous, Arrogant, Abrasive and Abusive Leader. They lie on a continuum of increasing severity and are all related to how the leader tries to keep his or her power:

- *Absent Leaders* typically do not communicate well with their employees. Messages are inconsistent or mixed and they don't respond much to events. They don't confront bad behaviour, and tolerate issues for far too long. They like to make decisions behind closed doors and will dole out information in unhelpful drips. Information is hoarded as a way to consolidate power. Staff are kept in the dark, and do not know what is expected of them or what to focus on. This generates uncertainty, hesitation and worry about doing the wrong thing. The fear is of losing a good reputation or of not being able to get things done. With the leader rarely giving feedback, staff also fear not being appreciated, or losing status and ultimately their job.

- *Ambiguous Leaders* do not show consistent behaviours. Even when they have approved their actions, these leaders may not stand behind employees, often letting them down in public, or they can over-react to problems instead of treating them as learning opportunities. Ambiguous leaders are not clear about roles, work targets and expectations, and the people who work for them feel unsure about what to do. As with absent leaders, ambiguous leaders generate fears related to loss of reputation, competence and position in the workplace.

- The *Arrogant Leaders'* main focus isn't 'How can I do the right things for my customers and employees?' They are more interested in keeping their status and job intact at any cost. Arrogant leaders will not hesitate to be rude to their staff; they believe that they are far more important than anyone below them in the hierarchical ladder, and should be treated as such. They have no concept that leadership may involve serving the organization as well as leading it. Arrogant leaders may well indulge in unethical behaviour to get what they want or believe is theirs by virtue of their position. Employees don't feel valued working for an Arrogant Leader, and fears related to loss of reputation, competence, relationship or status are common.

- *Abrasive Leaders* and *Abusive Leaders* are always having uncontrolled emotional outbursts; they behave abrasively and/or abusively to staff, and don't show that they trust or respect their employees. Abrasive leaders will tend to blame their subordinates, and snub, ignore or insult them in public, for example by pointing out mistakes in front of others. Abusive leaders go one step further: they will be aggressive, often shouting to gain control. They may threaten the employee with job loss or even physical violence. Whilst abrasive or abusive behaviour may be intentional or unintentional, it always leads to the employee feeling anything from insulted or humiliated to bullied or threatened.

Mirroring the leader behaviours described above, we have identified the same five typical ways that *staff* behave when they have to work in an organization full of fear:

- *Absent Staff* will not speak out for fear of repercussions. They will avoid robust, open debate, and are afraid to admit mistakes. They tend to fall silent when the boss walks into the room and not share with him or her what their animated talk was about. They are not willing to try new things, be creative or experimental, and will not assert their own, or their organization's needs. Paradoxically this creates the state of 'presentee-ism' – staff are there in body but are safeguarding their souls.

- *Ambiguous Staff* tend to show a pattern of blame or denial of responsibility rather than take accountability. They lack courage, and pre-meetings are the norm, with any ideas or proposals being reviewed endlessly before being presented to a senior leader. Ambiguous staff think that is it better for the boss to hear the 'right' answer rather than the truth, for fear of repercussion. Everything must be 'good news' and difficult e-mails are never sent.

- For the *Arrogant Staff* there is a focus on status. These employees tend to spend a lot of time talking about who is rising and falling in the organization; there is excessive gossip and blame permeates teams. Appearances are everything: employees stay in the office later than their boss to try and impress. Those who get on best are good at managing upwards, and only tell the boss what he or she wants to hear.

- *Abrasive* and *Abusive Staff* tend to bully their peers, or those subordinate to them, and have the same effect as abrasive or abusive leaders on those around them. Their behaviour may be a defensive reaction against being bullied or threatened themselves.

The types of *systems and policies* in place in organizations are also symptomatic of fear being present. There are three key things to look out for:

1 *HR systems are not people-led:* the HR systems in place operate to maximize the organization's bottom line and the power base of HR employees and/or the leadership, instead of focusing on the individual and what is best for the business as a whole.

2 *There are too many processes and systems:* there is an over-dependence on processes and policies, instead of thinking and common sense. There are too many rules, resulting in employees feeling as if management doesn't trust them.

3 *Performance is data-led:* leaders judge performance by numbers and, because everything is measured, not many questions are asked and many assumptions are made that are not challenged. People spend a large amount of time juggling data to avoid repercussions from management. Rewards and promotions are only based on results, and do not take behaviours into account.

Fear is never healthy in an organization. It doesn't encourage positive action; instead it destroys motivation and productivity, and undermines your confidence and morale. Ultimately fear stifles creativity, decreases trust, and willingness to speak up or take risks. Fear also prevents you from learning from your mistakes, so it condemns the organization to making the same errors again and again. Fear-based cultures foster short-term thinking: you become defensive, seek to avoid confrontation or reprisal and focus on eliminating any threats instead of working together to deliver shared targets and outcomes. Fear causes you to change your behaviour: you'll be careful about what you say and to whom; you won't speak up when something is wrong; you'll act as if all is well even when you know that it isn't; you'll try to please the boss even if you disagree with him or her; you'll avoid asking questions in case you upset someone. Overall, fear leads to reduced business performance and a stressed workforce. Having a fear-free organization makes all the difference.

In a company that thinks sticks and carrots are the way to motivate behaviour, remember that the recipient's brain remembers first of all the stick. The carrot only feeds the system for long enough to get the next stick.

References

The American Institute of Stress (2014) *Workplace Stress*, available at http://www.stress.org/workplace-stress [accessed on 10 April 2014]

Ashforth, BE and Humphrey, RH (1995) Emotion in the workplace: A reappraisal, *Human Relations*, **48** (2), 97–125

Austin, J (2000) Fear in the workplace: Symptoms, sources, solutions, *Potential At Work Inc*, available at http://www.potentialatwork.com/articles/fear.html [accessed on 10 April 2014]

Burke, E (1756) *A Philosophical Inquiry into the Origin of Our Ideas of the Sublime and Beautiful*, Oxford University Press, New York

Casey, L (2013) Stress and Wellbeing in Australia Survey 2013: The state of the nation two years on, and special feature on working Australians, available at http://www.psychology.org.au/Assets/Files/Stress%20and%20wellbeing%20 in%20Australia%20survey%202013.pdf [accessed on 10 April 2014]

European Agency for Health and Safety at Work (2013) European opinion poll on occupational safety and health (May), available at http://osha.europa.eu [accessed on 10 April 2014]

Gallie, D, Felstead, A, Green, F and Inanc, H (2012) *Fear at Work in Britain: First findings from the Skills And Employment Survey 2012*, Centre for Learning and Life Chances in Knowledge Economies and Societies, Institute of Education, London

Greenleaf, RK (2014) Getting fear out of the workplace, Greenleaf Center for Servant Leadership, available at https://greenleaf.org/winning-workplaces/ workplace-resources/ask-an-expert/getting-fear-out-of-the-workplace/ [accessed on 10 April 2014]

Health and Safety Executive (2012) Annual statistics report for Great Britain, available at www.hse.gov.uk [accessed on 10 April 2014]

Health and Safety Executive (2013) Stress and psychological disorders in Great Britain 2013, available at www.hse.gov.uk/statistics [accessed on 10 April 2014]

ILO (1992) Preventing Stress at Work, *Conditions of Work Digest*, **11**, 2/1992, International Labour Office, Geneva

Jacobs, K (2014) How to build trust in organizations, *HR Magazine*, available at http://www.hrmagazine.co.uk/hr/features/1142257/build-trust-organisations

Kuppler, T (2013) The 8 clear signs of a workplace culture of fear, *TLNT The Business of HR*, available at http://www.tlnt.com/2013/11/14/the-8-clear-signs-of-a-workplace-culture-of-fear/ [accessed on 10 April 2014]

Lennon, D (2013) Living in fear at work? Why? Overcoming the killer consequences of suspicion, *Business Fitness*, available at http://www.dawnlennon.com/2013/05/22/living-in-fear-at-work-why-overcoming-the-killer-consequences-of-suspicion/ [accessed on 10 April 2014]

Llopis, G (2013) Getting past 4 common workplace fears, *Forbes Magazine*, available at http://www.forbes.com/sites/glennllopis/2013/06/24/getting-past-4-common-workplace-fears/ [accessed on 10 April 2014]

McPherson, T (2010) 5 ways to deal with fear at work, *Talent Alley*, available at http://talentalley.com/2010/02/10/5-ways-to-deal-with-fear-at-work/ [accessed on 10 April 2014]

Nixon, PG (1982) The human function curve: A paradigm for our times, *Activitas Nervosa Superior*, suppl 3 (Pt 1), pp 130–33, available at http://europepmc.org/abstract/MED/7183056 [accessed on 10 April 2014]

Potter, M (2013) Beat the fear culture at work, *Psychologies*, available at http://www.psychologies.co.uk/work/beat-the-fear-culture-at-work.html [accessed 10 April 2014]

Rock, D (2008) SCARF: A brain-based model for collaborating with and influencing others, *NeuroLeadership Journal*, **1**

Ryan, KD and Oestreich, DK (1998) *Driving fear out of the workplace: Creating the high-trust, high-performance organization*, 2nd edn, Jossey-Bass, San Francisco, CA

Ryan, L (2010) Ten signs of a fear-based workplace, *Bloomberg Businessweek*, available at http://www.businessweek.com/managing/content/jul2010/ca2010078_954479.htm [accessed on 10 April 2014]

Sadock, BJ, Sadock, VA and Ruiz, P (eds) (2009) *Kaplan and Sadock's Comprehensive Textbook of Psychiatry*, Lippincott Williams and Wilkins, Philadelphia, PA

Welford, C (2013) Fear in the workplace, *HR Magazine*, available at http://www.hrmagazine.co.uk/hro/features/1076556/fear-workplace [accessed on 10 April 2014]

WHO (1998) *The World Health Report 1998: Life in the 21st century – a vision for all*, World Health Organization, Geneva

The nature of energy

07

Introduction

In the western world the 20th century saw the development of psychology as a body of knowledge, managing an uneasy relationship between philosophy and science. Models and theories abounded, many of which we can now see were belief systems rather than real sciences. Freudian thinking about the unconscious nature of sexual drives is a good example of this. In the absence of experimental data, models that were theories were taken to be facts.

What seems to have passed psychologists by is that the human system is like every other system in the known universe, which is that it runs off energy. And the way that energy is managed throughout the body by the brain, and within the brain, has a profound effect on behaviour. This energy is directed by basic emotions, and these are themselves the source of motivational energy (we call them 'e-motions').

In this chapter we explore the nature of energy in the brain. We observe that energy is key to how the brain organizes itself as well as the body, and that it may also be an essential part of understanding how the mind works.

We describe two models. One is a model of the organization in which the key element of energy can be mapped and tracked. The second is a working model of the mind, which postulates that it is an emergent property of the brain, managing and expressing the interplay between information, relationships and energy.

We conclude with some thoughts on what this means for organizations and leadership.

Energy and the brain

How do our brains manage connections that rival the trillions possible on the internet?

The brain does it, say Sejnowski and Delbruck (2012), through 'energy efficiency: when a nerve cell communicates with another, the brain uses just a millionth of the energy that a digital computer expends to perform the equivalent operation'.

There are two kinds of energy we need to think about when it comes to the brain: *physical energy* (how the brain cells themselves fire and wire) and *motivational energy* (how the brain motivates the body into action).

The source of *physical energy* for the brain is, as it is for the rest of the body, the glucose and oxygen that circulate in the blood. The body as a whole requires in the order of 95–100 watts to function well. Although only around 3 per cent of a person's body weight, the brain needs up to 20–25 per cent of the body's available energy to function: an enormously disproportionate amount (Harmon, 2009). The brain is one of the most continuously energy-hungry organs in the body, and is vulnerable to its energy supply being cut off. Brain cells do not have back-up energy sources – they create energy locally – so they depend on a second-by-second supply of food and oxygen by the blood; it only takes about 10 minutes with no food or oxygen to produce irreversible brain damage. Most of the brain's energy consumption goes into sustaining the electric charge of neurons as they fire. Active regions of the brain consume more energy than inactive ones, and this fact forms the basis for brain imaging methods such as fMRI.

But even when a person is at rest, the brain remains active. In normal life the brain never stops working and never sleeps. Performing a particular task, or responding to an external stimulus increases the brain's energy consumption by less than 5 per cent of the underlying base activity (Lives, 2010). Some 60–80 per cent of all the energy used by the brain is consumed by activities unrelated to any external event; the brain is active even when a person appears to be doing nothing, be it daydreaming, sleeping or even under anaesthetic. This ever-active messaging is known as the brain's default mode network (DMN). Its exact role is unclear, but it is thought to be related to the way the brain organizes memories, and may play a role in synchronizing all parts of the brain (Lives, 2010). David Rock (Rock, 2009) speculates that the DMN plays an important role in 'telling the story' about yourself, a key to sense-making. Experiencing the world through the DMN means you take in external information, filter it, and add your own interpretation.

During goal-oriented activity, the DMN is de-activated, and another circuit, the task positive network (TPN) starts up. The DMN and TPN are mutually exclusive. Rock (2009) suggests that when using the TPN, you are not thinking about the past or the future, but rather you experience information in real time. It is a very efficient use of energy.

How energy is allocated in the brain is still a mystery, but it is clear that this is an important mechanism. When one particular part of the brain needs more energy, food and oxygen has to be moved from another part of the brain to where it is more urgently needed. Like a squad of soldiers, the brain's energy cannot be in full strength in two or more places at the same time. It can be divided, but then efficiency where it is most needed declines. It is thought that a part of the brain called the right ventro-lateral prefrontal cortex is involved in some way in this process (Brown and Brown, 2012). This is the area of the brain that is important in sorting out competing demands.

Imagine that you are coping with high levels of stress due to a stressor you cannot control: it could be not getting on with your boss or partner; or you are in charge of a major project that is not going well; or you are anxious about a physical symptom that won't clear up. In any case, you are worried, can't sleep, and feel a sense of impending catastrophe. You need to find a solution to your problem.

What is happening in your brain? Most of the available energy is being used to manage the stress you are under, and there is not much left available for the area of the brain that may have the ability to sort out your problem. The more your boss rages, the more your adaptive system closes down because the energy is being diverted to the parts of the brain that help you cope and survive. The more the project fails, the more you are frozen into inaction, and your capacity to find new solutions gets shut down.

The brain's best bet under conditions of stress is to do what it knows best – to regulate everything for survival. The consequences of ignoring a survival emotion are likely to far outweigh the consequences of ignoring any other emotion.

The brain primarily operates emotionally before rationally, but these two parts of the brain sit in delicate balance, competing for precious energy resources. They act as drivers and braking systems to each other.

In any situation, it is the brain that directs the body's energy systems to do something. But an individual will only get the impetus to take action from the energy that is created by an emotion. Emotions are the source of mobilizing the body: the *motivational energy* in the human system is underpinned by emotion. In this sense, we can think of them as *e-motions*, because they create movement.

The *direction* of motivational energy depends on the emotion that triggered it. Survival emotions (anger, disgust, shame, sadness, but above all fear) divert the body's energy into self-preservation: energy is only available for actions serving the survival interests of that person, and flows inwards. When we are feeling threatened, we narrow our focus, our concentration is inhibited and our cognitive abilities decrease. Attachment emotions (trust/love, excitement/joy), on the other hand, allow energy to be used for activities beyond that person: energy can flow outwards. When we are feeling upbeat and happy we perform better on cognitively demanding tasks, and we are more inclusive of others.

In effect, the management of energy, organizationally, is the management of emotions. But of even more significance, perhaps, is the way the brain's energy is itself directed into behaviour.

Imagine attending a professional meeting and as you walk into the meeting room you see across the other side a person with whom you had a great friendship but with whom, in the circumstances of life and job moves and distance, you have not been in contact in recent times. Both of you spot each other at the same time. Both your faces light up, you immediately move towards each other, you both express delight at the unexpected chance of meeting and conversation carries on from there.

Imagine now exactly the same situation of going to a meeting and, as you arrive in the room, you see the last person on earth you would wish to meet. It is a person who has done you serious organizational damage in the past, whom you have never forgiven, and for whom you harbour deep feelings of resentment. Your behaviour is completely the opposite of the first encounter imagined. Nothing would encourage you into any expression of the delight at an unexpected meeting.

In both cases your immediate reactions *and behaviours* are triggered without any conscious thought. There is no *I think, therefore I am.* The thinking comes *after* the 'I am' (thrilled to see you/furious to have to be in the same room with you, never wish to clap eyes on you ever again, should I leave right now?). But how does the body organize itself so immediately and effectively?

In the first place, of course, it is as the result of experience. No one else in the room is reacting just like you to the presence of either person. We are, in the immediate present, the product of our past relationship with other people and, indeed, with everything else in our world. We actually *have* nothing other than the uniqueness of our own brain sculpted by the individuality of our own experience. But how does that guide our behaviour? How is the energy in our brain directed into the specifics of behaviour in our body?

The defining of the double helix in 1953 and the subsequent determination of the genetic code has created the general assumption that it is genes that control our behaviour and that genes are fixed by our heredity. Whilst it is true that genes are fixed by heredity and that they also control our behaviour, it is also true that the gene can express itself in a wide variety of ways. About 20 years ago, some cell biologists started to ask themselves: 'What is it that tells the genes how to express themselves?' In answering this question, the new science of epigenetics – what happens around the gene – began.

In *The Biology of Belief* the cell biologist Bruce Lipton (Lipton, 2007) vividly describes his excitement as he began to be certain that it is the neurochemistry of *perception* that tells the gene how to express itself. The way we see and sense things governs the way we respond. 'If only you could see things differently everything would be all right', we might say in a slightly exasperated way to someone who seems hopelessly stuck in the way things are. And it's true – though changing someone's perception has been an inexact science at best. *Managing* perception is what publicity people are trying to do all the time. Magicians are, too. Very good magicians have an extraordinarily developed capacity for managing perception and attention. As do con artists – confidence tricksters, to give them their full title.

On 6 December 2014 the *Daily Telegraph* was one of a number of newspapers that carried the story of how a shopkeeper in north London had, in full view of his own security cameras, been relieved of his wallet and several hundred pounds by having his trouser pockets picked. In a skilfully managed encounter, face to face, the thief had so engaged and directed the shopkeeper's attention that he was not aware of his pockets being emptied. He felt he had been mesmerized, though in fact he had been invited nonconsciously to cooperate with the thief in having his attention misdirected while his pockets were invaded.

It subsequently transpired that the shopkeeper had had one previous experience of being held up in his previous shop by an armed robber. That experience made him perhaps especially susceptible to the attention-directing skills of a thief who knew how to manage an invasion of the shopkeeper's personal space, to the extent that the shopkeeper seemed deprived of his own will to act otherwise than as led to act by the way the thief engaged with him.

It turns out that how we see things sets up an electrochemical charge, based on the whole accumulation of our own experience, which then floods the cells containing the genes. That charge then instructs the gene to tell our body how to respond. *It is the way we perceive things that counts.* There is nothing that happens without an underlying neurobiology. The science of epigenetics is beginning to show us the neurobiology of why this is so.

And the reactions can happen very quickly. Under threat the body can organize itself to respond within 80 milliseconds. That's what happened when you (hypothetically) met the person you least wanted to meet. But the awareness of what happened doesn't get up into consciousness for 250 milliseconds. By that time, the brain has already decided what actions it is going to provoke. The body and brain together *know* what the actions are going to be before what we think of as 'knowing' has got into our consciousness – our emotions have motivated the body to do something before we have had time to think. And the brain has done that by making sense of what is happening – by using data from the body itself.

Take this set of observations straight into the boardroom. Let's imagine no one present really trusts the chairman, though no one confronts that issue. He's the majority shareholder and likes getting his own way even when decisions are being made that, outside the boardroom, members of the board really doubt. Whatever is said verbally at the board meeting, there is another set of reactions that is going on inside each person around the table. It is each person's emotions that are guiding his or her actions.

Managing the brain's energy

As we have seen, the brain uses up enormous amounts of energy; to be effective it needs to be as efficient as possible.

Physical energy available to the brain can be depleted by the body's physical state and quality of food: for example, by virus infections using as much energy as possible to support the immune system dealing with the infection, leaving an overall feeling of being weak and unable to direct intention properly; poor sleep; too much alcohol the night before; poor diet; or a leaky gut. This has a knock-on effect on the brain's activity, familiar to many as feeling lethargic, sluggish or experiencing out-of-control emotions.

The brain needs access to good quality food and plenty of oxygen to function well. Research has shown that the effects of starvation on the brain can cause a lack of concentration, loss of motor skills and increased likelihood of anxiety and depression. Poor diet, including fast food and too much sugar, can impact cognitive function and mood (Anon, 2012), as well as lead to other problems.

Keeping fit and healthy, eating well, getting enough sleep, all help to ensure the brain has enough physical energy to perform well.

Motivational energy available to the brain when one wants it to focus in some particular direction can be massively affected by emotions engaged elsewhere. Worrying about what is happening at work can prevent you from going to the gym; overwhelming grief can result in apathy; blind anger can stop you seeing what is obvious to others. Stress causes the part of the brain that is responsible for the human capacity to integrate new information, make complex decisions and creatively adapt, to shut down. Under stress, the blood supply to this part of the brain gets diverted to the stress management parts of the brain: there is no energy available for other parts. People become ineffective under stress. The more people are stressed the less adaptively they function: it is not a function of will or intention, but the way the brain is organized. It is the fight/flight/freeze emotions that divert energy to deal with real or 'imagined' threats. If they are being imagined, to the brain they are real.

Emotions can also increase motivational energy. Being excited about a new project unleashes creativity and productivity; doing a job you love is no effort at all; feeling safe to be yourself allows you to bring the best you can to everything you do. When you do something you greatly enjoy, hormones and neurochemicals flow through your body with a beneficial effect on your heart, brain and nervous system. Glucose stored in your body is released into your blood and flows to your muscles. Oxygen increases in your body and you experience a surge in energy. It is the attachment emotions that energize.

For the brain is a dynamic organ: it has a property called 'neuroplasticity', which means that it can change both structurally and functionally. Changes can occur at cellular level, for example when experiences and learning change neural pathways and synapses, and they can occur at larger scales too, for example when injury leads to remapping of functions to different areas in the brain.

Neuroscientific research also shows that the energy of the brain can be deliberately managed, for example when practising meditation or mindfulness. Many authors (eg Davidson and Begley, 2012; Medina, 2009; Siegel, 2007) describe how meditation or mindfulness training can profoundly change the way different parts of the brain communicate with each other – and therefore how we think – permanently. MRI scans show that after an eight-week course of mindfulness practice, the amygdala (associated with fear, emotion and the body's response to stress) appears to shrink as if it becomes less activated. At the same time, the prefrontal cortex (associated with awareness, attention and decision-making) becomes thicker. How these two areas are connected together also changes: the connection between the amygdala and the rest of the brain gets weaker, whilst the connections between the areas associated with attention get stronger.

The scale of the changes directly correlates with the number of hours of practice achieved. For very expert meditators their resting brain looks similar to the way a 'normal' person's does when meditating: their brains are permanently changed.

Different types of meditation or mindfulness seem to have different effects on behaviour. Although there are many different practices (including physical ones such as yoga and t'ai chi), we describe the three main ones and their effects as follows (Ricard *et al*, 2014):

1 *Focused attention* practice involves concentrating on an object, word or concept, and aims to centre the mind in the present moment, developing the ability to remain vigilant to and effectively manage distractions. It seems to improve attention and decrease stress.

2 *Open monitoring* practice does not involve focus, but rather increases an awareness and acceptance of what you experience in a non-judgemental way. This seems to cultivate a less reactive awareness to emotions, thoughts and sensations occurring in the present moment, and reduces the 'internal storytelling'. It de-activates the DMN and activates the TPN.

3 *Compassion and loving-kindness* practice involves feeling unconditional benevolence and love for others. This refines empathy and promotes a selfless attitude to others. It enhances capacity for relationship building.

Research shows that meditation or mindfulness practice helps people to regulate their emotional responsivity; it helps them get in touch with their inner world of memories and emotions as it is in the present; and helps them to develop empathy for others. People who regularly practise can appreciate and value the effects of their emotions better; they can be present – let their emotions rise and fall – and not be swept up by them. It also changes the way they experience themselves in the world. Instead of spending a lot of the time telling themselves their own story, obsessing about the future or dwelling on the past, they live life in the present moment, how it actually is.

Practising meditation or mindfulness improves the way the brain manages its energy.

According to Siegel (2010) there are three ways in which the brain seems to use its motivational energy. One is chaotically. One is in rigidity. And one maintains the mind within what Siegel calls 'the plane of possibilities,' where its natural agility is available for maximal effectiveness.

In the *chaotic* state, and presuming it is not the clinically chaotic disturbance of a manic state, a person can appear very active, very energized, throwing out ideas continuously, creating a great deal of enthusiasm. But what the state lacks if not managed very well by organizational structures is focus, completion, and the kind of output that comes from sustained attention.

There are of course some parts of many organizations where this kind of restlessness has some value if well managed and contained. The more expressive ends of the advertising and events-organizing parts of an organization are such settings. When an individual has this kind of style, however, and starts moving into leadership roles or finds him- or herself promoted to being a CEO, then the lack of focus and directional clarity risks wasting a huge amount of both their own and others' energy.

Rigidity, the second condition of the way the mind works, is very much more familiar organizationally and, in left-brain societies, is often held to be a virtue. Playing everything by the rule book, wanting order and systems that stifle adaptation, having all boxes ticked whatever the value of so doing, are marks of rigidity being taken as a virtue.

A large local authority in the UK was concerned that around 100 problem families were costing the authority nearly £250,000 each, per annum, in providing crisis support services. Whatever the crisis, resources would be rushed in to manage it and then melt away again until the next one. The families were functioning chaotically with relationships that were very poorly regulated within the family. As social services, the police, fire services, school staff, benefits authorities, and so on and so on became engaged the chaos was managed but not regulated.

The authority decided to try a pilot scheme to see what could be done to change the situation. Choosing six families, the services of a small independent consultancy were hired to work with the families. Over a two-year period this consultancy, which had a profound understanding of attachment patterns, helped the families become self-regulating systems. Chaos was turned into caring within the family systems. 'Couldn't care less' was replaced by a sense of increasing autonomy and effectiveness within each family system that resulted in a reduction of costs to less than £10,000 per annum per family.

The consultancy had established one basic rule with the authority. It was that if any member called on the services of the authority during the processes in which they were engaged, whatever part of the system became involved would act according to the rules being established by the consultancy not by the prescribed rules of the authority. This was a hugely courageous decision on the part of the authority, but it paid dividends.

The real problem arose, however, when the authority wanted to take the pilot project out into wider use. Bound by all kinds of rules, many of its own making, the way to change the whole system defeated the authority. What the small consultancy had shown was that redefining relationships practically within the families allowed energies to flow very much more productively. But redefining a whole bureaucratic system was a daunting task. It was feared that an attempt to do so would be quickly sabotaged by the system that was so well established and able to spend upwards of £25 million a year completely unproductively – other than keeping all its services busy on crises.

A subsidiary discovery during the pilot programme arose from the question being asked: 'How do social workers – the front-line troops for problem families – spend their time?'

It was discovered that 80 per cent of a social worker's time was spent in administrative tasks – feeding the system. Of the remaining 20 per cent, 8 per cent was spent in inter-professional collaboration. The final 12 per cent was spent in client contact.

But what happened in that contact was that a front-line (and often quite junior) social worker was interacting with the family simply to acquire the information that could be used for filling in all the forms and protocols that the system required to show that social workers were involving themselves with the family in their professional care. Nothing was happening that was of direct benefit to the family. The rigidity of procedure and protocol had overwhelmed professional interaction, judgement and capacity to care.

This is the brain's energy operating in organizational rigidity. It is often induced by sub-acute, perfusive and unspoken fear generated in organizations.

The third state is known as *operating within the plane of possibilities*. This is most easily induced deliberately by mindfulness training. With its principles of attentiveness to the present and observing without criticizing, mindfulness is known to calm the chatter of self-talk and allow for clear thinking.

The concept of the brain's energy has many ramifications for organizations. As the master controller of the way the individual uses his or her energy, the brain is an organ to which leaders need to start paying serious attention. Properly directed energy can have a direct and positive impact on profits. Misdirected energy can erode value.

Tracking energy in the organization

But there is an unsolved problem, organizationally. Corporate systems like to be able to externalize their knowledge and track what is happening. They need to have business processes to see if the direction of travel fits with the stated strategic and operational goals. An energy model requires a supporting metric.

In the same way that in organizations there has been no generally agreed view of 'the person', so there has been no generally agreed view of what 'an organization' is. The noun is used very easily but its meaning is rarely pinned down. Not that there are not multitudinous attempts. Organizational theory has as many options on offer as psychotherapy – lots of ideas, no underlying agreement.

It is the same as medicine in the 18th century. With no agreement on what the vital organs were, what each one actually did, and how they were interconnected, any quack was almost as good as any other. More admired than the physicians were the surgeons who had remarkable dexterity. Under extreme battle conditions in a ship being raked by gunfire, let alone the elements, a leg could be taken off and sutured and the stump dipped into hot tar within 12 minutes. Physicians in the 18th century can be compared to the leaders of today, having imperfect knowledge of the organization and the human being within it with which they are dealing.

In the 19th century medicine started on the long and slow process of developing a scientific understanding of the body. The process of working out what the vital organs are, what each one does, what system each organ is part of, and how all the systems are interconnected, has been the province of scientific medicine for the last 200 years. Around 70 years ago it created the modern pharmaceutical industry.

There has been no similar approach in the management sciences. There is no agreement as to what the vital organs of 'the organization' are. In the absence of such agreement any consultant – like any 18th-century physician – is likely to be as good as any other with whatever management remedies are being offered. One consultancy says leadership is this; another says it is that; another says it is something other. Like the doctors who competed for the treatment of the mad King George III, consultants attend beauty parades in competition for their own brands of belief.

But now it is beginning to be possible to see a new direction of travel for management thinking. If it is human energy that creates profit, and the modern neurosciences are beginning to unravel the means by which that energy is translated into action, then understanding where energy flows within the organization and where it is blocked becomes an imperative.

Bringing the science of epigenetics (how we perceive things is the neuro-biological beginning of how we act) and knowledge about the way the brain manages energy together, suggests that one way of perceiving what is happening to energy flow inside an organization would be to create a metric that relied on individual perception to track action.

Such an attempt has been made by a husband/wife consulting team in Miami, starting more than 20 years ago when they were both postgraduate students in the School of Education at Harvard under the professor of education and organizational behaviour, Chris Argyris, one of the founding luminaries of the concept of the learning organization.

On the basis of a semantic reductionist approach using 100 data sets from managers within one organization, Phillip Cousins and Diane Downs derived an 11 element model that they proposed was the necessary and sufficient means of describing any organization or any part of it. In subsequent beta-testing over a large number of organizations and situations it has proved remarkably robust. A description of it in use has been published by Brown (2010).

Named 'Sofi' for 'Spheres of Influence', the model describes how an organization works using 11 different elements, or spheres (Figure 7.1). In the model, all the spheres influence each other, and a well-functioning organization will have strong and balanced relationships between all spheres. The strongest influence is exerted between spheres closest to one another.

Five of these spheres form the core of the organization, and are all related to people (the central line in Figure 7.1). They are:

- leadership;
- culture;
- staff skills and competence;
- staff;
- customer (the end-user of the organization's deliverables).

A successful organization delivers from the leadership's strong vision at the top to the engaged customer at the base, through the organization's healthy culture and its skilled staff, all of whom have effective relationships with each other.

FIGURE 7.1 Sofi model: Basic definitions

Three spheres are related to the internal workings of the organization (left side of Figure 7.1). These are:

- strategy (*what* the organization does and should be doing in the future);
- work processes (*how* the organization goes about executing the strategy);

- organization (*how* the organization is set up in all its systems, from governance to greetings on arrival to facilitate delivery of the strategic and operational goals).

The last three spheres are to do with the external aspects of the organization (right side of Figure 7.1). These are:

- relationships and communications (including internal as well as external relationships and communications as these are always interlinked);

- finance, resources and economics (how the organization is funded, including budgets, and what the key economic criteria are for decision-making);

- commercial and negotiations (how the organization positions itself externally for success, including sales).

Figure 7.2 illustrates how the model can be used to describe the three key forms of delivery: strategic, operational and tactical.

Data collection relies upon a 66-item survey structured around any focal point question that is of immediate management concern. Respondents are asked to make a judgement on the relative state of each of the 11 spheres (as if each were a vital organ in a diagnostic examination) using traffic light colours. Green means that area of activity is seen as functioning well. Amber/yellow means that there is some uncertainty about how well it is functioning. Red means that the respondent sees that part of the organization as being in need of remedial attention. Blue can be used if the respondent does not have sufficient information upon which to make a judgement.

The responses of all participants are accumulated to create a four-colour response sphere (shown in Figure 7.3 in black and white, with appropriate labelling). The focal point management question being addressed is: 'How does the workplace affect our organizational performance?' It will be seen that the names of some spheres have been altered to reflect the focal point question of interest. In the same way that the 'heart' is called something other in Chinese than in English, but does the same job, so a sphere can be differently named as long as its essential function remains the same within the model. Changes in names can also reflect specific organizational language usage. *Function* has to be maintained under such changes, however.

Responses from 89 individuals to the survey provided the data from which the model in Figure 7.3 was derived, in a situation where the director of an internationally renowned art gallery wished to work out how the limitations of the gallery workspace, back-of-house, might be affecting

FIGURE 7.2   Sofi model: Definition of organizational delivery

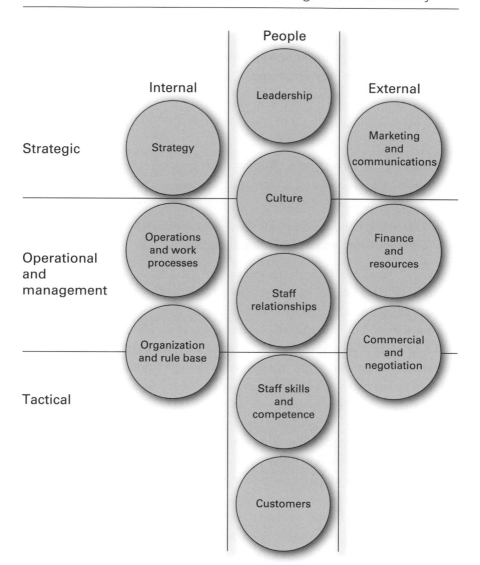

SOURCE: Cousins (1986)

organizational performance. Note that, among other changes, the 'leadership' sphere's name (top of the middle column) has been changed to 'exemplary workplace', as it is being assumed for the purposes of the enquiry that an exemplary workplace would give the lead to work performance as the opposite of the current management observation that a poor environment seems to be having an adverse effect on performance.

FIGURE 7.3   Sofi model in use

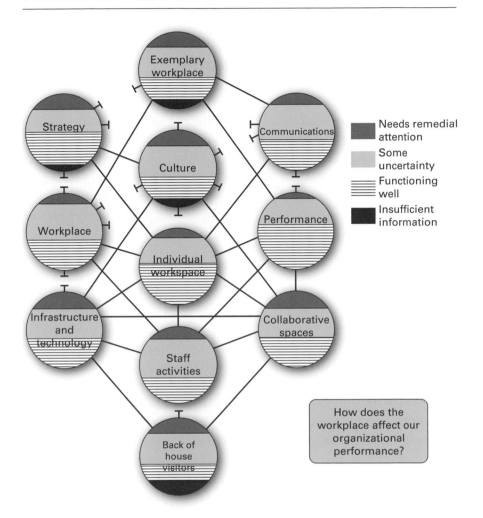

In Figure 7.3 the lines linking the spheres are accumulations of respondents agreeing with survey statements appropriate to the two spheres linked by any connection. They represent positive 'energy flow' between the different vital spheres. The hammerheads record a preponderance of disagreements. These show where energy is likely to be blocked. In a developed model, the thickness of the lines and hammerheads is a function of the strength of agreement and disagreement.

Within the perceptual framework of behaviour that has been described earlier, it is apparent from such models that it is possible in principle to map and track perceptions of energy flow. This is done in such a way that apparently soft data can be reliably and systematically accumulated in evidence of hard decisions, showing organizational energy flow as if an fMRI scan had been conducted.

The 'mind': A working model

Understanding how the brain works is important. But probably more important is understanding what the 'mind' is – the essence of who a person *is* – and what role that plays in an organization.

In the explosive shift coming from the neurosciences that is happening in our practical understanding of human behaviour, brain-as-behaviour is about to leapfrog all other ways of understanding human endeavour. Since 2010 three UK institutions – the Royal Society, the Royal Society for the encouragement of Arts, Manufactures and Commerce (RSA) and the Royal Institution – have all established programmes of enquiry about modern neuroscience to increase public and policy understanding of what is happening with regard to new knowledge about the brain and how the information can be used. Answers about what the mind is are emerging.

But there is no *unifying* concept yet. The brain seems to be so extraordinary – the most complex structure in the known universe, it is often said – that the excitement about the fact that its secrets are being slowly revealed, as the technology to do so also increases wonderfully, seems to overwhelm even an early attempt to make some widely general sense of what is known. It is also the case that most neuroscientists are not essentially interested in free-range human behaviour, or what the mind is. Not surprisingly they are focused on the brain and the nervous system, mapping how and why it works. But for those of us interested in the complexity of the human condition, of which working in an organization is a special case, being able to find some means of making general statements about the mind that have particular applicability would be very helpful.

At a 'Conversation' in Hanoi in August 2014, an event modelled on the work of the Gordon Cook Foundation (http://www.gordoncook.org), economist Professor Vu Minh Khuong of the Lee Kwan Yew School of Public Policy at the National University of Singapore presented his thoughts on what it is that is needed to make an emerging country great. There are three, he proposed. The first is that the right 'emotions' are in place. The second is that 'enlightenment' needs to be actively developed and promoted. The third is that 'coordination' at very senior government levels and then down through the system – what elsewhere is called joined-up government – needs to be highly effective.

That could be an equally good statement for any organization. If the emotions are right, *energy* flows. If enlightenment exists (*information*), then discovery takes place. If there is effective coordination (*relationship*), then the parts support each other. It is also a model of how the brain manages all its complexity – and perhaps an insight into what the mind is.

For many years, people working in the fields of mental health, psychiatry, psychology, social work, nursing, occupational therapy and educational therapy were not agreed on a common definition of what the mind was. This might have been thought to be rather a serious lack for mental health professionals for whom, arguably, it would be important to have a common professional understanding of what was meant by 'mental health'. Neuroscience is starting to provide a working answer as to what might be an operational model of the mind. Dan Siegel, the founding father of interpersonal neurobiology, has suggested that 'mind' is an emergent property of the way the brain works and is an embodied and relational process that regulates energy and information flow (Siegel, 2012). The mind is embodied because there are important components of mind that are contained within the body: the brain and the central nervous system. It is relational because a healthy mind is dependent on having healthy relationships with other people.

So information, energy and relationship are in a continuous dynamic flow with each other. What seems to have happened in the later part of the 20th century is that organizations have been swamped with information, ignored energy, and commercialized and systematized relationships with protocols of behaviour. In consequence organizations become 'mind-less'. And that induces fear, for then nothing can be relied upon: nothing is safe. The fear-free organization needs to reclaim the essence of the dynamic interdependence of information, energy and relationship.

If the brain is the organ for making sense of the five senses, for managing relationships and for directing energy, the mind, then, is an emergent phenomenon that tries to *make sense* of the brain that creates it, as well as assigning sense-making properties to other sentient beings. For a mind to be working well the three key elements of *information*, *relationships* and *energy* need to be in a continuous dynamic relationship with each other, each supporting and feeding off one other. The model is depicted in Figure 7.4. (For a fuller description of this, see Brown and Brown, 2012.)

The mind needs *information* to make sense of what is happening both in the outside world and within. Too little information and it is difficult to make much sense. Too much information, however, and it is overwhelmed.

FIGURE 7.4   Siegel's representation of 'mind'

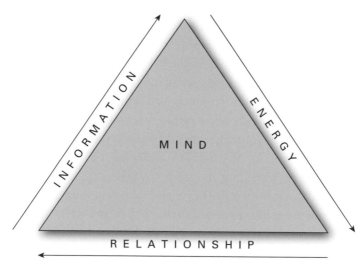

SOURCE: Siegel (2012)

As we have seen in Chapter 4, the brain is the organ of *relationship*. People can create emotional conditions in each other that can either result in amazing things happening, or can end up with a survival response in one or both individuals. In a relationship, one person's state of mind is influenced by that of another.

In this chapter, we have discussed how the brain plays a key role in managing *energy*. It does so not only for itself and the body, but also in giving impetus to action. The state of a person's mind is shaped by energy flow.

The fear-free organization

We believe that for the first time in the management literature this chapter has proposed that the modern brain sciences have the potential to create an entirely new way of thinking about organizations. It is that the management of information, relationships and most crucially energy, aligned as they are to how an individual's mind works, should be the basis for organizational theory and leadership development. Organizations and leadership could be redesigned around managing information, relationships and energy in such a way that they flow in the service of the strategic and operational goals of the organization.

The fear-free organization is one in which information flows unimpeded, relationships are trust-based and energy is freed to focus on organizational goals, not survival.

Information and relationships can be readily tracked in organizational systems, and techniques are emerging that make it possible to map and track how energy is flowing.

References

Anon (2012) This is your brain on food: Studies reveal how diet affects brain functions, featured research from the Society for Neuroscience, *Science Daily*, available at http://www.sciencedaily.com/releases/2012/10/121017091724.htm [accessed on 1 December 2014]

Brown, PT (2010) *Synergy in Buildings: Towards developing an understanding of the human interface*, Proceedings of the International Solar Energy Society, 23–24 June 2010, pp 149–54, Freiburg, Germany

Brown, P and Brown, V (2012) *Neuropsychology for Coaches: Understanding the basics*, McGraw-Hill Education, New York

Cousins, P (1986) *The Mapping Spheres of Influence: A visual typology of responses to rapid technological change in a large organization*, Harvard University Press, Cambridge, MA

Davidson, RJ and Begley, S (2012) *The Emotional Life of Your Brain*, Hodder and Stoughton, London

Harmon, K (2009) Earlier model of human brain's usage underestimated its efficiency, *Scientific American*, available at http://www.scientificamerican.com/article/brain-energy-efficiency/ [accessed on 10 April 2014]

Lipton, BH (2007) *The Biology of Belief: Unleashing the power of consciousness, matter and miracles*, Hay House, Carlsbad, CA

Lives, S (2010) The Brain's Dark Energy, *Scientific American*, **302** (3), pp 44–49

Medina, J (2008) *Brain Rules*, Pear Press, Seattle, WA

Ricard, M, Lutz, A and Davidson, R (2014) Mind of the meditator, *Scientific American*, **311** (5), pp 38–45

Rock, D (2009) Your brain at work, *Psychology Today*, available at http://www.psychologytoday.com/blog/your-brain-work/200910/the-neuroscience-mindfulness [accessed on 10 April 2014]

Sejnowski, T and Delbruck, T (2012) The language of the brain, *Scientific American*, **307** (4), pp 54–59

Siegel, DJ (2010) *Mindsight*, Oneworld Publications, Oxford, UK

Siegel, D (2007) *The Mindful Brain: Reflection and attunement in the cultivation of well-being*, WW Norton and Company, London

Siegel, D (2012) *The Developing Mind: How relationships and the brain interact to shape who we are*, 2nd edn, The Guildford Press, New York

Sofi system website, copyright 1985–2014, Sofi Executive Systems LLC, Sofi Logic LLC, Spheres of Influence International, All Rights Reserved, www.asksofi.com

Leaders and HR

08

Introduction

In this chapter we describe how the human resources (HR) function in organizations has evolved from helping staff with administrative tasks related to their employment some 75 years ago, to the present-day situation where the roles of the leaders and HR are often blurred and confused: it is unclear who is accountable for the decisions about people in the organization. This sets up conflicts and power games in which fear runs riot.

HR policies are designed to give structure to decision-making about staff to ensure consistency and fairness. It is important therefore that the HR team developing the policies understands the business and its environment, as well as the people working in the organization. If the policies are inflexible or are not adapted to changing circumstances they become liabilities, getting in the way of delivering success and generating a toxicity that saps the organization's energy.

What should be an HR team that supports staff to deliver the organizational goals in the best way possible becomes an HR function that despatches fear permeating the organization from the leadership down.

Who is accountable?

How can organizations rid themselves of the debilitating fear factor, and focus the energy, not on self-defensive strategies, but on winning success? Who is accountable for the 'people issues' that will make the difference in ridding the company of fear?

We believe that *leaders* are accountable for getting the very best from the people in their organization – unleashing the potential that exists to impact the bottom line. Furthermore, this is achieved by working through others: the individuals themselves. Leaders have the accountability to create the environment around them in which their people can thrive, in which they can bring the best of themselves to the job at hand, so that together they can produce great results. Leaders must remove the barriers that block and divert energy unprofitably, so that all can profit.

That is an easy and obvious statement to make. But it is surprising how much confusion there is around this simple premise. Many leaders feel accountable only for delivering 'the business', measured by widgets sold or financial accounts achieved. This is what they really understand; it is all they talk about and are interested in; these are the items covered on management agendas. But delivering a business can only be done through people – widgets and financial accounts do not appear on their own, they are made and lost by people, *and the way energies have been focused in pursuing the strategic and operational goals of the organization* – and it is only through really understanding and managing that most valuable of assets, the human resource and the way emotions direct how energy is used, that companies can achieve lasting success.

US General Colin Powell once observed that 'Organizations don't really accomplish anything. Plans don't accomplish anything, either. Theories of management don't much matter. Endeavours succeed or fail because of the people involved. Only by attracting the best people will you accomplish great deeds' (Powell, nd). In many organizations, leaders don't see the people – the human resources – in their departments as assets who add value to the organization. People issues are invariably disconnected from business ones, and in many organizations, they are expected to be dealt with by a separate HR department.

People issues are often viewed as the most frustrating part of a leader's job, just to be tolerated, or passed on as quickly as possible to someone else. At first sight, 'difficult' or 'non-performing' people are more easily replaced than sorted out (that is if you don't count the cost and time it takes to recruit and re-train the replacement). People issues are considered to be the soft stuff, easy to ignore, OK to be ignorant about. But in reality, there is nothing harder to deal with, and nothing more important.

Without a good understanding of the people within an organization, there is little chance of unleashing their energy to create success for the company. Without dealing with those people issues adequately, there is a risk of opening the door to fear, and wasting precious energy that should be channelled to ensure the enterprise success.

We have said that it is the leaders who are accountable in any organization, but that they often hand over responsibility for people issues to HR. Let's investigate how that happened and what the consequences have been.

The role of HR in organizations

That people issues are considered to be soft and irrelevant is not just prevalent amongst leaders. Ask almost anyone in an organization, and most will tell you that people issues are in HR's remit, not theirs. 'Find the local HR adviser,' they will tell you, 'and he or she will solve your problem.' Frequently, the conversation ends there.

So how did this come to be? We think that we can trace an evolution of HR alongside the redefinition of leadership in businesses that has contributed to the current lack of accountability for people issues in organizations – a quiet revolution largely misunderstood, frequently unnoticed, and – if noticed – mainly resented.

First let's look at how HR has evolved.

The most senior people in organizations have been in business at least since the 1960s and 1970s, so at a minimum, we need to consider what has happened in HR over that time – although the HR of today has its roots in the Industrial Revolution of the late 19th century (Jamrog and Overholt, 2004). Corporate memory is long, and many of the senior people in organizations still relate to HR in the shape it had several decades ago. Like finance and IT, HR has undergone a remarkable evolution over the past 40 years, and is still in active transformation. Many of the changes really impact the way firms are organized and run, but are not understood by those in charge of organizing and running them.

In the early 1960s, 'human resources' departments did not exist – 'personnel' or 'staff' departments were the norm instead, and had been since before the 1920s. The personnel department was seen as a purely administrative function, managing the payroll and time-keeping for staff working in the organization. Tracking of manpower numbers was also a key part of their tasks. In some companies, separate 'welfare' sub-departments had been set up in order to oversee support activities like housing, medical, and education, and 'labour relations' sub-departments headed off any trouble caused by employees or the unions.

Following the passage of the US Civil Rights Act of 1964, top business managers started to realize that improper people management could result in costly litigation, and began to pay more attention to the personnel function. Considerable resources both within the function and outside of it were devoted to compliance activities to minimize the risk of losing lawsuits brought by disgruntled employees.

During the turbulent years of the late 1960s through to the mid-1980s when labour unrest was prevalent and legislation rapidly changing, personnel departments were even more at the forefront of policing industrial and employee relations than ever before. Confrontations with unions and individuals were common as established industries declined and new ones took their place, driven by rapid changes in technology and society itself.

Throughout this whole period, personnel professionals remained essentially reactive, responding only to direct requests from their customers (line managers), and staying well out of the day-to-day delivery of the business. The competences that they developed were essentially in administration, manpower planning and reactive industrial relations management. We could call this the *administrative and employee relations expert* phase of how HR has evolved.

In this phase, accountability for any form of people management lay firmly with line managers, not personnel. People management wasn't much of a conscious effort however: relationships developed over time as most employees stayed their entire careers in the same company.

Recalling his time as the head of a local branch, one retired bank manager said:

> You grew to understand how the boss liked to work and you adapted to that or were miserable, and if it got bad enough, you left. He got to know you – your strengths, weaknesses – and he could make allowances for you and help you out. He often knew what he could get away with within the culture of the organization, and frequently did so. People didn't move much in those days and everyone got to know each other well.

It was only in the mid-1980s that human resource management as a discipline really began to develop, based on a wide range of disciplines all concerned with human behaviour (industrial and organizational psychology, organization theory, organization behaviour and sociology, Jamrog and Overholt, 2004). Academic research in these disciplines was beginning to lead to a better understanding of how the way humans behave in organizations is affected by their relationships, the organization's structure and culture, and the job and technology requirements.

The application of human resource management started with the recognition that experts in the personnel department could link their activities directly to the firm's business strategies and outcomes through people's behaviour. Early attempts were focused on policy (Hunter *et al*, 2006). Then came the work of Fombrum *et al* (1984) who mapped out how personnel interventions could influence the behaviours of employees in support of the business strategy. This included personnel getting involved for the first time in, and frequently being responsible for, staff selection, staff performance and appraisal, and staff remuneration and reward. The thinking at the time did not go as far as explaining how exactly the interventions affected employee performance or how the company's bottom line was impacted, but it was the start of personnel becoming proactive in contributing to the business.

At about this time, there was also a shift in thinking about the people in the organization; the focus on them as 'employees' became one of 'human resources'. This meant that people in organizations were seen as having the potential to develop and express individual needs (Hendry, 1995), which led to an increased focus on development and training, as well as what some have called the 'happy worker/productive worker' approach. This manifested itself in some firms by high attention on activities like company picnics and pay bonuses to keep staff motivated, happy and – hopefully – more productive. Let's call this the *change agent* phase in HR's evolutionary story.

Throughout the 1980s and 1990s, the focus of human resource management continued to move away from working with just HR transactional processes and systems to managing people in order to drive business performance – for example by working on changing behaviours and developing commitment amongst employees. Staff development and training became important, as did organizational development and change.

All this opened up the means for personnel – now called 'human resources', or HR – to impact performance, and ultimately the business, but it started to blur the line between the leaders and HR as to who was ultimately accountable for managing people.

It was during this period that people management started to be a much more conscious, proactive process for both line managers and HR, though it was still largely a hit-and-miss affair. The underpinning research of what affected human behaviour was new, complex, and the language difficult, so leaders often felt unsure of themselves. It was like working in the dark in a different language, and they wanted the expert input from HR to make sense of it all. It was at this time that the focus of people-related activities moved away from 'output' to 'process'. It became more important to comply with the process and for it to be seen to be fair, than what the outcome of that process was, fair or otherwise.

Key to all this was the assumption that the basis upon which HR practices were based was soundly researched and verified. As the field was so new, many of the interventions were experimental or not thought through thoroughly enough, HR personnel were new to the discipline and inexperienced, line managers were unclear as to what they wanted, and the results sometimes did not end up as predicted.

An example is the story of Jonathan, an enthusiastic young HR graduate, who joined a small family-run retail company based in the north of England in the early 1980s.

Jonathan had been hired by Michael, the CEO of the firm and son of the firm's founder, who was keen to modernize what he perceived as antiquated HR practices first put in place by his father some 20 years before. Jonathan had studied all the latest theories and was excited about the prospect of putting into practice all he had learned at college. Finally, he was going to get away from studying books and really see some action.

The first area that Michael wanted Jonathan to focus on was the pay and reward structure for staff in the business. When he told the management team that this was the area Jonathan would tackle first, there was great concern. To date, the management team had simply rewarded all staff equally at the end of each year, in line with the government's published rate of inflation, regardless of actual performance. The heads of three of the four departments were particularly worried, as they felt that the system in place was fair, and supported the culture of equality – the family feel – that was the particular strength of the firm. They couldn't visualize how the decisions would be made as to who would get more and who would get less. They thought there was a risk that it could be perceived to be unfair, and might probably end up costing the firm more money both in administrative and employee costs, as well as in staff turnover.

Jonathan started by proposing an appraisal system: all staff had to be appraised by their manager. There was grudging support for this by the management team, pushed by Michael. No questions were asked, no implications discussed; Jonathan was simply told to make it happen. He went ahead and designed the appraisal forms, laid out the timetable for this to happen, and gave rudimentary training to all managers. He wrote memos informing staff of what would be happening, and answered any queries as best he could – though some of the questions were quite unexpected, and he had difficulty giving a good response.

The appraisals were completed over an anxious three-week period – all staff were nervous and spent a lot of time during their tea breaks discussing the conversations they had had with their supervisors. Productivity was noticeably lower. The management team got together to determine who were the high performers that would be paid more, and the poorer performers who would get less. It was the hardest meeting that Michael had ever chaired. During the session, it became clear that not everyone on the management team had used the same assumptions for what would be rated 'good', 'average' or 'poor' on Jonathan's forms. Worse still, evidence for the ratings was patchy and often biased. They ploughed on and eventually settled on a ranking of staff that would be used to allocate the year's pay awards.

Once the news of the awards was told to staff, many were outraged. The feedback supporting the pay award was often poor, inconsistent and sometimes simply unsubstantiated. Line managers were not used to having difficult conversations with staff and were not good at it. Many had managed to work around any tricky people issues for a long time, and they didn't want to confront them now. Some succeeded in steering clear of the whole business, fearful that it would damage working relationships and ultimately the business. It left both staff and line managers frustrated and angry. The mood at the company, once so family-like, degenerated to confrontation quickly, and Michael's next assignment for Jonathan involved his industrial relations expertise – the workers wanted to strike.

There was a lot to learn.

The 1990s were a white-knuckle ride, according to Jack Welch, former CEO of GE (Tichy and Sherman, 2005). Not only were organizations becoming increasingly complex as firms merged, formed alliances or joint ventures, but industries also started to globalize. What happened on another continent impacted your business locally and, with the advent of internet technology, this could occur almost instantaneously. The pace of change had never been faster and the sober world of work became a gossipy village. Social and demographic trends accelerated demands for making the workplace more attractive, for managing diversity and for continual learning in order to keep up. And the combined impact of high interest rates, international competition and shrinking productivity forced companies to cut overheads and costs.

Employees no longer expected to stay at companies for life, and job-hopping became common. The bedrock of working together in an organization – relationship building – was put under enormous strain as new teams were put together and dismantled over weeks not years, and were expected to deliver more, not less. In many cases, cross-border, virtual teams were required to deliver a global business – individuals had to learn to work together without being together or seeing each other. Building effective relationships in that environment was new territory for everyone.

Line managers didn't have the skills to cope with the rapidly shifting people issues all these changes generated. The role of HR became more important as the source of advice and expertise, lending stability and consistency to a fast-changing world.

As human resource management grew as a discipline, the models started to get more sophisticated and complex, and so did the language around them. Confusion about who was accountable for people issues in organizations became prevalent, but was not expressed. Leaders began to remove themselves from active participation: they didn't understand the concepts in detail and couldn't see the point, or outcome, that was required – it all seemed to be about process. They didn't have the time to invest in developing relationships that were fast-moving and changing all the time. They didn't have access to the research in the language they could understand that could have helped them, and so often it took too long to deal with, time they thought was better spent 'on the business'. In any case, many were glad to have someone else on board willing to run with it, and to take the rap if things went wrong. As line managers abdicated accountability for people issues, HR became accountable by default.

In the late 1990s, many HR experts (notably Dave Ulrich and his colleagues at Michigan University) began to urge HR professionals to adjust to the times by changing their roles once again (Jamrog and Overholt, 2004). The HR function had to be seen to add value to the business or risk being abolished altogether ('Should we do away with HR?' asked Dave Ulrich in his 1996 watershed book *Human Resource Champions*). He strongly advocated a place for HR at the decision-making table – a role with strategic input to the business.

From *administrative and employee relations expert* to *change agent*, HR now evolved to the phase we can call *strategic business partner*.

At the heart of HR as a strategic business partner was the stated aim of delivering a competitive workforce (Ulrich, 1996): ensuring that the right staff are in the right place, with the right tools and the right skills to deliver the corporate purpose. This meant having the ability to understand the business purpose, drivers, issues, external environment, and to translate these into actionable people strategies that gave the company a competitive edge in the market place.

It is, however, not easy to align HR strategy to business strategy: business strategy tends to change very fast, whilst long time-cycles and stability are essential for successful HR practice. In 1999, Gratton *et al* noted:

Time-cycles for people resources are considerably longer than those for financial or technological resources. Consider the following: it takes 10 to 15 years to select and develop an international senior executive cadre; a minimum of 3 years to pilot and implement a reward system refocused on supporting a new set of competencies; 5 years to reshape the technological skill base of employees. In sum, for the crucial people issues, the temporal perspective is not just months, and could even be decades, so the planning cycle for people resources must be capable of creating the foundation for skills and behaviours far beyond the one-year cycle favoured for many business strategies.

Gratton *et al* (1999)

The new HR professional was being encouraged to be able to play four roles all at once. In addition to the (by now traditional) roles of administrative and employee relations expert, and change agent, he or she was expected to be able to operate as a strategic business partner. This remains an enormous challenge, not only for the traditional HR professional, but also for the leaders in the organization, many of whom were not aware of the changing role of HR and the implications of that.

As global economic competition continued in the first decade of the 21st century, pressures increased on companies to reduce costs. Transactional and administrative activities in service functions such as HR, finance and IT became targets for outsourcing and off-shoring. Shared service centres became common. Application of technology such as web-based transactions offered the promise of dramatic cost reductions through standardization and automation, and contributed to more change in the in-house HR departments. These were significantly downsized, and HR staff were encouraged to spend more time on their strategic partner role, which more often than not required acquiring new capabilities. Local HR support for people issues became scarce.

The transition from in-house HR provision to outsourced HR was a major change for staff and line managers alike, as they were expected to help themselves to HR support, most usually through online portals, or via help desks located in different time zones. Help desks were frequently manned by staff trained to follow a 'script', who were not able to handle the everyday subtle changes in details of people's personal circumstances. The rapid implementation of these changes often left gaps in execution and performance, which were frustrating for all concerned.

Not all line managers and staff were happy with the transition as they deemed doing what they had for years regarded as HR responsibilities as outside the scope of their position, and simply added to their already overloaded work schedule. In many cases, line managers struggled to understand what was required of them. The changes foisted on them were unexpected and fast; they were given little time or support to adjust. At the same time, both line managers and staff often despaired that the systems and processes were too prescriptive and inflexible, and failed to address their particular situation. Managing sensitive people issues remotely or online, or with the help of scarce local HR support, became a nightmare. Focus on the individual became lost.

Whilst there have been some reports of successful HR outsourcing initiatives, there have been some disasters too. Some failures can be attributed, for example, to handover of complex or poorly understood processes and systems, or a lack of ensuring that the prospective provider has the necessary capabilities. These failures resulted not only in significant loss of value to the company, but also a drop in morale of the employee, and a subsequent loss of confidence in the management team's ability to manage effectively.

Nowadays, in the early part of the 21st century, leaders in organizations are expected to act as mentor, champion and one-person HR department to each of their reports – along with all the business responsibilities that they may have. Despite numerous attempts at leadership training, it remains the case that leaders are often not confident in their ability to tackle the difficult and sensitive issues around people development and management.

Indeed, many leaders find it harder to have a difficult conversation about performance or career potential with a member of staff than to take a tough business decision, or to negotiate a complex deal. Their experience is that having a great, motivating conversation with an employee is a highly skilled task, which often takes years to master, however good their relationship with that employee is.

HR professionals have begun to recognize that attempts to develop leaders by building line manager skills on short training courses are not enough. Furthermore the 'war for talent', particularly in a globally connected marketplace, has become very real as businesses compete to attract and retain the best people. As a discipline, HR is responding to this by suggesting that it play a bigger role in managing and developing talent in organizations. HR practitioners claim to have the skills to have the difficult conversations about performance, to guide and mentor employees towards career goals and greater career satisfaction. How HR will develop in this potentially new role as *talent and development expert* to meet these requirements remains to be seen. Key will be engaging with leaders to decide who plays what role in ensuring that people issues are properly handled, and that the leaders and HR work together as a team to put the focus back on the individual in the organization.

The role of leaders

Just as HR has changed significantly since the 1960s both in practice and in concept, so too has leadership. Indeed, being a leader *of* an organization in the 1960s had a quite different meaning to being a leader *in* an organization today, some 40–50 years later.

In the 1960s and 1970s, there was only one leader in any company – the top man (or woman), the leader *of* the company. The leader was special, distant, and unique. Everyone else in supervisory roles in the organization was referred to as a line manager or supervisor – there was a strong hierarchy that everyone understood. Generally, there were many line managers and supervisors; they were close to their staff, they got involved in the day-to-day work, they *supervised*. What people expected from leaders and line managers was very different – and has remained the same to this day. In 1999, Kotter defined the difference between what line managers and leaders do in a very simple way:

- Line managers are busy with activities that produce *predictability, order* and *consistency*, such as planning and budgeting, organizing and staffing, controlling and problem solving.

- Leaders are focused on activities that produce *useful, dramatic change*, such as establishing a new direction, aligning people, motivating and inspiring.

The leader provided the direction, and delegated the daily implementation of that to the line managers or supervisors. This included full accountability for the management of all staff in the organization. Let's call this the era of the *hierarchical leader*.

During the 1980s and 1990s, companies changed shape considerably in response to the tough, roller-coaster economic climate. Cost-cutting led to hierarchies being dismantled and organizations becoming 'flatter' – layers of line managers were removed, and workers became closer hierarchically to the leader. Self-managing teams were popular, in which the role of the line manager or supervisor was phased out altogether, shared, or done as part of another job. All this led to there being fewer line managers or supervisors in the company, and almost no one had 'managing others' as a full-time job. Quality time with subordinates became scarce, as there were simply not enough hours in the day to double-check everything that employees did, so staff empowerment or self-help became the default. The span of control of the single leader at the top of the company grew disproportionately, as he or she tried to run a flat organization with little, and sometimes no, full-time line management support. Attempts to delegate to a defined cadre of line managers or supervisors became complex and ineffective, and with many of those line managers or supervisors busy trying to do more than one role, confusion about roles and responsibilities became widespread.

The daily, close supervisory relationship between line manager and staff got lost. There was little time left between meetings and responding to the changing environment to pay real attention to the people who actually made things happen in the company. People moved between project teams – and companies – quickly, so the team bonding that used to take place over weeks and months had to be cemented in an away day or two, run off-site and facilitated by experts who didn't know any of the participants and would most likely never meet them again.

Many line managers and supervisors responded to the pressures by presuming that their employees were competent and hoping that they were self-reliant. They only stepped in after things had gone wrong. Whilst this worked in the short term, it was recognized that the approach was simply setting up problems for the future when a new generation of line managers needed to be in place. During the 1990s, compliance to governance require-ments became very important, and many companies spent millions ensuring that the people working for them could be verified as competent. Organ-izations strived to become places of learning. Staff were no longer supervised by their bosses; they were coached and mentored, intermittently, 'in the moment' when staff happened to be in the same place as their boss. The buck no longer stopped with the line manager, but was the responsibility of each and every individual in the company. This was the era of the *self-managing team*.

The idea of leadership as a more common role in an organization be-came popular towards the end of the 1990s. Not only was the head of the company expected to (in Kotter's words) 'produce useful, dramatic change', this was now expected to happen throughout the company.

> Leaders are people who
> *make sense for others*
> about what is happening.
>
> *Good enough leaders* do that by
> giving direction
> providing a map for action
> helping us master uncertainties

creating order out of chaos

creating a sense of excitement

providing a sense of purpose

Kets de Vries (2009)

Malcolm Higgs in his 2003 paper 'How can we make sense of leadership in the 21st century' advocated that a focus on 'sense-making for others' is the way forward for successful 21st-century leaders. In this case, the key measure of a successful leader is not just the impact on financial performance, but more importantly, the impact they have on their followers.

Everyone had to understand that change was now the constant in corporate life, and become part of making it happen. Everyone could be a leader – and everyone wanted to be one. We call this the *everyman leader* stage.

Being a leader became commonplace – and was tough. In the fast global pace of 21st-century business, many were ill-equipped to truly lead their staff. Once again, the individual got lost. It became really difficult to have both the time and the skill to really pay attention to each person, to help each member of their team unleash their potential, so that together they could deliver extraordinary results.

Many began to look for support and help from their HR departments. But what they found there was not what many expected, as we have seen. Instead it seemed that HR was asking for leaders to do more work – administering processes – rather than take work away. The expert advice was often not easily available quickly and locally, and leaders were left to deal with complex people issues on their own.

By the late 2000s, there was a realization that the key to success in the competitive business world was the talent in the organization, and that there needed to be a focus back on the individual.

Fred Hassan, CEO of Schering-Plough, said: 'The CEO has to see himself as the chief developer of talent, no matter how large the company' (Green *et al*, 2003).

What is developing talent if not unleashing the energy and potential locked up inside each individual? In order to achieve this, Jack Welch believed that it was necessary for him to spend at least 40 per cent of his time with the people who worked for him.

Relationships are the foundation upon which people interact, and these need time and energy to be nurtured. Let's call the leaders of the future *relationship leaders*. They need to be able to develop the talent in their organization through coaching and mentoring, to inspire loyalty and commitment in others, and to be great role models.

Leaders and HR working relationships

Looking at how both HR and leadership have evolved in different ways over the past 40–50 years, we can see how the relationship between them has become strained (Table 8.1).

In recent times, there has been open conflict between leaders and HR. From the leader's perspective, this was exposed by *Fast Company* Deputy Editor Keith Hammonds in his August 2005 paper 'Why we hate HR'. He describes the frustration that leaders have about HR: that processes seem duplicative and wasteful, and in the end appear to have no clear output; that the focus of HR is to find 'ever-more ingenious ways to cut benefits and hack at payroll'; that HR communications 'so often flout reality'; that they 'pursue standardization uniformity in the face of a workforce that is heterogeneous and complex' simply because it is easier and cheaper to do so – from the HR perspective; and that they always work in the interest of the organization rather than the individual. He complains that HR staff are not fundamentally interested in business, and invest more importance in activities rather than in outcomes.

If HR processes and rules are too prescriptive or complex – perhaps unintentionally so – staff and leaders alike will indeed perceive them to have been designed by HR without any consideration for the business needs and drivers. Whilst there is no doubt that there are fundamental processes and products that are required to ensure the organization is efficient in managing its people and doesn't flaunt local legislation, it is really important that the design and implementation of these doesn't come solely from the HR perspective and in the HR language. Instead, the design and implementation of key products and processes should be built on the specific business and emotional needs of the company and its staff, and be communicated in the way normal business is done.

HR staff feel equally frustrated about leaders. Among their complaints is that they frequently exclude HR from the decision-making table, so ignoring the valuable insights that a people-focused approach can give. Indeed, the position of HR in a company is still set by the top man or woman. If the CEO of the company is not a champion of people initiatives, then HR will have a difficult time securing and keeping a respected place on the management team. This subordinate position for the HR function will then be cascaded throughout the organization, and the HR department will be just tolerated as a necessary overhead. Many will consider it expensive and difficult to justify and it will sometimes be lumped together with the administration and/or finance departments.

TABLE 8.1   Overview of working relationships between leaders and HR

Year	Business context	HR role	Leader role	Observations
1960s–1980s	• Local • Stable • Certainty • Clear roles • Hierarchical • Organized unions • Confrontations • Focus on supervisor and individual	Administrative and employee relations	Hierarchical leader	• Leader and HR strategy and organizations are aligned • Roles are clearly defined • Leader and HR work well together
1980s–1990s	• Fast-changing • Instability and uncertainty • Flat teams • Staff empowerment • Lack of time • Focus on cost	Change agent	Self-managing team	• Leader and HR not dealing with changing environment together • Gaps in managing people emerge
1990s–2000s	• Global • Highly competitive • Flexible resourcing • Outsourcing • Focus on competition	Strategic business partner	Everyman leader	• High pressure on Leader to manage both business and people with not enough time or HR support • Focus on the individual is lost
2010s+	• As above • Skills gap emerging • Focus on skills	Talent and development expert	Relationship leader	• Realization that individual is key to success • Focus is back on individual

HR are also frustrated that leaders appear to abdicate their responsibility for managing their staff, often asking HR to step in to have the difficult conversations they are not prepared to have, and that they appear slow to accept change and reluctant to enable progress. There is much concern that leaders do not take time to understand the employment legislation that underpins most of mandatory HR processes, and can therefore run the risk of serious litigation, so that HR have to police these mandatory processes to ensure compliance, rather than rely on promises kept that this would be done within a certain deadline.

Having reviewed how HR and leaders in business have changed over the past 40 years, it is not really surprising that there is much confusion and frustration about who is accountable for 'people issues' in an organization. Inevitably this absorbs energy from people that can be more profitably used to the benefit of the organization as a whole.

Underlying the modern HR dilemma is that it lacks a coherent professional understanding of 'the person'. In the way that 18th-century medicine did not really understand the body, yet nevertheless some physicians made beneficial decisions even though trust in medicine as a whole was not high, so modern HR seems to have got itself into a position where it is driven by trendiness or compliance rather than systematic knowledge.

If HR were a mechanical engineering department, it would seem to have lots of tools and bits of kit but be uncertain how to put them together in an orderly fashion that would produce a reliable working vehicle. So uncertainty amongst line managers as to what HR actually contributes professionally to the bottom line of the business, which is every line manager's most pressing concern, creates doubt about HR. And this doubt is often itself a source of fear. HR then becomes, paradoxically, the source of the fear that drains energy: hence its potential for toxicity. Our experience tells us that in many organizations there is low trust for HR. That is not a happy state for a profession that, as Colin Powell proposed, ought to be at the heart of the organization.

References

Fombrum, CJ, Tichy, NM and DeVanna, MA (1984) *Strategic Human Resource Management*, John Wiley and Sons, Canada

Gratton, L, Hope Hailey, V, Stiles, P and Truss, C (eds) (1999) *Strategic Human Resource Management: Corporate rhetoric and human reality*, Oxford University Press

Green, S, Hassan, F, Immelt, J, Marks, M and Melland, D (2003) In search of global leaders: Perspectives, *Harvard Business Review*, **81** (8), pp 38–45

Hammonds, K (2005) Why we hate HR, *Fast Company*, available at http://www.fastcompany.com/53319/why-we-hate-hr [accessed 10 April 2014]

Hendry, C (1995) *Human Resource Management: A strategic approach to employment*, Butterworth-Heinemann, Oxford

Higgs, M (2003) How can we make sense of leadership in the 21st century?, *Leadership and Organization Development Journal*, **24** (5), p 278

Hunter, I, Saunders, J, Boroughs, A and Constance, S (2006) *HR Business Partners*, chapter 1 (The Evolution of HR), Gower Publishing, Aldershot

Jamrog, JJ and Overholt, MH (2004) Building a strategic HR function: Continuing the evolution, *Human Resource Planning*, **27** (1), pp 51–62

Kets de Vries, MFR (2009) *Organizational Paradoxes: Clinical approaches to management (organizational behaviour)*, Tavistock Publications Limited, Abingdon

Kotter, J (1999) *On What Leaders Really Do*, A Harvard Business Review book, Harvard Business School Press, Boston, MA

Powell, C (nd) *A Leadership Primer*, available at http://net.ucar.edu/nets/intro/staff/jcustard/jc-la2004/powell-leadership.pdf [accessed 15 June 2014]

Tichy, NM and Sherman, S (2005) *Control Your Destiny or Someone Else Will*, Harper Collins, New York

Ulrich, D (1996) *Human Resource Champions: The next agenda for adding value and delivering results*, Harvard Business School Press, Boston, MA

PART THREE
The future of organizations

The role of leadership

09

Introduction

In this chapter we explore the role that leaders play in their organization; how their own fears can be projected into the organization; and how the way they themselves deal with their own fears affects their teams. We discover how critical leaders are in developing relationships in the organization, in creating its culture, and in setting its strategy.

We conclude that crucial to creating the fear-free organization is having leaders who are self-aware and understand the impact they have on others, as well as having the ability to generate and maintain trust.

> The river moulds the banks and the banks guide the river. Similarly, the ethos moulds the cultural structure and is guided by it.
>
> Gregory Bateson (1987)

What makes a good leader?

Edward had worked for over 30 years in the same company. He was an expert in his field and much sought after for advice. But he had been in the same team for almost 10 years, and was starting to feel stale. Worse than that, the business environment had rapidly deteriorated and the company was struggling to meet its targets. There were rumours that head office was getting ready to make major changes, so the local leadership team felt increasingly under pressure and began to approve projects that, although profitable in the short term, would really damage the business in the longer term.

In this situation Edward was often asked to sign the projects off from the technical and commercial perspective. His boss made it clear that he had no option. Edward realized that it would be his reputation that would be damaged if anything went wrong, not his boss's. He became very stressed – there was no one he could turn to at work with his concerns. He couldn't sleep at night, became unfit and started to put on weight, and developed stress-related migraines.

Eventually Edward decided he needed a change and applied for a job in the same company but in another area. He wanted to work for someone with integrity, someone who would inspire him so that he could deliver his best. And he wanted to work in a team that would make a positive difference to the business and have fun whilst doing so. His application was successful and he was really excited about working for his new boss, who was dynamic and had a great sense of humour. It then came as quite a blow to discover that his new boss would be leaving soon and Edward would be working for another 'wooden administrator'. His mood plummeted again.

As part of his induction he had to attend a department meeting at which the new head of department, David, would be speaking. It felt like more hassle, and not worth the effort. No one had heard of this guy, and no one was enthusiastic about going to the meeting. When he told his colleague in a different department, her face lit up. 'Wow – David! You are so lucky to be working that close to him – he is amazing!' Intrigued, he went to the meeting. For days afterwards, he couldn't stop talking about it – in the short half hour that David had spoken to a room of over 50 staff, he had connected with each one, shone with integrity, and inspired them all to do their best. He left them with the feeling that each one of them would be deeply appreciated for their efforts, and could contact him at any time to discuss problems they had – he was there to listen and to help. Never had Edward seen the impact of leadership as powerfully as he did that day. The experience stayed with him for a long time and helped him to settle well into his new job.

There are a great many good people who fulfil leadership roles at the top of and throughout organizational structures. There are also others who are not so good, or perhaps are just 'good enough'. Good leaders are rare. Great leaders are rarer still. And they are all very easy to recognize.

Leaders are the people who *make sense for others* about what is happening in and around the organization. *Good enough* leaders do that by giving direction and providing a map for action (Kets de Vries, 2009). They help to master uncertainties, and create order out of chaos. They make key decisions and in doing so consciously or otherwise direct everyone's efforts onto what they value. They create the climate, culture, and mood within which others either flourish or fail. And they provide a sense of excitement and purpose to the organization. Leaders sometimes use the HR function as an instrument to implement how they want the organization to be, but this does not dilute the important role leaders themselves play.

Emotions and feelings attached to experience create meaning expressed in language. Without emotion there would be no meaning. And emotions underpin all decisions. The key source of influence between one person and another is the way emotion is transmitted and received between them. Relationship is the key carrier signal between people for effecting any change, development, or even ordinary everyday action.

Leaders also help their teams improve their thinking – not to do the thinking for them, but to create conditions for people to think better for themselves. People don't want to be managed: they want to be unleashed.

People follow leaders for different reasons – some conscious, some not conscious. Lao Tzu 2,500 years ago described the best leader as the one who helps people so that eventually they don't need him. Next is the leader who is loved and admired. Next, the one who is feared. And worst of all is the one who lets people push him around – who is no leader at all.

People and organizations do best following leaders that generate the attachment emotions of trust/love and excitement/joy in them. Leaders who generate fear may produce results in the short term, but ultimately they corrode organizations. Leaders who let themselves be led by others or their opinions should not be called leaders at all. It is perhaps interesting to note how some modern politicians may be an example of Lao Tzu's lowest order of leadership: they allow others to find out what the electorate wants and then promise, realistically or otherwise, to deliver it to them.

How do leaders lead?

As we have seen in previous chapters, people's motivation to do something or to change is triggered in the first instance by their emotions. If they feel angry, they will shout and maybe lash out. If they feel sad, they may grieve or cry. If they feel fear, they will go into survival mode. If they are surprised, they may create unexpected solutions to a nagging problem. And if they feel trust they will be open to possibilities.

It is only through the impact that the leader has on a team's emotions that any changes can be made to the team's behaviour and motivation. It is by engaging with people's emotions that the culture of an organization thrives. From a neuroscience perspective, the essential skill of leading is to facilitate motivation and change in people in such a way as to get their brains working in constructive, and perhaps even in new, patterns that achieve corporate goals. Getting things to happen in an organization relies on the leader deliberately and consciously creating opportunities based on how people feel – not directing *how* they act, but creating conditions under which they can use their own energy and adaptive capacity to reach the goal. Leaders need to direct people's energy to *thrive*, not just survive.

The only way to engage people's emotions is through relationship. Understanding that the brain is the organ of relationship is essential for leaders. And understanding how the brain works enhances leadership capacity.

It is through the emotional system that the brain is the organ of relationship, as well as the primary organ of making sense of what is going on in the outside world. The emotional system is for experiencing; the intellectual system is for understanding. The brain puts those two together, making cohesive sense of them and integrating them into a whole. The right brain is mainly focused on the emotional system and possibilities, while the left brain deals with facts, however complex, and what is known.

An organization really is impacted by how its leader's brain works. What happens within the leader, emotionally, generates conditions in others and they respond in kind. Special brain cells called 'mirror neurons' facilitate that exchange. The whole system controlled by the amygdala is effectively a transmitter as well as a receiver.

When you see someone hurt their finger you immediately flinch in sympathy; or when you spot a friend wrinkle up their face in disgust at tasting some food your stomach reacts right away. When someone smiles at you, you smile back. This ability to instinctively and immediately understand what other people are experiencing is called being in sync – and it's related to the brain's mirror neurons. They are a special class of brain cell that fire not only when you perform an action, but also when you see someone make the same action, or you imagine the action to be taken.

An organization operates best when people's brains are in sync with the leader's brain: it's what good communication and high morale are all about. It is almost as if there is a 'resonance' between the leader's brain and the brains of the people in the rest of the organization.

Because the brains of all the people in the organization are trying to make sense of the signals that the leader's brain sends out, a leader's ability to understand and regulate his or her own brain first is essential. Leaders need to be acutely self-aware – they need to understand what they are feeling and why, and be honest about it. When a leader is fearful or angry about a situation, it is contagious; this type of behaviour appears threatening to others in the organization, initiating in them emotions of fear or anger as well. When a leader is excited about a project, or trusts the people in the team, this too is infectious; fears are calmed and people are inspired to do their best.

Being honest about what the leader is feeling is essential – emotions can't be faked. Authenticity in a leader is difficult to simulate. Other people are very good at picking up on insincerity, and that quickly leads to distrust.

At some level, the leader is also the person upon whom everyone in the organization feels reliant for his or her own survival; leaders can dilute or divert threats and they can show how to overcome obstacles.

This explains why the leader's capacity to 'be the change they want' and 'walk the talk' is critical. It is the best way for people to understand – at an emotional level – what is expected of them. It creates the safe environment for people to adapt to changes.

Leaders need to avoid – consciously or unconsciously – demonstrating behaviour that will be perceived by people's reptilian brains as creating risks or threats, because when this happens, their deep-seated response is to focus on survival, not on creative action. It results in people being defensive and suspicious; they use all their energies to endure and not to thrive.

Instead, leaders need to consciously create conditions that will generate the attachment emotions – trust/love and excitement/joy. This will ensure that all available energy is used positively in pursuit of the organization's goals: there is a clear path from the emotional part of the brain to the cognitive part.

Excitement/joy and trust/love underpin all the great human experiences. They are the stuff of poetry, drama, art and fundamentally enduring relationship and anything at all worthwhile hanging onto in life. But strangely, they have no primary survival value despite having enormous human, cultural and social value. They are what most people struggle for, most of their lives. They are what distinguish a great organization from a mediocre one. They create the best kind of sustainability.

Of the two attachment emotions, the most important one to motivate people in organizations is trust. It allows energy to flow, unhampered by the destructive side of stress or performance anxiety. This is because the primary danger-seeking function of their amygdala quietens down. When trust exists between leader and team, extraordinary things can happen – whatever goals are set can be achieved. But trust is not a commodity subject to transactional organizational rules. It is an emotion that underpins behaviour. Trust essentially originates in leaders in organizational systems.

For more creative enterprises, leaders need to focus on generating an environment where surprise/delight is prevalent, and give enough quiet space and time for the brain to generate unexpected connections that lead to 'eureka' moments.

Leaders therefore need to be able to calm their own fight/flight/freeze emotions of anger, disgust, shame and sadness, but most especially of fear so that they don't get passed on to others. As we have seen in Chapter 7, neuroscience research shows that leaders can change their brain's activity by practising mindfulness, a form of meditation that focuses attention. This quietens the amygdala allowing the brain to regulate emotions better, and can much improve the way the brain is working. It can also enhance feelings of compassion and empathy, which underpin trust.

The SCARF model introduced in Chapter 4 provides another framework for building leadership self-awareness. Leaders need to be acutely aware when they reduce people's:

- *sense of status* by providing too much direction and not enough feedback; leaders need to help their subordinates feel better about themselves;

- *certainty* by not providing clear expectations; establishing clarity and commitment about what is expected helps people focus and provides certainty;

- *autonomy* by micro managing their staff; trusting people and letting them make their own decisions improves autonomy;

- *relatedness* by maintaining a hierarchical relationship;

- *fairness* by treating others without due consideration.

Finally, the model of the 'mind' we discussed in Chapter 7 gives an overarching framework for leadership development, in which leadership is organized around managing information, relationships and energy.

Leadership and the Sofi model

How does what a leader's brain does fit in with the Sofi model of an organization that we introduced in Chapter 7? Remember that in the Sofi model, all the spheres influence each other, just as the vital organs of the body are interdependent; and a well-functioning organization will have strong and balanced relationships between all spheres. The strongest influence is exerted between spheres closest to one another, and the three closest spheres to the 'leadership' one are 'communications', 'culture' and 'strategy':

1 *Communications*. Leaders lead others through all kinds of communication that establish and maintain relationships. Having high-quality *conversations* is the core skill in building good relationships and communication.

2 *Culture*. Leaders shape the organization's culture and its beliefs and values. He or she must encourage behaviours that are *trust-based* in order to allow the best to happen.

3 *Strategy*. Leaders set the organization's direction and goals – *what* needs to be done. Clear cognitive thinking is required, unimpeded by any of the five fight/flight/freeze emotions, but most especially fear. In order to deliver on the agreed strategy however, leaders need to gain the individual's *commitment*.

It is in these areas that leaders need to truly excel in order to be great and make a real difference to their organization. The next three sections examine these three areas in more detail.

Relationships and communications

Relationships and communications are the essence of leadership. They are how the leader engages his or her team and unleashes in their brains the power and energy to deliver extraordinary things.

Coping with complexity in an organization and succeeding in a changing business environment depends critically on how the people in that organization relate to one another, and how sense is made together. Relationships between people are more important than the people themselves. As we have seen, any time you interact with another person, both you and the other person are tapping into each other's brains.

Relationships build on the interaction between one person and another: one person acts, triggering a response in another. That response in turn acts as a trigger on the originator. And so on. Good sense is made, and relationships have a chance to become trustful. Then great things can happen.

Sense must be made and shared, meaning understood, before the best action can be decided upon and taken. But frequently the response is modified by the person's internal landscape – determined by their experiences in the past and their hopes for the future. They don't see straight. So sense is not made, nor is it shared. The interactions are flawed, the actions are not appropriate, and the outcomes are sub-optimal.

At the core of interactions and sense-making between people in organizations are *conversations*. Thoughts, feelings and meaning are conveyed through words, gestures and body language. Conversations can spark ideas, start projects, monitor and steer them. They can postpone, reschedule, and stop work. Conversations can excite and motivate others; they can depress and upset too. They are needed to explain, to teach, to learn. People learn to think together through conversation. Change can only happen if there is an effective conversation.

When we use the word 'conversation' we mean the two-way interaction between people in order to deepen meaning *together*: it is both talking and listening deeply – *properly*. Some authors label this process one of 'dialogue'. In the context of our book, conversation and dialogue are one and the same.

Feedback is one special form of conversation that allows a check to be made. Was the impact of the action or statement in line with the intention, or not? And if not, then what was the impact? Feedback is all about learning how others view a situation – understanding how someone else just made sense of what happened. It is critical in building trustful relationships; incorrect assumptions are undone, replaced by honest understanding.

Telling stories is another special form of conversation. Facts can be connected with values and feelings all at once, and understanding of meaning can be much more profound.

According to Complexity Theory (Stacey, 1996), diversity and ambiguity are critical to succeed in an unpredictable, uncertain world. The best sense is made when as many different conversations and stories as possible are heard and understood – the 'collective intelligence' of the group enriched by the diversity within the group.

Mastering the skill of having good conversations is key to quality interactions and relationships in an organization. It is the most important skill humans have to stop fear in its tracks and to create the environment where people can thrive. It is the capacity that is needed to allow solutions to emerge.

Good leaders can't do without it. Indeed, according to Ronald Heifetz (1999), 'the work of a leader is to lead conversations about what's essential and what's not' in order for everyone to achieve great results.

There are many books available that help individuals acquire the skill of having a good conversation. Amongst the best are *Crucial Conversations* (2002) and *Crucial Confrontations* (2005) by Patterson *et al*, *Difficult Conversations* (2000) by Stone *et al*, and *Dialogue and the Art of Thinking*

Together (1999) by Isaacs. Nancy Kline's 1999 book *Time to Think* is outstanding in helping to create the environment for good listening – the essential component of good conversations. Most recently, *5 Conversations: How to transform trust, engagement and performance at work* by Cowley and Purse (2014) emphasizes that good leadership is based on conversations which build relationship and trust.

In all these books, the fundamental keys to good conversations are to be able to see beyond what is going on inside you, to step out and understand the world as it is, not as you are. Work through your thoughts and feelings – the stories that you tell yourself – and determine whether these are true or not. Learn how to suspend, and to be present in the 'now'. Check the reality of that 'voice inside your head' – be self-aware, be 'mind-full', solicit feedback. And really listen to what the other person is saying; sense their meaning; help them to get underneath their own stories.

With practice, this type of 'suspension' can be done in a matter of seconds in any given situation. It's all about being conscious of our own feelings in the present, being aware of our own assumptions and verifying them in that moment, in order to ensure that the response that we choose to make is an appropriate one for that situation. This is one way to tame the fear that automatically takes hold.

Conversations can sometimes turn to *confrontation*; emotions ride high and much is at stake. So many of us fear confrontations at work – we are afraid to speak up against the manager who is breaking the rules, who is giving us too much work to do, who has the power to wreck our career. Fear is unleashed, and the right outcomes so often fail to materialize. In facing a confrontation, Patterson *et al* in their book *Crucial Confrontations* suggest that the key is to work together with your potential adversary to reach a shared understanding on what happened, before deciding *together* what to do next. Key to resolving a confrontation is relationship, and the brain that plays a significant role in that.

To deal with a person who 'becomes emotional' – who is angry, frustrated, afraid or worried – we have to get to the source of their feelings. Highly expressed emotions are triggered by events, thoughts and emotions, shaped by perceptions arising from their internal world. We all tell ourselves stories about what has happened to us, so we need to try to understand the original trigger and the story the person is telling him- or herself behind their emotional outburst.

Dilemmas can get people stuck in organizations, unable to decide the way forward. They arise from deep-seated values, powered by the emotions, and are often difficult to articulate simply and tough to negotiate. The problem in resolving dilemmas arises because people can sometimes see the value in the opposing arguments, and so find it hard to choose. A conversation to uncover the nature of the dilemma is the first step in resolution. The next step is to explore whether or not there is a deeper, more fundamental value that encompasses the two conflicting values – something that allows everyone to accept the way forward whole-heartedly.

Building a trust-based culture

The culture in an organization sets the tone about 'how stuff gets done around here' (Deal and Kennedy, 1982). It includes the organization's values, beliefs and norms, as well as its language, systems and habits. It is the pattern of collective behaviours and assumptions that result in how things are perceived, and it affects the way people think and feel at work, as well as how connected they are to the organization.

Cultures at work are primarily shaped by the leader (Schein, 2010; Brown and Hales, 2012). But cultures also exist in a context – other factors, including company size, nationality, history, industrial sector, power structure and risk appetite have an influence, partly because they influence the leader as well, but also because they shape the cultural cues that are acceptable.

In the literature, there are many models that describe different organizational cultures (eg Hofstede, 1980; Deal and Kennedy, 1982; Kotter and Heskett, 1992; Handy, 1976; Schein, 2010), but none explicitly recognize the significant impact that fear at work has. As we have seen, fear diverts energy away from the purpose of the organization in order to safeguard survival, and a culture full of fear negatively impacts the company's bottom line.

Times have changed. In the past, fear was the predominant way leaders had of operating in the workplace. Even as recently as the 1950s and 1960s, leaders imposed rewards and punishments based on a strict adherence to rules. At home and at school, corporal punishment was acceptable to impose discipline. During the 1970s, however, the shift in employment from factory or industrial worker to knowledge or service worker meant that culture at work had to change. It became essential to encourage creativity and innovation, and to encourage good relationships, especially with customers and clients. Diversity started to become appreciated, and people expected to be treated fairly at work. It was no longer necessary to impose strict adherence to rules through fear, and it started to become recognized that leadership through fear was counter-productive. But cultures at work can persist for many years and are difficult to change without strong leadership. Remnants of an old fear-based culture can remain, often perpetuated by long-serving staff who find it hard, or don't want to, make the changes.

George's first job after graduating from university was to join a large multinational financial services company. In the past, the company had a terrible reputation for bullying its employees to make them work very long hours and drive hard bargains with their customers to maximize its profits. Although the pay was high, many people had left as they buckled under the pressure, and the word on the university campus was that this was not a great place to start a career. After the 2008 financial crisis, numerous practices at the company were exposed as unethical, and a significant drive to change the culture was launched. George joined four years on. On his first day, he met his new boss Alan, a veteran of the company who had survived the purges of the past four years. Alan's first words to George were, 'Wipe that smile off your face, and don't pay attention to the pandering that is being peddled. It's all window dressing. You're here to make the highest profit you can. Here are your targets. I expect you to deliver them, or you'll be in big trouble.' George's first day at work was already full of fear.

In a fear-free organization, it is the leaders' primary role to create a culture of trust. When an organization's culture is built on trust, staff don't have to fear that changes, including losing their job or status, are the result of the unpredictable impulses of an uncaring leader.

To create a culture of trust, it's not enough to behave ethically; people will only trust someone who shows that he or she trusts them. The leader must be open and honest about what is happening around him or her, and why. We all tend to fear the unknown. The antidote is accurate and true information – the factual kind. In the absence of information, we all tend to fill in the blanks, creating stories that become reality. So leaders must fully communicate with their employees, especially about key decisions, and if possible include key staff in decision-making. Honest, open conversations are key.

We believe that the culture in a fear-free organization is underpinned by *honesty*, *openness* and *trust* (HOT); we like 'HOT' teams.

Leaders need to be able to listen and understand their teams' concerns, their mistakes and their problems. They must acknowledge what has been said, then collect the facts. They need to create a safe environment for employees to speak up about issues that concern them, even if those issues are sensitive or exasperate the leader. They must especially allow people's worst fears – however far-fetched – to be vocalized so that they can be dealt with quickly and publicly.

Fear of talking about mistakes breeds lies – if leaders cannot admit to errors, how can anyone else in the organization? Embracing errors constructively engenders trust. When mistakes happen, the leader needs to first look in the mirror to determine what their role has been in the failure. It's no good getting upset with the employee if the leader hasn't made expectations clear enough, or the expectations were unrealistic, or perhaps if the systems or processes in place were faulty. Working out what went wrong and how to prevent it happening again in future is best done together with the employee in an open and honest way. If the leader has made a mistake, they should be willing to share it – always tell the truth.

Oliver was doing a gap year job on a very large livestock and arable farm. He had no intention of becoming a farmer, but the chance had arisen of doing something quite different before university took him back to his history degree. Liking to be fit and the summer just beginning, three months leading up to harvest, board and lodging all found, sounded fun.

James, the co-owner of the farm, asked Oliver to drive a tractor out of the barn. Having passed his car-driving test a year before and feeling himself a perfectly good driver, Oliver jumped at the chance. Off he went, only to find as he approached the wall of the barn where the tractor was housed that he couldn't find the brake pedal. Modern tractors being powerful things, and this one being in a low gear after just starting, it drove itself straight through the panel structure of the barn, Oliver being lucky not to have been hit by heavy shards of brittle panelling raining down around him.

Running up to him and alongside as he struggled to find the brake, James pointed out the brake pedal to Oliver and the tractor came to a sudden halt in the farmyard, the pedal pressed with all the pent-up energy of fear and confusion.

Covered in confusion and seeing the damage he had caused, Oliver started apologizing profusely. 'Stop it,' said James. 'It's my fault. I didn't check properly whether you knew enough to drive a tractor. It's second nature to me and the other lads. I had forgotten you hadn't been on one before. And I'm glad you're not hurt.'

James could have laughed at Oliver or otherwise belittled him. The barn was going to cost some time and money to repair. But in a moment he acted like a true leader – saw the source of the error and allocated it fairly. Such a boss gets a huge psychological gain from an employee. Trust grows.

In creating a trust-based culture it is good to remember that employee status matters – more explicit kinds of behaviour are required to encourage openness and trust at different levels in the organization. Lower-status employees need clear social and organizational cues. Higher-status employees may not need explicit permission.

Not only does creating a trust-based culture remove fear, it also increases information sharing, openness, and cooperation. It boosts the quality and quantity of ideas exchanged and shared. It also helps to change and co-ordinate people's values, ideas and behaviour.

Setting strategy and getting commitment

Leaders are accountable for setting the company direction and strategy. How they do that is covered in many other books (eg Johnson *et al*, 2010; Hrebiniak, 2013; Henry, 2011; Mintzberg *et al*, 2008), and we will not be covering the subject. What we are interested in, however, is how the leader delivers on his or her *accountability* and enlists the *commitment* of staff to deliver, in such a way that fear is kept at bay.

Let's look first at what we mean by the term 'being accountable'. Accountability is a term often used in organizations, but it frequently has different meanings for different people – leaders see it as the key to getting things done, but staff can see it in a much more negative light.

Ask leaders about what they mean by accountability, and they will tell you that it's the basis on which things get done – it's the bedrock on which trust is built. It's their team's performance contract for the year.

Ask a team about what accountability is, and they will tell you it's about whom you blame when things go wrong. Ask them how it feels, and they'll say that mostly it doesn't feel good. Ask them if they want more accountability. If they feel free to be honest with you they will more than likely say no: they fear retribution, punishment, exclusion, if they don't deliver. They will tell you that their leaders often use the magical phrase 'you are accountable' when they want to get something done, though they have not the faintest idea of *how* it will be done, nor the intention to give the structure and support to ensure that it *can* be done. Furthermore, if you ask them how clear their leaders are with them as to what they have just been made accountable for or the context around that, most of them will say, 'not very'. When the boss says, 'just get it done', many people will – through sheer willpower, long hours and brute force. And they will burn themselves out in the process.

Accountability is usually defined as the 'state of being liable to answer for one's conduct; to give account, and to receive reward or punishment for actions' (Webster, 1828). Accountability is often used synonymously with such concepts as answerability, responsibility, blameworthiness and liability. In effect, it is 'doing what you said you were going to do, when you said you would do it'.

Numerous books deal with accountability (eg Kraines, 2001; Bustin, 2014; Patterson *et al*, 2013; Worrall, 2013), and all identify the lack of it as one of the biggest blockers to delivering an organization's strategy.

Accountability is effectively a 'contract' between the individual and the leader to deliver what the organization needs (Kraines, 2001; Bustin, 2014). It is committing to a personal promise – on both parts. Effective accountability is not about defining the carrots and sticks to make someone achieve a target: it's about establishing a trustful relationship with clear, common expectations and the ability to tell each other when things are starting to go wrong so that the commitment can be restated if necessary. It is not only the individual that needs to commit to delivering what he or she promises on time; the leader must also promise to ensure the success of the individual performing the task, including for example ensuring a clear goal, and that there is enough time and resource to do the job well.

Delegation of accountability, authority and resources threads throughout the whole company – from the shareholder to the board, then to the CEO or MD, senior leaders, and so on, to every person in the organization. In order for this to work, each leader and each member of staff must be held mutually accountable for delivering their individual obligations – the chain is only as strong as its weakest link.

If not well defined, accountability can fail. Holding employees accountable for achieving a goal that isn't clear can lead to mistakes, wasted effort, or rework. Holding employees accountable for tasks that they haven't been given the resources or authority to complete, results in stress, frustration and resentment. Holding employees to account when the context isn't clear will possibly result in a sub-optimal outcome in the context of the rest of the organization: even if a result is obtained, there could be an erosion of value. All failures of accountability impact the bottom line.

Failure of accountability is full of excuses: the individual who claimed that the project scope increased, or that there wasn't enough time to do the work properly; the leader who insisted that the team wasn't up to the job, or that the budget allocated was too small. In many companies, it is acceptable, instead of delivering 'results', to deliver 'no results plus a good story'. Put another way, failure along with a plausible story is seen as success.

But the bottom line is that if a task is not delivered as agreed – if accountability is breached – then this is a basic violation of trust. The person (either the leader or the individual) failed to live up to their commitment – they didn't do what they had promised to do. The relationship between individual and leader becomes strained, and one of the flight/fight/freeze emotions may well be triggered, leading to even more lack of delivery.

Consequences can be used to help reinforce accountabilities – to modify actions and behaviour. Positive reinforcements mean that the individual's actions and behaviours result in getting what they want. This enhances trust, builds commitment and accountability. Negative reinforcements on the other hand, mean that the individual's actions and behaviours result in them avoiding what they don't want. This introduces fear into the environment, and builds compliance instead of commitment. It's always best to provide positive rather than negative reinforcements.

Being a limbic leader in a brain-focused organization

To implement a brain-focused approach, leaders need to understand enough about how the brain works to apply that knowledge to themselves and their teams. Critically, they need to understand the role that emotions play in improving performance, and that building relationships based on trust is key. Furthermore, they need to be authentic and model the behaviour that they want others to follow.

Brown and Brown (2012) have defined six necessary qualities for a brain-focused leader. They call this the *limbic leader*. The first five of these qualities arise when the leader trusts him- or herself. For the sixth quality, others trust the leader, who has the capacity to:

1 *Connect*. This means that leaders have empathy; they can tune into others and factor that into their own reactions. They are great listeners and understand the importance of trust-based conversations. They believe in others, and are not cynical. They invest in other people's growth and know that error is often the basis of growth. They are good at giving feedback. They know how to be persuasive and influential, whilst taking others along with them.

2 *Be courageous.* This means that leaders are secure in themselves and have the courage of their convictions. They accept that they may have to go against the prevailing orthodoxy, or that they may make mistakes. They lead by example and confront inadequate behaviour quickly.

3 *Be clever enough.* These leaders are intellectually competent, and can filter the irrelevant or the unnecessary. They like to learn. They understand that being a leader is like conducting an orchestra – you don't have to know how to play all the instruments, but you do have to create the conditions for others to play their best.

4 *Walk their own talk.* This means that the leaders are self-aware, authentic and congruent; they encourage feedback from others to develop themselves further. They can weave the different strands of their life together in a coherent whole, and the sense is that they have a good work–life balance. They have integrity, often taking a moral perspective and going for a win–win.

5 *Inspire others into action.* These leaders have passion, vision and purpose. They enjoy being creative: synthesizing complex variables and taking into account diverse views. They understand that people don't want to be managed; they want their energies and talents to be unleashed. They work with the person, not with the problem. They understand how to gain commitment and what their role is in setting accountability.

6 *Be worth following.* These leaders have others' trust. They create HOT teams.

Leadership and gender

It is not possible to leave this chapter, however, without opening up an area that is hardly discussed at all in the management literature. It is the difference between men and women as leaders. Just as we start to define what neuroscience might tell us about the kind of leader who could create a fear-free environment, neuroscience itself develops and starts offering new insights and possibilities. There was one such occasion in December 2013.

The University of Philadelphia released the composite results of the brain scans of a thousand boys and girls, men and women. What they showed for the first time in great detail was how very differently male and female brains

FIGURE 9.1 Different patterns of male and female connectivity between (on left) and within (on right) brain hemispheres

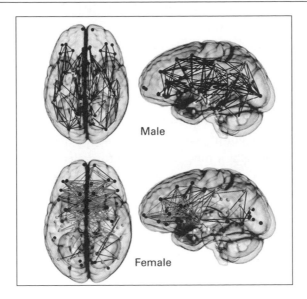

SOURCE: Verma, University of Pennsylvia (2013)

function (see eg BBC News, 2013). The way energy flows along and creates pathways between and within the two halves of the brain is remarkably gender specific.

The female brain composite showed rich interconnections *between* the two halves of the brain, as if the whole of the brain was busy talking to and engaging itself. The male brain, on the other hand, showed relatively little connection between the hemispheres but a great deal of activity *within* each half (Figure 9.1).

As Trimble (2012) suggests, it seems as if the male brain is organized to be pointing and propositional, while the female brain is organized to be integrating. The male brain likes problems. With a problem available a man can take action. The female brain likes solutions. When solutions are known a woman can get on with being.

Furthermore, there is evidence that men and women may process certain emotions differently (Medina, 2009), though this remains to be proven. It is based on the observation that men appear to have a larger amygdala (the areas that control our emotions and some types of learning) than women, whilst women have larger front and prefrontal cortex areas (where decision-making takes place) than men. Men also produce serotonin (which helps to regulate emotions and mood) faster than women. Professor Gina Rippon believes, however, that these differences may be related to environmental factors like stereotyping (Knapton, 2014) rather than underlying brain structure, and so can change.

What is the significance of these differences for leadership?

The first big and long-term implication is that men and women are likely to approach solutions in quite different ways. Robinson (2014) speculates that it is likely that women prefer to gather more details and integrate them faster into complex patterns. They like to generalize and synthesize, and to take a broader, more holistic view. Men on the other hand are more likely to focus on one thing at a time. They seem to prefer to compartmentalize information, discarding what they consider to be irrelevant, and analysing data in a more linear way. It may also be that women will remember the details of an experience related to emotion, whereas men will only remember the gist of it (Medina, 2009).

A second important implication is that men and women are likely to prefer different organizational structures. Men may be more comfortable in hierarchical structures that have clear goals and a directive communication style. Women on the other hand tend to excel in multifaceted flat organizations that allow open discussion and involvement.

Requiring women to function within male-defined operational systems may be a stressor that could begin to acquire serious legal attention as these findings start filtering into commercial consciousness.

When one major international private equity firm had a class action brought against it some years ago by women who took the view that they had been very badly treated interpersonally in the system, a view not infrequently expressed in the press was: 'If they didn't like the rules of the game, why did they get into it?'

That view is going to be less and less supportable in these corporate days of gender equality. Equality of opportunity does not *de facto* require similarity of action. Diversity is not a solution if it is not backed up by differences in options.

The scientific evidence seems now to indicate that men's and women's brains do work differently. When this is more fully understood, it will be reflected in the workplace and include acceptance of appropriate and proper leadership styles, and a new revolution regarding organizational behaviour cannot but occur. Gender specificity, the opposite of diversity, is coming to the corporate world and will not go away. These matters will require a very sophisticated and creatively adaptive response from leadership and the HR community.

At the same time it has to be recognized that not *all* men's brains are profoundly different from all women's brains, or vice versa. There is a spread of male-ness and a spread of female-ness about the brain. It may well be that, along with so many biological characteristics, the range is contained within a normal distribution. If that is the case, then the majority, being in the middle, may not show much in the way of differences between male and female brains. But the evidence at the moment suggests that this is a bit unlikely. The composite differences that the University of Philadelphia have shown are so remarkably different that the tail ends of a distribution cannot easily account for them. The best working hypothesis at the moment is that men's and women's brains are very different indeed, even though the basic biological building blocks are the same.

After all, the same is true for body shape and function, which we can observe clearly. The biological building blocks are exactly the same in men and women but the outcomes are very different – just as bricks and mortar in 19th-century London produced buildings that were identifiably different from something Frank Lloyd Wright might have created using bricks and mortar too.

Alas, in normal everyday life we cannot observe the brain as clearly as the physical differences between men and women.

Or could we?

If we really changed our organizational perceptions of male/female into ones of real *equality* plus a profound *difference*, we might – for then we could start observing accurately, free of non-conscious assumptions, instead of from the usually-projected position of expecting others to 'be like me'. We might also start to recognize that working together, as in a family unit, men and women's differences complement each other so perfectly that the total is easily greater than the sum of its parts.

A 2014 blog from Peter Diamandis, one of the founders of Singularity University and an extraordinary innovator, quoting Lynn Tilton (Diamandis, 2014), offers the beginning of a clue as to what the profound difference might be about.

Lynn Tilton is CEO of an $85 billion revenue holding company, Patriarch Partners. Talking of women executives, she writes:

> This unrivalled quest to 'have it all', to 'excel at both', or the unbearable compromise to 'sacrifice one for the other' should bind us [women] and unite us in the awe and appreciation of modern womanhood. But instead, few of us find the support system, the sponsors, or the advocates to drive us forward when the darkness envelops us, and the battles overwhelm us.

It need not be this way. It should not be lonely, but the path lively with the laughter and love of female friendship. I have often stated in speech and written word that our destinies, as women, will change when we begin by being kind to each other. We can then expect men to take their cue from us... We live in a country where we can embrace every liberty, gain admission to every institution of higher education, and find entry into every professional field. We, as women, graduate at the top of our classes in undergraduate, legal, business, STEM, and medical educations. And yet, when we look to the top echelons of our respective field, so few of us sit at the top...

Of one inalienable truth I am certain: together, standing shoulder to shoulder, women are the greatest force of nature. I also know that when we cease to dilute our power in the name of politics, religion, and male attention, we will be introduced to the best version of collective self. The Dalai Lama has opined that women will be the salvation of the world in the communal power of their compassion. And compassion is contagious.

Diamandis (2014)

A 2014 book by Nancy Kline, called *Living with Time to Think,* echoed Lynn Tilton's thoughts remarkably. Writing to her 18-year-old god-daughter, on the threshold of adult life, who at aged 10 had asked her the question, 'When I get to be a woman, how can I have a good life?', Nancy, as godmother and long-standing observer of the corporate life, wrote:

You can happily live with men, marry them, work with them, make love, dance, cook, create children, set policy, make decisions, stock shelves and accumulate a fortune with them...

... you do not need to emulate the rigid, destructive behaviours in their culture. You don't need to confuse leadership with competition and control. Or let admiration for men lure you down that 'we must do it the way they do if we want to be successful' road. The world is haemorrhaging because of that model of leadership... (p 32).

... choose joy, having considered all the facts (p 70).

Kline (2014)

We tentatively conclude from this newly emerging field of scientifically supported gender differences that a fear-free organization modelled by a woman might look quite different from one modelled by a man; its energy flow might also feel quite different. The test would be, of course, seeing to what extent differently modelled organizations met their strategic and operational objectives – in which the outcomes might not only be quantitative (bottom line) but qualitative (sustainability).

In the next chapter, we discuss how change happens in organizations in the process of reaching towards a fear-free organization.

References

Bateson, G (1987) *Steps To An Ecology of Mind*, Jason Aronson Inc, available at http://www.edtechpost.ca/readings/Gregory%20Bateson%20-%20Ecology%20 of%20Mind.pdf [accessed on 15 November 2014]

BBC (2013) Men and women's brains are 'wired differently', BBC News, available at www.bbc.com/news/health-25198063

Brown, P and Brown, V (2012) *Neuropsychology for Coaches: Understanding the basics*, McGraw-Hill Education

Brown, PT and Hales, B (2012) Neuroscience for neuro-leadership: Feelings not thinking rule decision-making, *Developing Leaders*, issue 6, pp 28–37

Bustin, G (2014) *Accountability: The key to driving a high-performance culture*, McGraw-Hill, New York

Cowley, N and Purse, N (2014) *5 Conversations: How to transform trust, engagement and performance at work*, Panoma Press, St Albans, UK

Deal, TE and Kennedy, AA (1982) *Corporate Cultures: The rites and rituals of corporate life*, Addison-Wesley, Reading, MA

Diamandis, P (2014) Please... We need more women in technology, *LinkedIn*, 3 November 2014, available at https://www.linkedin.com/today/post/article/ 20141103165518-994365-please-we-need-more-women-in-technology [accessed on 1 December 2014]

Handy, C (1976) *Understanding Organizations*, Penguin Books

Heifetz, R (1999) *Leadership without Easy Answers*, Belnap Press, Harvard University Press, Cambridge, MA

Henry, A (2011) *Understanding Strategic Management*, 2nd edn, Oxford University Press, Oxford

Hofstede, G (1980) *Cultures and Consequences: International differences in work-related values*, Sage Publications, Beverly Hills, CA

Hrebiniak, L (2013) *Making Strategy Work*, Pearson Education, Upper Saddle River, NJ

Isaacs, W (1999) *Dialogue and The Art of Thinking Together: A pioneering approach to communicating in business and in life*, Doubleday, New York

Johnson, G, Scholes, K and Whittington, R (2010) *Exploring Corporate Strategy, Text and Cases*, 8th edn, Prentice-Hall, Harlow, UK

Kets de Vries, MFR (2009) *Organizational Paradoxes: Clinical approaches to management (organizational behaviour)*, Tavistock Publications Limited, Abingdon

Kline, N (1999) *Time to Think: Listening to ignite the human mind*, Ward Lock, UK

Kline, N (2014) *Living with Time to Think: The god-daughter letters*, Octopus Publishing Group, London

Knapton, S (2014) Men and women do not have different brains, claims neuroscientist, *The Telegraph*, 8 March 2014, available at http://www.telegraph.co.uk/news/ science/science-news/10684179/Men-and-women-do-not-have-different-brains-claims-neuroscientist.html [accessed on 1 December 2014]

Kotter, J and Heskett, JL (1992) *Corporate Culture and Performance*, The Free Press, New York

Kraines, GA (2001) *Accountability Leadership: How to strengthen productivity through sound managerial leadership*, The Career Press Inc, Pompton Plains, NJ

Medina, J (2009) *Brain Rules: 12 principles for surviving and thriving at work, home and school*, Pear Press, Edmonds, WA

Mintzberg, H, Ahlstrand, B and Lampel, J (2008) *Strategy Safari: Your complete guide through the wilds of strategic management*, 2nd edn, FT Prentice-Hall, Harlow, UK

Patterson, K, Grenny, J, McMillan, R and Switzler, A (2002) *Crucial Conversations: Tools for talking when stakes are high*, McGraw-Hill Education/Open University Press, New York

Patterson, K, Grenny, J, McMillan, R and Switzler, A (2005) *Crucial Confrontations: Tools for talking about broken promises, violated expectations, and bad behaviour*, McGraw-Hill Education/Open University Press, New York

Patterson, K, Grenny, J, McMillan, R, Switzler, A and Maxfield, D (2013) *Crucial Accountability: Tools for resolving violated expectations, broken commitments and bad behaviour*, 2nd edn, McGraw-Hill Education/Open University Press, New York

Robinson, D (2014) Neuroscience and the natural leadership talents of women, *EvanCarmichael.com*, available at http://www.evancarmichael.com/Sales/4500/Neuroscience-And-The-Natural-Leadership-Talents-Of-Women.html [accessed on 15 October 2014]

Schein, EH (2010) *Organizational Culture and Leadership*, Jossey-Bass, CA

Stacey, RD (1996) *Complexity and Creativity in Organizations*, Berret-Koehler, San Francisco, CA

Stone, D, Patton, B and Heen, S (2000) *Difficult Conversations: How to discuss what matters most*, Penguin Books

Trimble, M (2012) *Why Humans Like to Cry: Tragedy, evolution and the brain*, Oxford University Press, Oxford

Verma, R (2013) Brain connectivity study reveals striking differences between men and women, *Proceedings of the National Academy of Sciences*, available at http://www.uphs.upenn.edu/news/News_Releases/2013/12/verma/ [accessed on 1 December 2014]

Webster, N (1828) *A Dictionary of the English Language*, Black, Young and Young, London

Worrall, D (2013) *Accountability Leadership: How great leaders build a high performance culture of accountability and responsibility*, Worrall and Associates, Carlton, Australia

Change, adaptability and flow

10

Introduction

Hamid isn't thinking, his instincts are now focused on acting without the interference of his brain.

Paul Coelho (2009)

The brain hates change but nevertheless has a remarkable capacity for adapting. We explore this seemingly contradictory statement in this chapter and assess what it means for organizations, especially those attempting to undergo change through organizational change programmes.

Making a change or adapting to a new situation is hard work for the brain and it takes a long time. But there are situations when the brain is working effortlessly and is at its optimal best – a state that neuroscientists call 'flow'. We investigate what happens when flow occurs, and what type of conditions set this up in organizations.

Finally, we discuss how change that is fear-free can be achieved in organizations.

Adaptability and change

There is clear evidence that social and environmental changes influence genetic function, and that the brain is constantly changing and adapting to its environment and what is happening to it (Hirsch and Hirsch, 2014). Indeed, the brain is remarkably good at adapting to external influences: it is constantly changing and learning. But these adaptive changes are always purposeful. Neural networks are formed for everything that we pay attention to and nothing that we don't (Vorhauser-Smith, 2014). Paying attention seems to be a prerequisite for neurons to be activated and neural networks to be built. And we have evolved to pay attention only to those stimuli that are interesting or meaningful to us.

Recent studies involving brain scans have shown how activities change the size and organization of the brain. Playing a musical instrument consistently over time increases the part of the brain responsible for hearing, and for keeping a beat and rhythm. Brains can also rewire to adapt to damage: blind people find a way of 'seeing' through sound and touch, and deaf people can transform lip reading into 'sounds' in their brains.

Creating new neurons or new pathways in different parts of the brain is hard work and takes time. In his book *Outliers,* Malcolm Gladwell (2008) suggests that learning a new skill well takes at least 10,000 hours of practice – that's almost 3½ years of 8 hours' practice every single day. Put more realistically, it's somewhere between 8 and 10 years to become really skilled at something. And that is under conditions of wanting to acquire the skill.

But if change is imposed upon it, the brain reacts quite differently. As we have seen, our brains have evolved to keep us safe from danger, and are constantly on the lookout for signals that threaten our well-being, responding with extraordinary speed to get us ready to survive through a fight, flight or freeze response. These reactions are triggered whether the threats are related to real life-or-death situations, or to a perceived threat like a potentially angry boss or an unknown but dangerous business competitor. Every change the brain detects is a potential threat, and the body reacts depending on our gene make-up, our history and our personal experiences. Unless we have evidence to the contrary or we receive more information, we are in general programmed to react negatively to any and all change. Our brains are organized to make sense of the world as we perceive it based upon our own experience, and to react accordingly – and we trust that reaction because, after all, it is the brain that has kept us safe so far, and in all likelihood will keep doing so in the future. The brain that got us here is most likely the one that will get us there.

Change represents a big threat to the brain. The best bet for the brain is always to trust its own experience rather than someone else's assumptions. Intellectually, whilst change may sound exciting or challenging or appropriate, to most brains it spells danger. And in any event, it is more economical – easier – for the brain to go on being the same.

The emotional reaction we experience when we get new information influences the way any subsequent information is perceived and processed – we are naturally biased. If we are frightened by a change, it colours the way we perceive any subsequent related change. If we are subjected to successive related changes, our brain will trigger more and more fight, flight or freeze responses; we will not be dealing well with the change, and can ultimately become ill with stress.

Seeing and flowing

It is the way we see things that makes the difference, and that is based entirely on our experience. It's worth exploring this a little further, and perhaps challenging currently held views, because the consequences are so profound.

In 1949 Canadian psychologist Donald Hebb made an imaginative leap about how the brain works (Hebb, 1949). The brain is, he suggested, an associative learning system: it structures itself and builds itself through neuronal pathways that are developed as the consequence of repeated stimulation. 'Hebbian learning' as it became known, is popularly summed up in the idea that *the cells that fire together, wire together.*

We introduced this idea in Chapter 2, and it is one that is repeated time and time again in the literature. Sixty-five years of repetition tend to establish a truth that becomes so familiar it acquires an orthodoxy all its own. But perhaps the time has come to revise Hebb's view. He did not, after all, have the extraordinary power of the electron microscope, as cell biologists have had, to see and measure what was really going on.

'Wired together' conjures up an image of pathways that are rather like a road system in a dense map – the A–Z of London laid out in one vast sheet, then (from a brain's point of view) crumpled into the small space of the skull where all the connections go on operating; or the wiring harness of a great aeroplane squashed into the smallest ball shape that can be made of them, but somehow still able to connect to the flaps and wheels and engines to make everything work the way it should.

But the brain isn't as mechanical as that. A new phrase is beginning to appear as a consequence of a shift of interest.

And it seems to be based on flow.

Now that the brain is being seen from the point of view of how it manages energy flow, and the mechanisms of decision-making are slowly being understood, the phrase that is beginning to be used is: *where attention flows, energy goes.*

What if, instead of being a *sequential* process, much that happens in the brain proves to be a *simultaneous* process? And that it proves to be as unfamiliar to us in its laws as the quantum universe?

Electron microscopy and immense computing power is slowly untangling the extraordinarily densely packed systems in our brains that contain those 86 billion neurons connected by thousands of miles of axons and dendrites – the senders and receivers of the electrochemical messages that operate within the brain's wetware. And rather like a quantum view of the universe, in which it is apparent that there are interconnections we can as yet hardly comprehend, the cellular structure of the brain itself may be supported by a just-beginning-to-be-noticed net-like structure whose purpose is not properly understood at all.

In practice what this means is that the old, rather mechanical, view of the brain as being a mass of wired connections is giving place to something that is much more fluid in its conception – though of course fluidity is in its nature difficult to fix. The working summary of the brain we are trying to reach for might best at this stage be summed up as *the cells that grow together, flow together.* Or even the other way round: *the cells that flow together, grow together.*

Alas, that reduces the rather comforting certainty of *the cells that fire together, wire together.* But in fact the cells don't fire together. They fire electrically only to create the conditions under which the neurochemicals are eased across the synaptic gaps. The brain is all the time reconstructing itself through the chemistry that is being activated within it. Despite apparent stability everything within it is being continuously regenerated through well-worn channels that are more easily used than creating new ones.

It is remarkable how extraordinarily small the spaces are within which the complex chemical reactions of neurochemical transmission happen in the brain. The gap that lies between any two connecting points – and a single neuron may have 10,000 connecting points – is less than 100 nanometres. To imagine that kind of smallness remember that a millimetre is a thousandth of a metre. Now take a millionth of a millimetre. That is a nanometre: one billionth of a metre or, more formally expressed, 10^{-9}. One hundred of these are not going to take up a very big space. That's the size of the synaptic gap.

Why a gap? It takes us back to the wiring image. If the brain really were hard-wired – everything connected to everything else with complex switching mechanisms to get the circuits right – then if we wanted change, a circuit would have to be broken. It would not be a clever way of creating adaptation.

(There are some circuits in the brain that are entirely electrical, in the sense that the axon and dendrite are fused together and the electrical impulse does not have to generate a neurochemical process to cross a synaptic gap. But they are relatively few in number and can be ignored from the point of view of this general argument.)

What seems to happen is that the fluid power of the brain can be channelled off in new directions. An old circuit, or channel, is simply left alone to dry up, unused, while the energy in the circuit is re-routed electro-chemically into new channels.

This may be the way that humans have acquired their extraordinary power of adaptation. We have the capacity to manipulate the external world in such a way that the world becomes a projection of the imagination of the inventor, entrepreneur, or child playing with plasticine. This is very much more than 'adaptation' in a Darwinian and evolutionary sense. While that's important, it doesn't distinguish us humans from other animals. Imaginative adaptation is some variable capacity to change the world around us in such a way that 'new-ness' emerges. And adaptive changes in the brain involve changes in how genes are expressed.

It could be argued that all possible and potential discoveries are in fact already present in the brain: that what we see as discovery is only a continuing journey of understanding about how this most complex organ works. There is an epistemological argument that says 'nothing can be known until it is known, because otherwise it could not be discovered'. Then the source of the knowing must have been (in) the brain that already knew.

In the history of understanding the brain, each stage of understanding has used whatever state-of-the-art mechanical metaphor was currently available to try to convey what was understood. In recent times clocks, steam engines and computers with hardware and software have been especially used to try to gain some practical understanding of the complexity of the system. But all fail because they only convey what has thus far been discovered, not what might be discovered. That is to say, they are a product of where discovery has got to ('Is this the source of the Nile or not?'), not what is inherent in the system ('Where did the rain come from?').

Attempts to create a biological computer turn this process through 180 degrees. They start not from mathematics but from living systems and the capacity of the brain to encode information in ways that are other than binary. They will have dense data storage, massive parallel computational power, extraordinary energy efficiency, and be based on DNA sequencing. One gram of DNA can store the same amount of data that would take 145 trillion CDs each holding 80 gigabytes of data. Laid edge to edge, that number of CDs would circle the earth 375 times (see **www.youtube.com/watch?v=UhGAK0LmCsQ**).

That's the power we already have in our heads; and most of it is entirely unknown to us while it operates every nanosecond of our existence. When the brain is operating as its best, it's known as being in a 'flow state'.

The flow state

Flow happens when individuals are really in tune with themselves and their actions, so that everything they do is effortless. Experiencing flow is one of the main reasons that people enjoy playing video or online games.

Flow can also happen when individuals are in tune with each other, and the collective transcends the individual. A fine jazz ensemble understands that very well. The best improvisation happens out of a shared understanding of what is possible yet can still engender great surprise at what unexpectedly emerges. The best sports teams improvise continuously within the certainties of members trusting each other and surprise themselves by their shared achievements.

Flow is experienced during periods of complete attention as feelings of high energy, motivation and focus (Csíkszentmihályi, 1990). Concentration is so centred that everything else falls away. Our self-consciousness disappears and we have a sense of personal control over whatever it is that we are involved in. Time seems to slow down (every second is noticed) as well as to speed up (three hours seem to pass by in three minutes). The experience of the activity is highly rewarding and wholly absorbing.

To happen, flow demands both attention and skill. It requires the ability to intensely focus and relax at the same time. Staying 'in the flow' is lost if feelings of apathy, boredom or anxiety arise.

At a fundamental level, flow is what allows the brain to allow adaptation or not to object to change. Studies show that during a flow state, the brain temporarily shuts down activity in the prefrontal cortex – the area related to higher cognitive function, self-monitoring and impulse control. With this area de-activated, we can be more courageous and less critical. Chemicals related to reward flood the brain, giving a feel-good feeling.

In *Trying Not to Try*, Edward Slingerland (2014) traces the Chinese history through Confucianism and Daoism of what might be involved (for an ancient Chinese man) in achieving some state of perfection. It is oddly modern.

Confucius, he observes, had a concept of carving and polishing – trying really hard for a very long time. Laozi, a Daoist, had more the sense that Michelangelo conveyed when someone marvelled at his *David*. He did not have to create the statue, he observed, only take away the stone that was hiding the statue already embedded there. Mencius, a later Confucian, encouraged 'cultivation of the sprouts'. Processes that are natural can be properly tended to give of their best. Zhuangzi, a later Daoist, wanted everyone to forget about trying and go with the flow – almost as if he were a Timothy Leary follower in the 1960s. There might even have been relaxing substances involved.

Whatever way might have been chosen, the aim was to achieve something called *wu-wei* and *de*. Both imply a state of 'effortless accomplished living' or 'spontaneous action' whilst apparently doing nothing. Both radiate some sense of power, however. The power is palpable and is of the kind that attracts others. The ancient Chinese were just as fascinated about what made an effective leader as is the modern corporate world.

A modern example of what Slingerland means comes in the introduction to his book. He describes a mind ball game at his local science museum. There is a single large metal ball on the surface of a long table that has a magnetic field under it. One player sits at either end of the table. Each player wears a headband that picks up electrical signals from the brain that can alter the magnetic field and so control the position of the ball. The objective of the game is to control the movement of the ball, by thought alone, so that it drops off the edge of the table into the lap of the opponent. That's the win.

What happens very often, apparently, is that the closer one person gets the ball to the opponent's edge of the table, the more that person who is about to win loses control and the opponent is enabled to take control. What is actually happening is that the possibility of winning creates signals of anxiety or anticipation that start interfering with the control that got the ball to an almost-win position. It is the same as the tension that stops a great soccer player scoring on the penalty shoot-out, despite perfection in hours of practice. Thought-controlled mind ball is a contest of who can keep the effective flow going by staying calm at the critical moments. 'Staying in the zone', professional sportspeople call it.

Timothy Gallwey was among the first of recent writers to observe this when he produced *The Inner Game of Tennis* (Gallwey, 1974). He did it without the benefit of modern neuroscience. But as captain of Harvard's tennis team in 1960 and then a disciple of Guru Maharaja Ji where he learnt meditation techniques, he discovered something special about focus and flow. His Wikipedia entry observes that:

> The 'inner game' is based upon certain principles in which an individual uses non-judgmental observations of critical variables, with the purpose of being accurate about these observations. If the observations are accurate, the person's body will adjust and correct automatically to achieve best performance. Gallwey was one of the first to demonstrate a comprehensive method of coaching that could be applied to many situations, and found himself lecturing more often to business leaders in the US than to sports people.
>
> http://en.wikipedia.org/wiki/Timothy_Gallwey

What he did was to *observe*, very accurately, which is the great primary discipline of all good science. In English eyes his crowning achievement was to have coached the women's tennis finalist Virginia Wade so that, after many previous attempts where a finals win eluded her before Gallwey's coaching, she won Wimbledon in the Queen's Silver Jubilee year, 1977. Gallwey has written:

> In every human endeavour there are two arenas of engagement: the outer and the inner. The outer game is played on an external arena to overcome external obstacles to reach an external goal. The inner game takes place within the mind of the player and is played against such obstacles as fear, self-doubt, lapses in focus, and limiting concepts or assumptions. The inner game is played to overcome the self-imposed obstacles that prevent an individual or team from accessing their full potential.
>
> Gallwey (1976)

High-performing teams often describe being 'in the flow' when work is going well. Achieving that state is something every leader wants his or her employees to do. Helping people to do that involves giving them well-defined tasks that they are capable of doing, and giving immediate feedback on how they are doing in order to encourage them (Csíkszentmihályi, 2004).

It is also important to create conditions for people's attention to be wholly focused and relaxed. But above all, the organization must be fear-free so that energy can be released to flow.

Different ways of thinking

Gallwey's work links closely to the more modern, neuroscience-derived ideas about the different ways there are of thinking: fast and slow, hot and cold. They in turn may link to predominantly right- and left-brain processes. Let's integrate fast–slow, hot–cold, with right–left.

In a lucid and thoughtful *New York Times* review of Daniel Kahneman's *Thinking, Fast and Slow* (Kahneman, 2011) entitled 'Two Brains Running', Jim Holt (2011) synthesizes Kahneman's essential thesis that one part of the brain works *fast* (System 1) and appears instinctive and emotionally driven, whilst the other is *slow* (System 2) and is more logical, deliberate and memory based:

> System 1 uses association and metaphor to produce a quick and dirty draft of reality, which System 2 draws on to arrive at explicit beliefs and reasoned choices. System 1 proposes, System 2 disposes.
>
> Holt (2011)

This may be linked to what has been termed hot or cold reasoning (Pillay, 2011). *Hot* reasoning is related to high emotional arousal and is thought to involve the reward centres in the brain, whilst *cold* reasoning is related to low emotional arousal and may be to do with short-term memory.

In his magisterial book *The Master and His Emissary*, neuropsychiatrist and Cambridge English don Iain McGilchrist simply asks the question, 'Are we each a metaphor of ourselves?' (McGilchrist, 2009). He then observes:

> Because the right hemisphere sees nothing in the abstract, but always appreciates things in their context, it is interested in the personal; by contrast with the left hemisphere, which has more affinity for the abstract or impersonal... The right temporal lobe deals preferentially with memory of a personal or emotionally charged nature, what is called episodic memory, where the left temporal lobe is more concerned with memory for facts that are 'in the public domain'.
>
> McGilchrist (2009, p 54)

And again:

> ... the affinity of the left hemisphere for everything it has itself made ('the fruits of human invention') is in contrast to the affinity of the right hemisphere for what exists before and after – and beyond – namely ourselves, nature.
>
> McGilchrist (2009, p 56)

The two halves of the brain do not work in isolation, however. Nor do the different ways of thinking and reasoning. They are all, at best, part of an integrated system. One part is focused. One part is searching. One part delights in order. One part wants to see the whole mess and wonder at the patterns that emerge.

Guiding how the brain operates and integrates fast–slow, hot–cold, left–right is the individual's sense of self: the sum of all that person's experiences, emotions, and thoughts that constitute his or her uniqueness and essential being.

What is the Self?

In their development, what human beings create is a remarkable sense of Self. And the Self – it's worth a capital letter – seems to be important in impeding or facilitating flow: in permitting or seriously objecting to change. Out of Self comes identity and out of identity comes action.

Good metaphors are not easy to construct – though once constructed they look very easy because they themselves facilitate flow. And this metaphor for the Self may be a bit clunky. But let's try it.

Imagine that on day one of life, all experience is being encoded on a disk, like a CD though not digital; and that the brain has the capacity to make an enormous number of these disks that can operate in parallel. So all experience gets encoded and the more any particular experience or closely associated experience gets repeated the more that channel and its associated pathways become a familiar pattern increasingly easily accessed.

Very early on a second disk is laid on top of the first, and then so on and so on and so on. A huge stack of disks builds up.

There has to be some mechanism for managing all the information and pulling it off and presenting it to the world in a consistent and coherent form. Let's call that a central integrator. Or let's call it the Self.

Imagine, in our metaphor, that the central hole of the stacked-high disks has the capacity to develop within it the mechanisms that can access all the information on the disks. It is built out of the experience encoded on the disks but also has the primary capacity of being able to access that data. As it develops in a dynamic relationship with the world (which in turn is the source of the data that creates the Self but also the setting with which the emerging Self continuously interacts), economically it chooses to access only some bits of information and in doing so creates patterns which, projected into the world, we then experience in another person as their individuality.

The way that person smiles, walks, speaks, reacts, dresses, decorates a bedroom as a teenager, strives, slumps, loves and hates – everything about that person whom we recognize as a consequence of some deep capacity in ourselves for pattern recognition – has been constructed and managed by the central integrator, or Self. Information flows.

That is what is at the core of the person. In deteriorating disorders, like Alzheimer's, when the flow within the brain is being continuously impaired by what are the brain equivalent of tree trunks laid across railway tracks to derail trains, the central core is no longer able to function and the person that we knew becomes lost to us. The same happens transiently under the influence of too much alcohol, recreational drugs, or severe stress. The Self is no longer able to be its Self.

Experience and attentional focus seem to be very important for the Self to function effectively. Experience is what creates the raw data that the Self can integrate. Focus directs the Self into what it is to do. That capacity – the focus on what to do – is itself a function of the continuously self-reinforcing structuring and maintenance of the Self. Dynamic biological systems interact in such a way that they continuously both consume and create. Digital systems, when switched off, are inert until they are switched on. Biological systems only switch off at death. The brain and the Self are intensely biological systems.

So we can experience this Self as variably integrated – coherent and cohesive at best, or maybe coherent in an un-cohesive kind of way (see **https:// www.youtube.com/watch?v=QnCTrq5siac&feature=em-subs_digest-vrecs**).

There are times when the Self cannot explain itself to its Self. Post-traumatic stress disorder (PTSD) can show this especially vividly. The following illustration is a particular example.

Brian was a young man of 28 who, when driving one wet and very dark New Year's evening, found himself arriving at a situation on a country road where a traffic accident had just happened. A car a little ahead of him had crashed through some poorly lit road work barriers and buried itself under some large piece of heavy machinery that was parked within the roadworks. He could see someone trying to get out of a jammed rear door, screaming through a half-opened window.

Jumping out of his own car, and perhaps without any thought for the danger to which he was exposing himself, he went to the boot of his own car to get hold of a big tyre wrench he had there and that he thought immediately would be useful in prising open the jammed rear door of the wrecked car. As he got it out of the boot and was just turning the corner of his own car to get to the wreck, another car came on the scene too fast, struck Brian from behind and hurled him into the air. It was subsequently thought that he lost consciousness for about half an hour.

Eventually the whole developing mess was sorted out by police and ambulance. Brian found himself in hospital with some serious injuries, though eventually recovered his physical capacities. What did not recover was his Self.

When serious physical trauma occurs accidentally, if the person suffering the accident has even a second's warning of what is about to happen the whole of the body immediately organizes itself with flight/fight/freeze responses. The body knows absolutely it is in danger. So it makes instantaneous sense of experience.

But when something traumatic occurs for which there could have been not a second's preparatory reaction, the body subsequently has no knowledge of what happened. In such circumstances experience does not get embodied. Intellectually a person may hear a description of the events. But the description has no more meaning than does the same repetition of events to a person who was not involved in the accident in any way at all.

And because the body has not encoded the experience, the Self has nothing on which to make any sense of what happened. Brian was continuously asking the question, 'What happened to me?' He had clear memory of everything up until the moment of the impact that threw him into the air. We can imagine him under a huge adrenaline surge in the darkness and wet rushing to the boot of his car, grabbing the tyre lever, setting off to rush back to the wrecked car... and then blank. His circumstances made no sense to him.

With the rise in PTSD in modern times, the question is often posed as to why, under the horrific conditions of 19th-century warfare, what is now recognized at PTSD as a result of battle stress was not more apparent then.

Among many possible answers, one very plausible one is that such battles happened within a very short space of time and within sensory range. Horrific though Waterloo was, it lasted only a (long) day and everything that happened took place within the compass of the immediate senses.

A drummer boy whose arm was shot off went on drumming with the other. In the closing stages of the battle Lord Uxbridge, sitting on his charger standing next to Wellington's Copenhagen, having had eight or nine other horses shot from under him during the day, had his leg shot off by almost the last cannonball fired. 'By God sir,' he is reputed to have said, 'I've just lost my leg'. 'By God sir', replied Wellington, 'so you have'. Neither would have thought it in any way incumbent on either of them to interrupt Wellington in the final flow of the battle to do other than notice one among many of the horrors of the day. Uxbridge took himself off to a dressing station, such as they were, and survived an above-the-knee amputation, complaining only that the instruments seemed a bit blunt. The amputation saw survives still.

The First World War, a century after Waterloo, produced a slow recognition of shell shock. That conflict took warfare into a phase where not only did it last for intolerably long stretches of time but happened beyond the limits of the senses. The battlefield could not be comprehended within sight, nor reactions made ready to deal with shells that might have been fired from many miles away. All the body could do was maintain itself on impossibly high alert and have no chance to expend its energies in effective action. Under such conditions the Self is put under maximum stress-test to cope. Neither experience nor focus may make any difference to unmanageable events. If the stress proves too great the Self can no longer structure the person's own sense of him- or herself.

All actors and singers and performing artists dread the feeling of anxiety that arises, not from the adrenaline flow of excitement, but the surge of cortisol that tightens the muscles that prevent real flow. They know they need to relax to give of their best, but trying hard to relax if there isn't a great skill already in relaxing only compounds the problem. In the event, sufficient performance skill may have got the performer applause enough. But the performer knows when he or she was or was not in flow.

So flow comes from within the Self: but only in a Self that has enough in it upon which to flow. The 10,000 hours of structured experience needed to give mastery of a skill only creates the conditions under which flow might then happen. It happens when the emotions are in place, and attention can be focused.

Organizations generally structure their processes around predictability and control, trying to reduce everything to what is known and can be comprehended. It is unlikely that every Self in the organization can align with these processes. And so such processes generally dampen down flow and thereby hinder it.

Organizational change programmes

Does this have any impact on our understanding of the way organizations manage change?

'Change management' seems to have been a bonanza for consulting firms but has often resulted in remarkably little benefit to those on the receiving end. There are many organizations that are weary of change, and corporate energies that are exhausted by it. Building on John Kotter's work (Kotter, 1996), Scott Keller and Carolyn Aiken of McKinsey's Chicago and Toronto offices respectively wrote a major report for the millennium year 2000, entitled *The Inconvenient Truth About Change Management* (Keller and Aiken, 2000). They noted:

> Conventional change management approaches have done little to change the fact that most change programs fail. The odds can be greatly improved by a number of counterintuitive insights that take into account the irrational but predictable nature of how employees interpret their environment and choose to act.
>
> Keller and Aiken (2000)

This was a great insight. It had been foreshadowed a decade earlier in a Harvard Business Review article on *Why Change Programs Don't Produce Change* (Beer *et al*, 1990).

More recently, a study by the Economist Intelligence Unit (Kielstra, 2011) found that 44 per cent of change initiatives have not delivered. The survey of over 600 managers found that 'people were the issue'. Failing to engage hearts and minds was reported as the main issue by 57 per cent of respondents, with 31 per cent saying that they had failed to take into account local issues and 27 per cent that they didn't allow for local culture.

One of the toughest challenges is to maintain employee motivation and engagement in the middle of the uncertainty created by organizational change.

It is only now that we can begin to understand *why* it is that employees choose not to have change imposed upon them, but prefer instead to act on the basis of how they interpret their environment.

And it is not irrational at all. For the individual concerned, it makes absolute sense. The emotional system has a clear logic of its own in directing our behaviours, and that logic is now slowly being recognized. The reason employees choose to act on the basis of how they interpret their environment comes from cell biology and the way perception, from second to second, creates the neurochemistry that instructs the genes how to tell the body what to do.

How often have you heard 'that'll never work' or 'there's no way I'm going to do that' when a change programme is introduced to a group of employees? How many times do change programmes fail because of active staff resistance and rebellion? What we now understand is that this is a perfectly reasonable response for every employee who perceived the proposed change to be in any way threatening. Their emotions limited their ability to accept the change – they could not adapt. Their Self guided their brain to respond protectively, and they were acting to protect themselves. Their attention was focused on survival, and they may not have felt they had the skills to make the change: their ability to 'go with the flow' was blocked.

Change in a fear-free organization

Managing change in an organization needs to take into account how individuals perceive the change – particularly if fear is triggered in them. Presenting the change in a fear-free way is therefore a critical success factor. According to Gordon (2000), minimizing danger and maximizing reward is an overarching, organizing principle of the brain, which David Rock used to develop the SCARF model (status, certainty, autonomy, relatedness and fairness). John Barbuto (2011) summarized the application of SCARF to successful change management as follows:

> A goal of good change management is therefore *to orchestrate delivery of change information such that emotional reactions within staff do not subvert the change effort* [author's italics]. This goal is promoted in its first instance by delivering information about change that is both powerful (leading to attention) and constructive (providing a path towards positive resolution)...
>
> ... correctly orchestrated, engagement is the first step in the process towards effective change.
>
> Barbuto (2011)

The first step in any organizational change programme is to help people not to feel threatened when talking about the future and the changes ahead. Based on David Rock's SCARF model, leaders need to avoid people perceiving that, as a consequence of the change, they will have a:

- potential loss of *status*;
- lack of *certainty* about the future;
- reduced *autonomy*;
- erosion of *relatedness* or trust;
- heightened sense of lack of *fairness*.

Furthermore, it is important to help people think in new ways for *themselves*. This means that leaders shouldn't rely on 'telling' their teams what to do, but should instead model the change: be the change they want to happen. They need to help teams identify what makes sense for *the teams*; and help them find ways to adapt to the new future. This may well give rise to surprising and unexpected actions, which should not be dismissed. Leaders should focus on regulating their own and others' emotions so that all 'stay in the moment', and stay fear-free, controlling any fight/flight/freeze responses which could jeopardize the change. Finally, leaders should help people to develop new habits – this means giving positive feedback, acknowledgement, and reinforcement.

References

Barbuto, J (2011) Engagement, emotion and change management, *LimbicZen*, available at: https://limbiczen.wordpress.com/the-neuroscience-of-emotions-for-change-management/engagement-emotion-and-change-management/ [accessed on 10 November 2104]

Beer, M, Eisenstat, RA and Spector, B (1990) Why change programs don't produce change, *Harvard Business Review*, **68** (6), pp 158–66

Coelho, P (2009) *The Winner Stands Alone*, Harper Collins

Csíkszentmihályi, M (1990) *Flow: The psychology of optimal experience*, Harper and Row, New York

Csíkszentmihályi, M (2004) *Good Business: Leadership, flow and the making of meaning*, Penguin Books

Gallwey, WT (1974) *The Inner Game of Tennis*, Random House, New York

Gallwey, WT (1976) *Inner Tennis: Playing the game*, Random House, New York

Gladwell, M (2008) *Outliers: The story of success*, Penguin Books

Gordon, E (2000) *Integrative Neuroscience: Bringing together biological, psychological and clinical models of the human brain*, Harwood Academic Publishers, Singapore

Hebb, D (1949) *The Organization of Behaviour*, Wiley, New York

Hirsch, MA and Hirsch, HVB (2014) The adaptable brain: Biology of social neuroplasticity, *Topics in Geriatric Rehabilitation*, **30** (1), pp 2–7

Holt, J (2011) Two Brains Running, *New York Times*, 25 November 2011, available at http://www.nytimes.com/2011/11/27/books/review/thinking-fast-and-slow-by-daniel-kahneman-book-review.html [accessed on 10 November 2014]

Kahneman, D (2011) *Thinking, Fast and Slow*, Farrar, Straus and Giroux, New York

Keller, S and Aiken, C (2000) *The Inconvenient Truth about Change Management*, McKinsey & Company, available at http://www.mckinsey.com/app_media/reports/financial_services/the_inconvenient_truth_about_change_management.pdf [accessed on 15 October 2014]

Kielstra, P (2011) Leaders of Change: Companies prepare for a stronger future, *Economist Intelligence Unit*, January 2011, available at http://www.economistinsights.com/sites/default/files/downloads/Celerant_LeadersOfChange_final%20final.pdf [accessed on 10 November 2014]

Kotter, J (1996) *Leading Change: Why transformation efforts fail*, Harvard Business School Press, Boston, MA

McGilchrist, I (2009) *The Master and His Emissary: The divided brain and the making of the western world*, Yale University Press, New Haven and London

Pillay, SS (2011) *Your Brain and Business: The neuroscience of great leaders*, Pearson Education Inc, Upper Saddle River, NJ

Slingerland, E (2014) *Trying Not to Try: The ancient art of effortlessness and the surprising power of spontaneity*, Canongate Books, Edinburgh

Vorhauser-Smith, S (2014) The neuroscience of learning and development, Pageup People White Paper, *PageUp People*, available at http://www.pageuppeople.com/wp-content/uploads/2012/06/Neuroscience-of-Learning-and-Development1.pdf [accessed on 3 October 2014]

The fear-free organization

11

Introduction

Writing specifically on the question of energy, to a god-daughter leaving college, Nancy Kline in her 2014 book *Living with Time to Think* makes the following observation on the book by her friend Bill Ford called *High Energy Habits* (Ford, 2002). 'You might want to read it every year just to make sure you are up to scratch in the energy department', she suggests. She goes on:

> My favourite of his insights is that you can test whether a decision you are about to make is right by noticing whether it gives you energy. If it does, you are probably on the right track. If it doesn't, you should probably take another turn at the drawing board.
>
> Kline (2014 p 85)

Then writing to her eldest god-daughter, now aged 42 and who has had to wait 37 years for an answer to her question as a 5-year-old about how can we be happy today, Nancy writes:

> Love is the text; all the rest is footnote... It quells fear. Safe, then the brain sends out hormones like serotonin, oxytocin and endorphins. Love, neurologically speaking, makes us happy.
>
> So what is so hard about deciding to love? What is so alluring about its opposites: fear, rage, resentment, retaliation?
>
> I think it is because, although generating love has helped human beings thrive, generating fear has helped us survive. Surviving precedes thriving.
>
> Kline (2014, p 127)

So that is what is at the heart of the organizational struggle we create when emotions are not understood. Fear. It helps us survive and is much easier to trigger than kindness, compassion, trust or love. Its signals are more immediate, impel action, force themselves into awareness, and persist on a 'just-in-case' basis. The attachment emotions do not persist in the same way. There are no stress disorders connected with an excess of work-generated excitement, joy, trust or love.

Fear is the wrecker of trust. Trust is the antidote to fear. It can only come from individuals who first of all trust themselves, understand their own strengths and weaknesses, do not exaggerate on either side of that scale, and have integrity. This is both the starting point and the continuous goal of a fear-free organization and is completely the opposite of corporate bullshit.

As with all the earth's resources, sustainability is a key concept for the 21st-century organization. It means having the knowledge and the capacity to not waste energy and, as applied to human beings, create the conditions where the supply of human energy is continuously renewed through the quality of relationships within the organization and between the organization and the whole of its wider environment.

This chapter concludes with setting out 10 design requirements for creating a fear-free organization as one early beginning way of creating sustainable organizational systems worldwide.

A useful reminder

We must always be kind to the earth and tread humbly upon it. We are transient particles in the mystery of creation. Happily or unhappily, however, we have been given a consciousness that makes us aware of that fact and, in the short time that we have to engage with the mystery of existence, we want to make sense in some way or another of why we are here.

The work we do and how we do it is a great source of making sense of our existence. In the Western world, especially, 'the organization' has acquired a purpose and existence of its own, yet despite its independent status at law it is worth bearing in mind that 'the organization' is not an entity that has human attributes. It only functions because of what is attributed to it by human beings. Organizations can be what we choose to make them. When, as is so often the case, 'the organization' is endowed with demands that have no moral basis to them but exist simply for the pursuit of profit, and means are always at the service of such ends, then as human beings we risk losing ourselves. For, in the end, meaning and our sense of place in the world only comes from the quality of relationships that we establish. How much we amass can be measured. How much we are loved and remembered for what we created between people can only be treasured.

The ways that we have constructed life in the Western world for the past two centuries or so have resulted in a tension between the demands of the organization and the demands of a meaningful existence. The danger is that the organization becomes superior, and we find our existence limited only to the demands of a non-human entity.

The special prerogative of human beings is to be sentient – to feel and think, and then to act. Or, if acting first, to make sense of thoughts and feelings afterwards. And we have evolved an acutely sensitive apparatus with which to do that. It is called the feeling system, backed up by the cognitive system. Together they make sense of whatever sense there is to be made.

This book has been about fear especially. But, despite its prevalence in Western organizations, getting to grips with fear, understanding it and finding ways of living a life not constrained by it, is not a Western prerogative. Because, worldwide, all humans share the same emotions just as we share the same basic biology, so other bodies of knowledge and thought have addressed the same subject.

The long-exiled Vietnamese spiritual leader Thich Nhat Hanh has written this on fear. It was *Huffington Post*-ed on 2 January 2013:

> Most of us experience a life full of wonderful moments and difficult moments. But for many of us, even when we are most joyful, there is fear behind our joy... So even when we are surrounded by all the conditions for happiness, our joy is not complete. We may think that if we ignore our fears, they'll go away... But we have the power to look deeply at our fears, and then fear cannot control us. We can transform our fear. Fear keeps us focused on the past or worried about the future. If we can acknowledge our fear, we can realize that right now we are okay. Right now, today, we are still alive, and our bodies are working marvellously. Our eyes can still see the beautiful sky. Our ears can still hear the voices of our loved ones.
>
> The first part of looking at our fear is just inviting it into our awareness without judgment. We just acknowledge gently that it is there... When we practise inviting all our fears up, we become aware that we are still alive, that we still have many things to treasure and enjoy. If we are not pushing down and managing our fear, we can enjoy the sunshine, the fog, the air, and the water. If you can look deep into your fear and have a clear vision of it, then you really can live a life that is worthwhile.

Further in the text, he says:

> Fearlessness is not only possible, it is the ultimate joy. When you touch non-fear, you are free. If I am ever in an airplane and the pilot announces that the plane is about to crash, I will practise mindful breathing. If you receive bad news, I hope you will do the same. But don't wait for the critical moment to arrive

before you start practising to transform your fear and live mindfully. Nobody can give you fearlessness. Even if the Buddha were sitting right here next to you, he couldn't give it to you. You have to practise it and realize it yourself. If you make a habit of mindfulness practice, when difficulties arise, you will already know what to do.

Thich Nhat Hanh (2014)

Perhaps practising being fearless might be a starting point for the fear-free organization. It is not that one somehow has to get rid of fear. It is cultivating the opposite that counts, which requires directed energy. The absence of fear is the presence of *fearlessness*, which comes through the practice of the presence of fearlessness. That takes us back to the second quality of the limbic leader: *courage*, built on the first quality of *connectedness*, but connectedness with oneself in the first instance.

The beginnings of a central unifying theory

The science of human behaviour is changing beyond all recognition. Instead of theory, with 20th-century 'schools' of psychology competing with each other but having no common shared understanding, the 21st century's neurobiological exploration of behaviour is beginning to open doors to understanding in ways that the 20th century had no expectation of at all. Unverifiable description is giving way to experimental explanation.

At the same time, and as we explored in Chapter 8, that part of the organization especially and widely responsible for people and their well-being, modern HR, seems to have got itself into a tangle of conflicting expectations of and ambitions for itself, resulting in a widespread sense of dissatisfaction, so that, at the heart of the organization, process has a strong tendency to trump possibilities.

Everything that happens to each one of us now, and that we imagine for the future, is framed by everything that has happened to each one of us in the past. We are unique, though we are also structured from within our family and cultural systems to make us more like those we are close to than like those to whom we are distant.

And all behaviour and every thought and feeling is underpinned by the specifics of the neurochemistry that are uniquely associated in each one of us. Our perception – the way we see things – tells our genes how to instruct us to behave. Then it is the emotions that provide the motivational energy for the direction of our action. Even inaction is a form of action, neurobiologically speaking, as it has its own brain circuitry.

It is also now quite clear that the brain is an energy system – as indeed is the whole of the body. Consciousness (our unique capacity to think about the fact that we think), and a sense that we make decisions that are both an expression and a confirmation of the fact that we have a Self (the central neurobiological integrator of our existence) are both expressions of that energy being organized in ways we do not yet fully understand. They are nevertheless manifestations of a central principle that, without energy properly organized, there is no structure to existence. That organizing capacity is evidenced through what we call the 'mind'. Without it, we are mindless.

So neuroscience is giving us the possibility of seeing for the first time a unifying and general theory of the individual and the organization. From this perspective what the brain is about is organizing and managing energy, while what the organization is about is transforming human energy into profit. The leader's primary task is to mobilize energy in him- or herself and then the whole organization; and to know how to do that in the service of the strategic and operational goals of the organization. Neuroscience lets us begin to see how all that can be done. And being free of fear makes it sustainable.

And neuroscience is also opening the largely unexplored field of how men and women might lead organizations differently. Chapter 9, on 'Leadership', brought some very recent information on this possibility to the fore. The essence of it is that equality of opportunity must not imply similarity of action – which it has done in the past. 'Playing it by men's rules' will, we believe, slowly give way – very slowly, probably, in the manner of such changes – to a dawning awareness that men and women have radically different contributions to make; and it is possible that sustainability through relationships is something that women understand and operate much more readily than men. So if, after the banking crisis of 2008–12, the Western world really is looking for a new organizational model, and there is arguably some likelihood that the new model is to be based upon relationships that generate sustainability in organizations, then we can see a more complex and richer interpersonal environment developing at work that may have huge benefits.

And of course, if it is to work, trust will be at the heart of this. And it won't be all plain sailing. There are women bosses who can be as manipulative, hurtful and selfish as men can be; just as there are some men who can be as relationship-aware as women generally are. What the new data are telling us, though, is that the differences between men and women in the way they harness brain energy is much greater than has previously been known for certain. And change will come from that knowledge.

En-couragement

In the way that we unpacked the word 'emotion' and saw huge implications in the hyphenated 'e-motion', it is worth unpacking 'encourage' in the same way. 'En-courage', pronounced in its French form emphasizing the last syllable, gives a great sense of an input of courage – something rather stronger than English usage of the word 'encourage' usually implies, with its hearty, cheerleadery overtones. So we are talking about how the human spirit is made courageous: en-couraged.

It will be obvious by now that it is through the quality of relationship that the human spirit is encouraged; that relationship is with oneself as well as others; that the absence of fear creates the possibility of trust together with endless consequential supplies of attachment energy in a continuously circular process where real trust abolishes fear; that mapping and tracking what is happening to energy flow through having an experimentally derived model of the vital organs of an organization creates a metric that allows people to 'see' what is happening, which in turn creates the possibility of perceptual tuning – *the capacity to be able to 'see'* – in a way that words and numbers usually don't.

At this stage of our understanding of the applied brain sciences, this is the beginning of an early-stage specification for a long-term, diffused set of ad hoc and purposely designed tests to show how it all might work. And it seems likely that applied feminine energies and applied masculine energies might arrive at different ways of doing it.

Proposed design spec for a fear-free organization

The following is a proposed design spec to build a fear-free organization:

1 Have a leader who is good-hearted; who is willing to go on testing and tuning the making of intelligent emotions within him- or herself and to use those as the source of data which reaches well beyond the numbers into reading people well and knowing what to do with that data; and who believes in the human spirit and its infinite possibilities to be both highly focused and reaching out into the unknown. Have the six qualities of the limbic leader well understood, practised and appreciated at all levels. Knowledge, competencies and skills are hugely important, but it is the delivery that makes the

difference. Trust makes full acceptance of the best delivery possible. Without trust not much will work. Therefore what the leader must have is the capacity to trigger the attachment emotions and understand that simply triggering flight/fight/freeze emotions is a cheap and, in the long term, unproductive win.

2　Back that with an HR department re-titled to reflect human energy as its main focus – 'organizational energy' (OE) perhaps – and organized around the way the mind works. The leader is essentially charged with managing information flow, energy and the quality of relationships throughout the organization. The OE department is a continuous resource to the leader in so doing, and at all levels of leadership. OE would have to do that in such a way that it evidenced, in its own practices, what it was supporting in others. The leader would probably abandon annual appraisals and performance-driven cultures in favour of a personal goal focus within a known strategic or operational framework. The leader's task is to continuously focus and integrate the energies of others. OE would track, enable, administer and help delivery. The leadership might have to encourage OE to be very brave and dismantle much of what it had previously erected in trying to over-specify how human relationships were to be conducted organizationally – much of which, like racism and homophobia, has found its way through into legislation that only serves to immobilize relationships. The leader would generate a climate that handed responsibility for all their actions back to well-integrated individuals and expect to see a real drop in conflict-driven complaints, with a corresponding rise in spontaneous and generously supportive acts. Personal responsibility, a sense of worth, integrity and opportunity for learning and personal development would necessarily be central to every aspect of the individual's organizational life.

3　Develop metrics that convey ways of *seeing* things accurately, perceptually, not just numerically and cognitively. Sofi is one such model. If the way we see – understand, perceive, figure – things is the key controller of our behaviour, then there is a huge premium on capturing perceptions. Making pie charts and histograms is not visual data as implied here. Mapping and tracking is what is required. Sofi captures dynamic flow, in the way an X-ray or fMRI does, and freezes it in time. Unlike a pie chart it is not constructing a way of representing numerical data but a way of capturing perceptions.

4 Design all systems around the principles of what is technically known as 'secure attachment' but which means, organizationally, that individuals know they are welcomed and respected as individuals, can make honest mistakes, can expect support for recovering from those mistakes, and can see their work as part of their own life's journey as they continuously offer to the organization the best of themselves in the knowledge we are all fallible, and can sometimes disappoint ourselves about ourselves, as well as surprise ourselves. The best regiments of the British army, when they are at their best, evidence this at all levels. The best fighting ships do too. Trust makes the best fighting forces, and it leads to profound attachments.

5 Begin to see that profit is the statement of how energy has been applied in the system and that there is a remarkably bountiful supply of energy in people if properly attached so that energy is outward-flowing, in the service of the organization, not inward-flowing, in survival mode.

6 Give great thought to the culture. Structure can be very variable, from strictly hierarchical to full 'coaching culture' flat. It's the dynamic of the way it works, not the design, that counts.

7 Let meetings be focused around the principles of embedding time to think.

8 Begin to live with the idea that organizational long-term sustainability is related to joy at work; energies are directed outwards to the goals of the organization, not inwards to personal protection. Happiness is a mood state that has no motivational properties in it. Joy is infectious and sees possibilities everywhere.

9 The test for the limbic leader is: 'Are joy and trust apparent round here?' But the limbic leader will *not* allow them to be measured. They are too important to be the focus of measurement, which will systematically destroy them. Good-hearted people will know so, and good-hearted people will create what needs to be created.

10 Remember there is no final state. Relationships are endlessly dynamic, and business of all kinds is a continuous and continuing journey. The high energy that can be brought into play through human beings in trusting relationships cannot be bought, it can only be gifted; but the conditions where the gift is freely given and honoured in the way it is put to use will make fear-free organizations infinitely satisfactory places to be and to work.

So if that is the high-level design specification for the fear-free organization, what is it at this stage of applied neuroscience that underpins the spec?

Throughout the book we have made the continuous antithesis between the escape/avoidance/survival emotions, in which energy is used to protect the person, and the attachment emotions, in which energy flows outwards, makes connections, and is creative. Fear is rooted in escape, avoidance and survival. Trust is central to attachment. So at the heart of the fear-free organization there is an organizing principle about the way emotions drive energy and the direction of motivation. Organizational theory has never had such clarity before about these basic processes. The exciting times ahead will depend on whether organizational practice can incorporate this knowledge and get the benefits it contains.

The biology of the brain, its neurochemistry, and the way it manages to operate as an effective mind or, if badly treated, mindlessly, is what underpins all profit-seeking behaviour. It is our contention that the best way to mobilize human capacity – energy – is to create the interpersonal conditions where that can happen and then to focus the outputs. Management becomes an energy-releasing task in the service of the strategic and operational goals of the organization. In such a way organizations will stop sapping energy, wasting it, creating stress disorders, and driving people to despair. They will instead stimulate and harness energy, enjoy its productivity, see how personal and organizational goals can be aligned, and watch stretch happen naturally.

What guides us in all our organizational actions is the way we each, individually, 'see' things. The source of how we see things is a compound of all our life experience and the meaning we make of that through the way our emotions build feelings and, attaching experience to language, create meaning. What great leaders manage to do – even great bad leaders, whose moral compass is deranged – is to so engage the minds of others that their actions propel the leader's ideas into action. That's the task of both men and women leaders, organizationally, though we have also suggested that they may need more room to do things differently than has hitherto been made possible.

At the heart of it all is trust, the great antidote to fear. Vulnerable though it is to fear, trust backed by quiet excitement and some joy creates possibility and stretch that no amount of demand can ever do because, spawned by the individual in response to the quality of relationship, trust generates the neurochemicals that sustain all bodily systems at their best, whereas fear systematically corrodes them.

So the biology of behaviour coming into organizational life tells us that relationships are the single key element to sustainability; and that key to relationships is trust. That is where the heart of the fear-free organization lies.

References

Ford, B (2002) *High Energy Habits: The busy person's guide to more energy (without diets or exercise)*, Pocket Books. Simon and Schuster, New York

Kline, N (2014) *Living With Time To Think: The god-daughter letters*, Octopus Publishing Group, London

Thich Nhat Hanh (2014) *Fear: Essential wisdom for getting through the storm*, Harper Collins, New York, available at: http://www.huffingtonpost.com/2013/02/01/thich-nhat-hanh-fear_n_2502265.html#slide=1613277 [accessed on 15 October 2014]

ENDNOTE

Since we sent the manuscript of this book to the publisher in late 2014 we have become aware of the remarkable work of Frederic Laloux in his recent book *Reinventing Organizations: A guide to creating organizations inspired by the next stage of consciousness* (Nelson Parker, Brussels, 2014). Without any particular reference to applied neuroscience, Laloux has found and described the workings of organizations that are creating and living the new 21st-century paradigm based upon relationship, trust and cooperating responsibility. He shows how process gives way to possibility and the hugely beneficial impact that has on the bottom line. Human energy is released to be wisely used, not wasted, in patterns of work that have purpose at the centre of organizational existence. It is a new perception that he brings, and perhaps as revolutionary as Darwin's was. Both start from restless enquiry rigorously pursued.

Had we seen Laloux's work before we finished writing, it might have stopped us in our tracks. Seeing it after we finished is a joy of discovery. Read it, test it, live it. He has coincidentally described the fear-free organization operating in real time. We are thrilled, as many others have been, by the joy his discoveries bring. As with so much in the emerging applied neurosciences, the science begins to underpin half-formed understandings that then reset individual experience and create informed knowing. Through Laloux's work we can begin to see an end to tick-box, performance-based cultures and the re-emergence of the dignity of real professional judgement at all levels in organizations. People find again that they can love what they do and do what they love.

Thank you, Frederic Laloux.

INDEX

Page numbers in *italic* indicate figures or tables